# 100
# First
# Dates

## A Collection of Encounters That Will Make You Laugh, Cry, and Cringe

## Desirée Kent

**100 First Dates**

Copyright © 2018 by Desirée Kent

Published by:
Desirée Kent
100FirstDatesBook.com

ISBN 978-1-7326943-0-9

Book Design: Carla Green, Clarity Designworks

Printed in the United States of America

To all the single ladies -
Don't give up. He's out there.


And to my future partner -
What the fuck took you so damn long?

# CONTENTS

# PREFACE

I've been on some great dates in my life.

I've also been on some really shitty ones.

The idea for this book originally came from my friends. I would be sitting with one of them, over coffee, over lunch, over drinks, recounting my dating stories since the last time I saw them, inevitably ending every story with how I was going to quit dating. How it was so hard to find a good guy.

Whatever story I told, they'd claim I had the craziest dating stories. Ones they couldn't believe. I didn't think they were the *worst*, per say, but the more I thought about it, the more I realized there were *quite a few of them*. They said I should write a book. I told them they were crazy, that I wasn't a writer. I'm a high school math teacher. I don't write!

I was in therapy for about five years, working on some issues that seemed completely unrelated to, and yet were completely seeping into, my dating life. I would complain to my therapist week after week about how I was never going to find the right guy. At the beginning of therapy, it was about how I was too fat (I'm not one of *those* girls that just thinks they're fat, I am actually about 40 pounds overweight, but I'm quite proportionate and pretty fucking gorgeous, if I do say so myself), too boring, I didn't know how to talk to men, and a thousand other insecurities that had arisen as a girl with very little experience who didn't like herself very much. During my work in therapy, my dating stories became more about how the guys out there weren't smart enough, or didn't have cars, cell phones, or a job. I started to take the blame off of myself, and turned it around to the guys that I was dating. Mostly because now that I liked myself slightly more, I was dating any guy who'd give me some attention. *Anyone.* No job? That's okay. Live with your parents? Oh, it's alright. You didn't graduate from high school? Well, you seem worldly enough working at this Starbucks. You only sell weed to your relatives? That's fine. *Ugh.*

I've grown a lot, though. Now I date guys who I consider potential mates. Most of the dates just don't work out because we don't click, not because they are (or I am) severely broken.

Somewhere along my path, when I was crying in my therapist's office about how I was never going to meet "the one," she told me some statistic she'd heard somewhere:

"You have to date about a hundred men to meet 'the one'!"

I told her through my sobs that I must be pushing a hundred, that it must be about time to meet this guy. I was *so* ready for him to be in my life.

It was at this point that I started to write down how many dates I'd been on. Every time I went somewhere, I'd think to myself, *have I been on a date here?* And inevitably, the answer was the same: *yes.* So, I'd take out my phone, write down who the guy was, and what had happened on the date — some sort of memory of what kind of guy I perceived him as, something that stood out to me, or how I'd met him. I realized that I was quickly approaching 100, and that I had some pretty interesting stories along the way. (Although, to be fair, don't we all? My friends and I talk all the time about our dating lives, and I always think we all have interesting stories.)

I reached 100 a while ago, and Prince Charming still hasn't appeared. But I haven't given up hope. I try to think of every date as practice for the last first date I'll ever go on. That every experience I've had prepares me to be a great partner, lover, and friend to my soulmate. He's out there. I just have to kiss a lot of frogs before I find my prince.

# WHY AM I SUCH A MESS?

*This chapter pretty much sums up how I'm a complete disaster: the fucked up way I talk to myself, the way I believe others perceive me, and the way those messages are reflected in my dating life.*

*Don't worry, the stories get less painful and more comedic over time.*

# 1
# John

I didn't know it at the time, but my first date foreshadowed the rest of my dating experiences for the next 12 years.

I was 17. My two best friends, Laura and Stephanie, and I spent all of our time at Stephanie's house. Stephanie's house had a pool, and Stephanie's parents were Parrotheads — obsessed with Jimmy Buffett. Stephanie's house was the hang-out spot, since her parents were so laid back. They were very accepting — the kind of house you could walk into without knocking, even when Stephanie wasn't home, and help yourself to something in the fridge.

Stephanie knew John through her brother, who had gone to school a few towns over from where we lived. Stephanie, Laura and I were sitting around, complaining about how we had never been on a single date, how we were lonely and pathetic, and we just wanted to go on a date! It was at this point that Stephanie decided she wanted to set me up with John: not because I would think he was cute, not because we were compatible, but because she thought we would make beautiful babies.

Let me explain: I'm blond. Not bleach blond, but legit pale skin, blue eyed platinum blond. My dad once asked me why I was wearing shorts in the middle of winter, and I had to explain to him that I was wearing tights under the shorts — he couldn't even tell. John, apparently, was one of those blonds with blue eyes, and freckles. You know the type, the ones where you can't see their eyebrows or eyelashes? Yup, that kind of blond.

So, Stephanie wanted to set me up with him so we'd have *beautiful* blond babies, all at the age of 17. Oh, did I mention that I was a virgin?

After coming up with this brilliant plan, Stephanie set up a group of us to go bowling, and invites John. We planned to meet at Stephanie's house and all carpool from there (of course, to save money on gas, since it was $1.08 a gallon and we didn't earn a lot of money). I showed up wearing jeans and a silk shirt, something circa Spice Girls, 1998. I think I even put on heels. When John showed up, he was wearing super huge raver jeans, a belt, and an oversized white t-shirt. I thought he was cute, and I had butterflies at the thought that this boy agreed to go on a date with me. It was at this point that Stephanie leaned over to me and whispered, "Soooo...I didn't exactly tell him it was a blind date...but I will!"

My heart sank. This boy that I thought wanted to be on a date with me wasn't actually aware he was on a date with me. And I didn't have enough self-esteem to show him how gorgeous I was, to show him that he should want to date me. Mostly because I don't realize for another 10 years that I am gorgeous.

So, we all pile into Stephanie's minivan, with John in the front seat, Laura and I in the back, and head to the bowling alley. Along the way, John talks to Stephanie about how upset he is with his mom. I sit in the back, palms sweating, racking my brain to figure out something cute and clever to interject into the conversation.

It never happens.

We pull into the bowling alley, park, and head inside. As we're trying to figure out how many games to play, John gets a phone call, and heads off by himself to find a place to talk. I, of course, think it's sooooo cool that he's got a cell phone, and not just a pager. It's at this point that John comes back, and tells Stephanie we have to leave.

"Why?" Stephanie retorts. "We just got here!"

John rolls his eyes and appears agitated. "My mom is throwing all of my stuff out onto the lawn. She's kicking me out of the house because she found some weed in my room."

Having never smoked weed before, I obviously think he's a bad boy, and am instantly attracted to him.

At this point, the "date" ends, Stephanie drives us all home, and I get away with saying about two words the entire date. Stephanie, Laura, and I spend the night watching tapes of Color Guard Shows from other high schools, still having never been on a first date. I never see John again. Oh well, back to square one.

# 2
# Liquid Kitty

The summer after I turned 21, I frequented bars quite a bit. One of my favorites that my former roommate took me to was Liquid Kitty. It's one of those places that doesn't have a sign, but is always packed. It's the place you take your third date to get liquored up before you seal the deal. Their signature martinis are tasty, but deadly. Two is guaranteed to knock you on your ass.

A friend and I were drinking cocktails when somehow I met a guy in slacks and a button down shirt. In a local bar filled with guys in t-shirt and jeans, it was a welcome change. We exchanged numbers, and decided to meet the next day at the bookstore in the mall nearby. I thought it was kind of a cool place for a first date — get to know each other at the cafe inside the bookshop, and meander through the books a bit? Sounds amazing!

Well, that's not what happened. I wore jeans, a nice shirt, and heels. He showed up in a hoodie. After being so well-dressed the night before? He wasn't hung over, because he'd only had one cocktail at the bar and then left after we'd chatted. Why would he show up in a hoodie? And another thing: we didn't sit at the coffee bar and chat. He walked through the aisles of books, and I followed him. Like a puppy dog. At this time, I was dumb enough to believe that this was a date, that this guy was actually into me. It's clear now that I've had much more experience, he wasn't.

Somehow the idea came up that we should go back to my place. I think it may have been to have a drink. He wanted me to hear some music that he liked, so I'm sure he used that as an excuse to come up as well. He followed me back to my house, and we put on his favorite rapper. We listened for a bit, and then he made his move. (Um, duh....not offering to buy me coffee or a meal, and now back at my house? Obviously a hook-up.)

He kissed me. I think we may have even moved to my bed, but at that point in time I wasn't ready for it to go any further. He got upset with me, and stormed out. I never heard from him again.

Note to self: don't take a guy back to your place on the first date. Also, let him buy you *something*. Coffee counts as something.

# 3
# Dark Web Puppy (aka DWP)

I started online dating somewhere in my 2nd year of college at UCLA. Online dating wasn't socially acceptable at this time. It was a thing that only "losers" did. And so, that's where I found myself.

I met DWP through Match.com. I forget the exact details, but I remember that he was a writer, and had a website called Dark Web Puppy. He lived in the Valley. Before we even met, he sent me a story he had written about a girl he'd met online — who'd asked him to hit her during sex.

Now that I think about it, that should have been a warning signal not to go out with this guy. Who sends a complete stranger a story about hitting a woman during sex? Who's the idiot who agrees to go out with this whack job? Oh right, me.

DWP and I chatted, and for some reason I agreed to go over to his house for our first date. I had never met this guy before, but I thought it was going to be a good idea to go over to his house? I had no sense of my own safety.

When I arrive, we sit on the couch and chat. He tells me how his dad was on an episode of *90210*. I'm impressed and think this is the closest I'll get to dating a celebrity. I share the mundane details of my life (because, back then, I wasn't nearly as awesome as I am now. Or, at least, I didn't think I was awesome. I thought I was boring, and dorky, and undatable. Unlovable. Ugly. Fat. Who would want to be with me? Of course, ask me that question now that I love myself and realize what an amazing woman I am. Who wants to date me now: everyone. Okay, maybe now I'm slightly narcissistic. I don't half-ass anything in my life. I'm either one extreme or the other.)

DWP suggests we watch tv, so we do. We're sitting on the couch in his parents' house. Because he lives at home. Although, he is 23, so I guess at that age it is slightly more acceptable to live at home.

Somehow, we start making out. And my shirt comes off.

And my chest is already covered in hickies. Oh, the college lifestyle. I had hooked up with a guy friend of mine the night before (hey, it happens) and had worn a turtleneck on my date because I didn't want DWP to see it. He admitted that he couldn't be mad, because we weren't dating exclusively.

I still felt whorish. Oops.

I also should have known that this guy was not the one — who invites a girl over to his house, doesn't even offer her any kind of dinner, and tries to make out with her? That guy.

Who puts up with that? This girl.

I think I might have even contemplated seeing him again after our initial meeting, but I don't remember why I decided against it. It's probably because he was geographically undesirable.

Even after we stopped talking, I found it necessary to be the crazy stalker girl that would visit his blog occasionally just to read up on what he was doing. Turns out the girl he met after me he ended up marrying, and now they have a house and a child together. Of course, part of me was sad about it. Another part thought I dodged a bullet on that one.

# 4

# Behar

I was on my high school dance team. I wasn't a great dancer, but the beauty of the dance program at my school was that they were really accepting of anyone who had a desire and a passion to dance. I had the desire, and the passion.....the skill? Not so much. It was sweet and adorable that our dance teacher allowed such a nerdy girl to be a part of the team. Sometimes I wonder if it was just because I brought up the grade point average of the team.

Through dance team, I met a group of girls who were not in my honors and advanced placement classes. They were kids that I thought were "too cool" to be seen with me. There was one girl, Brynn, who befriended me in 1999, that I thought was entirely too cool to even talk to me. She was into the raver scene — she dyed her hair different colors, wore body glitter, tiny t-shirts that barely contained her hickey-covered gigantic breasts. She wore big baggy jeans over her perfectly curved body. She carried her glitter lip gloss in her mini backpack and hung out with a bunch of totally hot guys who hung out at the mall and smoked cigarettes. I was in awe of her — her self confidence, her ability to talk to strangers, especially hot guys that were way out of my league.

I had no self-confidence. I thought I was too fat and too ugly for any guy to ever like me. I dressed like a boy, and had no idea how to do my hair so it ended up in a big frizzy mess on the top of my head. My make-up was over-the-top, so much so that one of the guys in my classes called me "Mimi" after the character on the Drew Carey Show.

Brynn took me under her wing, and tried to encourage me to talk to boys, and improve my self-image. Of course, when you're being helped by a totally hot chick, it's hard to feel sexy. We hung out a few times in high school, and managed to stay in touch when I started college. The summer after my first year at UCLA, I came home and we hung out a few times.

In August of 2001, we were hanging out, and she took me to a friend's apartment where we played video games and watched tv with her boyfriend and a few of his friends. I felt completely out of place — I was the only one pursuing a college degree, and I was obviously the only goodie-two-shoes in the joint. I chatted a little bit with a few of the people there, but really only answered questions that I was asked. After Brynn and I left, she told me that one of the guys, Behar, was interested in me. He told her boyfriend, and her boyfriend told me.

I looked at her incredulously. I was still in awe of the fact that anyone could like me, or have a crush on me. I told her to give him my number. I couldn't even remember which guy it was, but at this point I figured any guy would be better than being alone.

He called me when I was already back in the dorms on campus. We chatted for a bit, and decided to set up a date for the next weekend. He came down in his ripped up VW Rabbit convertible. I met him in our parking lot, and he drove me to the Denny's down the street.

At Denny's, we chatted. He told me about how he'd done every drug under the sun. I told him I'd never done drugs. He mentioned to me that the one that he thought was the craziest, that had given him the weirdest dreams and worst withdrawals was the one time he'd drank an entire bottle of Nyquil.

He also mentioned that once, when he was driving his car, he ran over a guy on a bicycle.

Somehow we got on the subject of tattoos, and he showed me that his whole last name was tattooed across his back. In Old English.

In the back of my mind, somehow, it was still going to work out with this guy. After I'd told him how I'd never done any drugs, and gotten straight A's in high school. We obviously came from different worlds.

I was sad when he didn't call me for a second date.

# 5
# **Billy**

My third year of college I was still spending a lot of time with my best friends Stephanie and Laura. Still virgins, we always placed bets on who was going to lose their virginity first. They both thought it was going to be me.

Spoiler alert: it wasn't (and that story belongs in another book).

Stephanie still lived at home with her parents, and was really getting into hockey. Stephanie was one of those girls who threw her entire being into her interest. In high school, she was in Color Guard, so the only thing we ever did when we hung out at her house was either watch Color Guard videos of other high schools, or spin flags in her backyard. Post-high school, she gained interest in ice hockey, so she spent all of her time and energy skating, hanging out with her newfound friends on the team, or watching hockey on TV.

One such friend was Billy. Billy was 25, a full four years older than us, and ate, lived and breathed ice hockey. He owned the movie "The Cutting Edge," along with "Mighty Ducks" and "Slap Shot."

Stephanie thought Billy and Laura would be really great together. Laura was one of those people who was super nervous around just about everyone — she was diagnosed with Social Anxiety Disorder in high school. She was particularly nervous when talking to men, and had chosen to go to an all-girl's school so she wouldn't have to deal with it (later on, it turns out Laura married the first man she ever slept with, which is what we all had predicted was going to happen).

Since Stephanie was intent on setting up Laura and Billy, she organized a night during Christmas break for all of us to go out together to a gay club, since Stephanie's gay best friend Ryan (who she knew from her previous obsession with Color Guard) loved to go out dancing. We all piled into two cars — Stephanie, Laura and I in one, and Billy and Ryan in the other.

We get to the club, and the group heads to the dance floor. We can't tell who Billy is trying to flirt with — it seems to me that he's showing attention to all three of us girls.

Since Laura is so nervous around men, I'm sure it appeared to Billy that she wasn't interested, since every time he looked at her or tried to dance with her she shrunk away like she wasn't interested. I knew that Stephanie was trying to set up Laura and Billy, so I wasn't going to let Billy make a move on me.

He made a move on Stephanie instead. They ended up kissing on the dance floor. Laura was kind of upset, but was quite forgiving in the car on the ride home.

Stephanie and Billy kissed once or twice more after that night.

Somehow in the not-too-distant future, Billy and Laura ended up making out. They dated briefly — I think they even went out on one or two dates.

By the time Spring Break rolled around and I went home again, Billy asked me to come over to his house to watch a movie. I figured we were all just friends, so there was no harm in it. He spent half the movie massaging my shoulders and trying to convince me to lay in bed with him. At the end of the night, he confessed to me that, "you know, that night at the club...you were the one I wanted to make out with."

I totally fell for it. My low self-esteem was just thrilled that someone wanted me. I agreed to go on a date with him. I *absolutely* believed that this man had wanted to be with me first. And whether he had or not isn't the issue. The issue is sharing men with friends. It's always a bad idea, and it never ends well.

Billy decided to come down on a Friday night so that we could hang out together. I had a birthday party to go to for a friend on campus, so he came with me. We shared a romantic kiss in the sculpture garden of the UCLA campus. Afterwards, I told him I wanted to have drinks at the bar.

That was a bad plan.

Of course, being newly 21, I wanted to binge drink. Shots! Long Island Iced Teas! It's a good idea, right? Great first date behavior.

I got so drunk that I threw up in my bathroom back at my apartment. I, of course, thought this was a fantastic time to try to kiss Billy. Being 25, and much more able to handle his alcohol, Billy quickly denied me. He did not, however, deny the chance to sleep in my twin bed with me.

When I woke up in the morning, I was completely embarrassed that I had thrown up the night before. What was I thinking? I showered and brushed my teeth. Billy woke up, and kissed me.

It was then that I realized that I liked the *idea* of a boyfriend, of dating someone, but Billy was not the one. I didn't want to date a guy who had been with two of my best friends (and of course, now that I have hindsight, this was the reason that I got so drunk and sabotaged the date in the first place). This kiss just wasn't working out for me, I thought, as he shoved his tongue further into my mouth.

*How do I break up with this guy? How do I kick him out of my apartment?* Oh, the struggles of growing up. I stammer to find some way to tell him that I am busy, I have homework I have to do, and he should go. He agrees, and leaves, I'm sure because he's feeling slightly hung over.

He tries to call me once, and I find some excuse as to why I can't date him anymore. I'm sure I used distance as an excuse, or the fact that I had a lot of schoolwork going on.

By the time I came home for summer break, Billy was hooking up with Stephanie on the regular. Turns out she'd lost her virginity to him and they were friends with benefits. Of course, she ended up falling in love with him, and he broke her heart, as friends with benefits are prone to do.

# 6
# Barney

I met Barney when I was a junior in college. My roommate's friend was throwing a party, and he was there, as a friend of a friend of a friend. We talked at the party, and he asked for my number.

He was tall, black, and muscular. He was a lifeguard at some pool in the Valley, and was currently attending Community College. As a junior in college without much dating experience, I was excited for a guy to take me out on an *actual* date.

After the party, he called me, and we chatted a bit. He set up a date for the following evening, which was a Friday night.

That should have been my first warning.

Although, I guess when you're in college, it's totally fine to ask someone out for the next night. (Is it? I certainly wouldn't say yes now.) And that was my unfortunate mistake to say yes to a date for the next evening — but this was back when I had no plans on any Friday night, never mind any other night, except to walk up and down the streets in an attempt to find a party to crash with my friends.

He came to pick me up in his 1986 cream colored Pontiac 6000. It was a hideous car, and we drove the streets of Westwood in it. He knew just where he was going to take me, he said. He was excited about it too. His favorite restaurant, he said.

**Denny's.** This guy took me on a date to Denny's. Alright, I guess since we're both college students, I can't really be upset about being taken to Denny's (stay tuned for another Denny's date, in my late twenties, with another guy who claims it's his favorite restaurant). I have a salad, and he orders from memory, without even looking at the menu — some burger special they had at the time.

We chat through dinner, and it's not a terrible date. He seems nice, even if he has terrible taste in restaurants. All of a sudden, I really have to pee. The urge builds and suddenly becomes overwhelming. As our conversation winds down, I think about excusing myself to the restroom. It's at this exact moment that our server brings over the check.

I take this as the time to excuse myself to the restroom. As it's early in my dating career, I don't think about what happens to the check and how the money situation is supposed to work out in this case. I was just thinking about how badly I had to pee. As I stand up, Barney says the worst thing I could possibly think to hear:

"Do you want to get this, or do you want to split it?"

Do I *what?* I don't know much about dating, but I know you shouldn't ask your date if she wants to pick up the bill! Because I understand that we're both broke college students, but dude, if you can't afford to take a girl out for a meal, you shouldn't be dating in the first place. And the nerve to ask me to *split* it? I mean, I certainly would have *offered* to pay, but for you to *ask* me? Unbelievable.

By now my eyes are practically floating. I'm so shocked by his statement that I whip out my wallet, and mumble, "I guess we can split it." I throw down my half of the check while dancing in my seat and race to the bathroom. I do my business, and come back to the table, where the check has been taken away, and we're good to go. He drives me back to my apartment, and tells me what a great time he had, and how he'd like to do it again.

Here's the kicker: *I say yes.* Because my self esteem is so low that *any* man, *anyone* who shows any interest in me, is better than being alone, so why not be with a guy who isn't going to spoil me?

On our next date, we go back into Westwood, but we decide to have dessert at Jerry's Deli. We snuggle in together at a booth in the back of the restaurant, and share a slice of chocolate cake. I am excited just to sit next to a man in a booth. He leans over, and gives me a peck on the lips. I am ecstatic. Not because I like *him*, per say, I just like the *idea* of someone wanting to kiss me. We make out in the booth for a few minutes — more cute, innocent kisses. As we head out of the restaurant (apparently he could spring for the check for a piece of cake), he tells me he wants to show me this amazing view.

We get in the car, and he drives me down PCH, along the Coast, almost to Malibu. The view just along the beach is gorgeous in the evening. The more we talk in the car, the more I realize that we have no common interests. He turns up some residential street, and parks near a house at the top of a hill. Next to the house is an empty field. He leads me out into the space to show me the view.

At least, that's what he tells me. The lot looks out onto the ocean. He spent more time turned around facing me, trying to put his tongue in my mouth than he did taking in the scenic view. I felt weird about standing in this empty space in a neighborhood that didn't belong to either of us. For a few minutes I went along with kissing him, and then finally spoke up in a timid voice.

"I think we should go."

He pulled back, and looked at me. "*Why?*" He inquired incredulously, as if I had just told him I wanted to jump out of an airplane without a parachute.

"Well...uh...this isn't our neighborhood, and uh..," I stutter and ramble my way through some excuse that is far from the truth, because at the time I can't even identify what the truth is: I'm not comfortable alone, at night, in a field, with a complete stranger, who (it turns out) I don't actually even want to make out with anyways.

He reluctantly begins to drive me back, but has completely stopped caring about what I want or what I'm interested in at all. Apparently he was more interested in making out with me than talking to me. I sulk all the way back to the apartment, and he doesn't even bother to talk to me the entire way home.

As he pulls up to my apartment building, I turn to him to make some sort of small talk, to say thank you for some part of the evening. Blame my mother for my ridiculous manners, for my ability to find the good in any situation. He doesn't even turn down the music. I try to thank him for the nice time, but I can't even hear myself over the music or his singing. I stop mid-sentence, get out of the car, and slam the door.

He speeds off, out of my life forever. He couldn't have driven away fast enough.

# 7
# Gareth

I met Gareth at a party at UCLA on a Thursday night. It was put on by the engineering sorority (of which one of my roommates was a founding member) and a bunch of engineering frat boys were there too. Engineering frat boys were NOT your typical frat boys — they had NO game, and most were pretty introverted, even with booze. I'm sure a good portion of the guys there were still virgins.

Somehow, I started talking to this guy that I thought was so completely out of my league, it was ridiculous. He was hapa — half white, half Japanese, and totally hot. He was tall, with dark slicked back hair, almond eyes, and beautiful skin. He was an engineering major, a junior in college, and had a car on campus, which was really rare to find.

We spent half the night talking about our childhoods, and how they were similar — how we didn't come from a lot of money, had younger siblings, and a lot of responsibilities growing up. How we were misunderstood by most of the people around us, no one could sympathize with our struggle and what we'd been through, growing up poor in a desert community. I felt a connection to him — he was one of the first guys that I had encountered that didn't try to grind up on me on the dance floor; he seemed to be an actual gentleman and truly interested in me.

At this point in time, I didn't know how to handle it when a guy showed any interest in me. I didn't believe that a guy would truly be interested in *me*, what *I* had to say, mostly because I didn't like myself very much as a person. I didn't think I was attractive, and I still only knew how to give myself to men physically, because I was afraid if they actually talked to me and found out who I was as a person, they would decide I was too crazy, boring, or uninteresting, and just leave me. It was a lot easier to make out with them, and then just leave. It was easier not to be vulnerable.

So, when Gareth gave me his number, I was ecstatic. We agreed to make plans for the following week, since we both had midterms that week. I left the party soon after that, floating on air at the prospect of dating this hot, smart guy...one of the first guys who I believed to be as smart as me, or smarter, and that I could relate to. Of course, the minute I got home I internet-stalked him, like any normal single girl would. However, in 2003 the only kind of stalking that was possible was through MySpace — and he looked amazing.

I obsessed about trying to call Gareth over the next few days. It was all I could think about. I gazed longingly at his MySpace photos, and wondered what it would be like to kiss him. When I finally got up the nerve to call Gareth, we chatted for a few minutes and he agreed to pick me up from my apartment for a date. He called up to the apartment when he was downstairs (one of those cool kids who actually had a cell phone), and I walked down to meet him. Palms sweating, I got into the car. I was so nervous, every time I spoke the words echoed in my head about how dumb I sounded.

"So...uh....where are you whisking me away to?" I tried to ask smoothly as we merged from the 405 freeway onto the 10 West. The words echoed in my head after I said them. I sounded like an idiot.

"Have you ever been to Swingers?" He asked smoothly, "They have great shakes there, a whole variety. It's a cool spot."

"No," I responded. I was so nervous I couldn't think of anything clever to say. My brain sped through a thousand thoughts, not sticking to any particular one, and wondered what the hell I could even ask him that would seem normal. Guys in general made me nervous, but this one was so hot that I just couldn't even form a sentence. By the time we got to Swingers, we hadn't chatted much. All the stupid things I said reverberated in my mind and I mentally kicked myself for sounding like a bumbling buffoon. When we sat down, he mentioned that he normally dated older women. I was a year younger. He fired away at a few questions before the waitress could bring us some menus.

"Have you been on many dates before?"

"No, not really," I murmured, when in reality the answer was, "Nope, never been on a date with a guy who's actually got a brain AND looks. And I've definitely never been taken to someplace that wasn't Denny's," but my mouth wouldn't form the words. He proceeded to ask me about my dating experience, and I told him that I hadn't really dated much in the past. I forget what I gave as the exact reason, but somehow the conversation turned, and my nervousness turned from level five to level fifty five....

"Do you think you haven't dated because you're attracted to women?" he asked me, and cocked his head in a sympathetic matter.

"No! I...I just...no!" My face turned redder than the vinyl booth I was sitting in.

The waitress brought us our menus, and we sat in silence for a minute. The worst part? I actually thought this was going ok, and that I still had a shot with him.....until he dropped the bombshell.

"Yeah, I'm not going to date you. Let's just be friends."

Seriously?!?! You say this BEFORE we order milkshakes??? BEFORE?!!? Is this a sympathy date? What the fuck? So now I have to sit with you, drink this FUCKING milkshake, and not even enjoy it because I want to cry. Because my dream of getting married and having babies with you has now been crushed. And THEN I have to ride back in the car with you?! I was angry, sad, and humiliated all at the same time. I wanted to melt into a puddle under the table. In my revisionist history, he flirted with the waitress when we ordered our milkshakes, and I sat in silence while I drank my shake. He was at least nice enough to pay for my milkshake.

Looking back on this date now, I don't blame this guy. I was a hot mess. If I didn't like myself, how the hell was I supposed to sell myself to someone else? This was one of the times in my dating career that I was the one who was the total disaster, and not my date.

I don't even remember the ride home. I'm sure it's one of those things I've blocked out of my memory because it's such a traumatic event. I was so devastated I didn't go on another date until after I graduated from college.

# 8
# Miller

Gay Best Friends will get you out of many a jam, trust me. (Every once in a while they'll get you into a jam, if you're lucky, and it will create an amazing story.) On this particular occasion, MrKnight saved my ass.

MrKnight and I had decided to go out drinking in Santa Monica. We stood outside at an English pub. The bouncer at the door asked for our ID's — I noted that he was adorable. Dirty blond hair, blue eyes, about 6 feet tall with a stocky build. He told me his name was Miller, and we hit it off right away. MrKnight and I went inside the pub, and ended the evening there. As we came out, Miller was just getting off of work. It was late, and I told him we were heading to Norm's to eat. Miller decided to join us.

We sat together in a booth, with MrKnight sitting across from us. Miller was super sweet, and I enjoyed hanging out with him. At the end of our late-night Norm's date, he kissed me, and told me he wanted to see me again soon. I told him I'd come back to the pub to see him soon.

The following weekend, my friend Ev and I went back to the bar. We chatted with Miller and his friend Scorpion who was hanging out with him. Scorpion. Not kidding. (For more animal named dates, see story 29.)

Anyways, Ev and I have a few drinks and laughs throughout the night, popping outside to flirt with Miller and Scorpion every once in a while. At one point they ask us to go back to Miller's house after he gets off work. Ev and I agree.

We all pile into Miller's car, and we drive for about twenty minutes along the freeway. I tried to pay attention to where we ended up, but it was a neighborhood I was unfamiliar with. I just knew it was off the 10 freeway somewhere. It's three in the morning. The four of us each grab a drink from the fridge, and head to Miller's room. Miller says his roommate will be pissed if we wake him up, so we can't hang out in the kitchen (whatever excuse you want to use to get us into your bedroom, bud).

Miller's room is sparse. He has a mattress on the floor, and a desk in the closet. There's nothing on the walls. As we all chat together, he tells me he has a second job, working as a pizza delivery guy. I think I was 24 at the time, definitely a full time teacher, and too old to be dating a guy who has the same job my brother had in high school.

After laughing and chatting for a while, Miller finally leaned over and kissed me. Scorpion kissed Ev as well. We're all making out while we're in the same room together. How awkward. (Remember those days? Oh, to be in my early twenties again. Nope.)

Eventually, all of that dies down, and we're all tired. We doze in and out of sleep. Around 7 am, Ev and I both wake up, and we decide we want to go home. Miller won't wake up. Scorpion doesn't have a car.

We're trapped.

This is pre-Uber and Lyft. I don't have the number for a cab, and besides, it'll cost way too much money for us to get home. (This is also pre-smart phone, so I can't even Google a cab company.)

What do we do? Ev and I start to panic a little.

And then I remember. MrKnight. He works nights, and is just getting home from work at this time. I text him. It takes forever, since I don't have an on-screen keyboard. I have to touch the 7 key three times to type the R for ride.

**Can you come get us? We're trapped at a house.** I type.

**Sure.** He replies. I breathe a huge sigh of relief. Gay Best Friends are the best. No questions asked. **Where are you?**

Shit. Where *am* I? My heart races. Where the fuck are we? **I don't know.** I text back. This is pre-Google Maps, so I have no way to electronically figure out where I am.

**Lol well I need an address if you want me to come get you.**

I tell Ev that MrKnight will come get us, but we need an address. "I think I saw some mail on his desk," Ev tells me. We raid his desk and find his Domino's pizza paystub with his address on it.

I send it to MrKnight. **I'll be there in 20 min,** he tells me.

Ev and I book it outside, never looking back. We wait for MrKnight to pick us up. He pulls up and we hop in the car.

"So, fun night?"

I grin. "Wait 'til I tell you what happened!"

He speeds off as I recount the story.

And I never heard from Miller again.

# 9

# Nate

Back in the early days of online dating, I thought it was more effective to search for a date on Craigslist than any other platform. (Yes, I know. This is a terrible plan. I was young, and didn't know any better!)

I answered an ad that a guy had placed, looking for a partner in crime. It sounded adorable. I emailed him, and sent him a photo of me. I was surprised when I heard back from him. This was back in the day when I didn't have much self-confidence to know that I am gorgeous. I couldn't believe he had emailed me back! After a few emails back and forth we agreed to meet up for coffee.

He was gorgeous. Caramel skin, dark hair, square jaw. He was about 5'10, and well dressed. He was Egyptian, an engineer, and had moved here after college from New York. We lived only a couple of miles apart. And I was very attracted to him.

Since this was before I had much self-esteem, I wasn't really sure how to approach dating him. Do I call him? Does he call me? Do we email back and forth? How often is he going to message me? How soon should I sleep with him to get him to go out with me again?

Hello, Needy. Not the most attractive quality.

We meet for coffee, and conversation is easy. At the end of the date, he asks if I'd like to go out again.

I am ecstatic. I jubilantly shout yes, and we agree to go out in a few days. He calls me (yes, this was still in the days of calling — pre-texting!) to set up the date. He says that if I meet him at his place, he'll drive us to dinner. At this point, I'm willing to agree to whatever he says. So hot. Oh, what's this on my shirt? It's the new fragrance by Calvin Klein: Desperation.

Once I get to his place, he drives us to one of my favorite little sushi spots. There is such a long line that we end up at the sushi spot across the street.

Rant: *sushi is such a weird thing to eat on a first date. I'm never sure if we're supposed to get rolls to share, or just eat our own. And how many do you get? Can we just share? Because two rolls per person is too many, but one roll is too few. So we're left sharing, but some people get weird about it. Also, sticking a whole piece of roll in your mouth is never cute.*

We didn't share anything that night. He was one of those "I order and eat what I want. You can do what you want." Clearly looking for a partner, right? Of course I ate daintily — God forbid he find out I'm a real person who is sometimes a mess and sometimes I spill on myself. Or he discovers I'm a fat girl who eats! And for the record, being myself is goddamn endearing. I'm so glad I'm over thirty and through with the bullshit of pretending to be someone I'm not. Take me or leave me. (And actually, with that attitude, I've gotten and kept many more men than I did when I was pretending to be someone I wasn't.)

After dinner, he drove us to a rooftop bar. It was a gorgeous space in Santa Monica — lights strung across the ceiling, gorgeous black decor and white cushions on the chairs. There were also space heaters, because it was cold. (Okay, like California cold. You know, like 65 degrees? No flip-flops for me!)

The waitress came by, and he ordered vodka on the rocks. I told the waitress to make it two.

Bad idea.

After my second one, I knew there was no way I was going to be able to drive home. We became affectionate at the bar — his hand on my leg, my hand on his arm, which then moved to his arm around me, and my head on his shoulder. He drove us back (pre-ride sharing days. I know, I know, bad idea).

I told him I wasn't able to drive home, and he brought me upstairs. To his room. We spooned while watching TV on his bed. It all seemed very innocent. At one point I turned around to look at him.

That's when we started kissing. Things got pretty heated pretty quickly. He unhooked my bra. I pulled my shirt over my head, and took off my bra. He went to take off my pants, and I stopped him.

"I just wasn't ready for all of that yet," I told him.

"Well, then, maybe you shouldn't have come back here with me," he snapped back.

I blushed, embarrassed that I wasn't making him happy. I couldn't communicate that I had only ever been with one guy, that I was fairly new at being physically intimate with anyone. I couldn't tell him that, of course, because we weren't at a point where I could be emotionally intimate with him. And he wasn't making that very easy for me, considering that he just snapped at me for not wanting to take off my pants.

Time has taught me that I should never have to justify why I don't want to take my pants off. If I'm not ready, you need to respect my decision.

Back in this day, however, I felt super embarrassed. I couldn't speak. He stopped fooling around, and went back to watching tv. I tried to brush it off, thinking that he was just being a respectful gentleman. In hindsight, I now recognize that he was rejecting me and hoping that I would get the hint to leave.

Well, I didn't.

I lay there, watching TV, until I fell asleep. I mean, he's clearly into me, right? We were just making out. And he stopped when I said I wasn't ready. Plus, I like him, so I'm going to see what I want to see, instead of what's really there.

When I awoke, the sun was just starting to peek through the curtains. I laid there for a moment, looking at Nate sleep. I moved around in the bed, hoping it would wake him. It didn't.

I got up to go to the bathroom, hoping that would wake him. It didn't.

Finally, I just decided to wake him up.

"Hey, I'm gonna go," I whispered as I shook him.

He looked surprised to see me as he awoke. Like he didn't expect to see me in his bed. I took that look to be that he was surprised anyone was in his bed. You know, since he obviously would never have anyone in his bed unless it was someone he really cared about.

Oh, how naive I was.

He walked me to the door of his apartment, and pointed me towards the stairs — no, he didn't actually walk me down the stairs.

We said our goodbyes, and I walked down the stairs, and drove home. I replayed the events of last night over in my mind. He was so great. Just so, so great. I was smitten.

I emailed him the minute I got home to tell him what a wonderful time I had.

The stench of Desperation is overpowering. I bet you can smell it from where you are.

I took a nap for a few hours, and when I got up, I checked my email again.

Nothing yet. Oh well, I bet he's still sleeping.

I proceeded to check my email about twenty more times that day. It was Sunday, and I'd guess that he was getting ready for the week. I'm sure I'd hear from him tomorrow.

Oh, the stories we tell ourselves. Poor Past Me, you have no idea what is actually happening.

I checked my email about a hundred more times on Monday. Still nothing.

On Tuesday, I emailed him again. This time, just to say hi and see if he wanted to chat sometime soon.

Still no reply. I started getting really anxious.

On Wednesday, I sent him yet another email, this time saying I really wanted to go out with him again.

I was beginning to lose hope. I logged on to Craigslist, looking for another potential date to distract myself.

That's when I saw it — posted yesterday. A guy looking for a partner in crime. Same age. Actually, same post as Nate's. Exact same language. Nate has re-posted his want ad.

I burst into tears. I was not that partner. But why?! Wasn't I great? Why didn't he want me? Didn't we have a great time together? Why didn't he answer any of my emails?

It has taken me a long time to realize that pretending to be someone I'm not and reeking of desperation and needy-ness is not the way to win over any man. They can smell it a mile away, and it is never a good place to be in when starting to date. I had to learn to be confident with myself before I could even consider dating anyone. They always say you have to "love yourself first," and it's true, to an extent. I needed to be confident with who I was as a person, and be okay with being single before I could go out and date — because then I could become invested in the right person, rather than just attaching myself to the first warm body that came along.

# 10
# Terrence

When I worked at my first teaching job I met my coworker, Jane. Jane was Indian, and very attractive. I was envious of her and the strong social network that she was involved with. We had both gone to UCLA so we bonded over our love of the school. One evening she invited me to go out with her and a few of her Indian friends.

We headed out to meet some of her friends at a restaurant in Beverly Hills. I have never felt so out of place in my entire life. And it's not because I'm white and everyone I'm with is Indian: it has to do with the amount of money that is surrounding our table. I don't feel well-dressed or pretty enough to be hanging out in such a fancy, high-class establishment.

Jesus, what an idiot I used to be. It's all about how you carry yourself. Fake it until you make it, you know? Nowadays I really do feel like I can fit in anywhere — and maybe that's just because I don't care what anyone thinks, and I'm going to go where I want to go.

Anyways, we left there and went to a bar/club nearby. As we stood around with our drinks one of her male friends and I began to make conversation. He was an engineer and loved horse racing. After he discovered that I had never seen *Stand and Deliver*, the quintessential mathematics teaching movie, he decided we needed to watch it. We exchanged numbers, and set a date to get together.

He called me to double check on the date and time for the movie, and I agreed. I went over to his place (his roommate was going to be out of town) and he let me in. His apartment was huge: he informed me it was a condo that his parents had bought just for him to use during college. There were plaques on the walls of different horse races he had attended. This guy clearly came from money.

He offered me a drink, and we sat down to watch the movie. I was so enthralled with the film that I didn't even notice that he had put his arm around me.

Once the movie was over, we made out a little bit, but nothing too intense. In fact, he was a total gentleman about the whole thing. Eventually, I excused myself since it was late. We left on agreeable terms.

I expected to hear from him the next day, or the next, or the one after that, but I didn't.

I tried to ask Jane about it, but she was vague. (Really, that's the only way you can be when you're the middle-man between two friends who have dated — you have to be Switzerland).

I felt sad. Again. Yet another date that didn't work out. I try my best in these circumstances to remember that what I'm feeling is temporary, that he is not the last man I am going to be interested in, and that a man who is interested in me is going to come my way sometime soon. In the mean time, I am going to continue living the life I love, spending time with people who make me happy, and making sure that every day I am the best version of myself. This is what brings me happiness, and this is how I know someday I'll attract the man I'm supposed to be with.

# 11
# Stu

In college, I took a course specifically designed for mathematics students to decide whether or not they wanted to be teachers. As a junior in the program, I did observations and designed and executed lesson plans with the thirteen other people in the class. One of those people happened to be Susan, who I managed to stay in contact with after college. She became a math teacher in Orange County a few years after I became a math teacher in

Los Angeles County. We decided after too long of not seeing each other, we needed to hang out, so she invited me to her coworker's house party in Newport Beach.

I drove to Susan's house in Fountain Valley, and she drove us to Newport Beach. As we pulled up to the party, I noticed that the house seemed close to the house where I picked up another guy two years earlier for our date — for all I knew, it could have been the house next door. All those beach houses look similar on those little streets.

When we walked into the house, I couldn't help but think of how frat-tastic it was. There was a couch in the living room, and a flat screen TV on the opposite wall. There were bikes in the hallway. Susan told me that five guys lived in this three bedroom house. As a twenty-six year old, I couldn't help but think that dudes my age should not be living like their college fraternity days.

Susan and I mingled with the guys in the house, and their guests. Some had just rolled in from the beach, and most were in board shorts or bikinis with cover-ups. I felt completely overdressed in my jeans and tank top with heels. Fortunately, Susan was also dressed in jeans and a tank...and flip flops.

The minute Susan introduced me to Stu, I knew I wanted to kiss him.

Stu was Susan's coworker — it was his first year teaching math. He was 6'2, about 250 pounds, with mocha skin (I found out later that he was half Japanese and half Black), and he had an amazingly warm smile that could melt even the coldest heart. Susan, Stu and I chatted in the kitchen for a while, and somehow we all ended up looking at something in Stu's bedroom.

Amid Bob Marley posters I glanced at the life of this guy I wanted to kiss so badly. House by the beach. Bob Marley posters...which implied weed smoking. A guitar in his room —

ok, so he's musical. And he's got a degree in math, a teacher, and pursuing a Masters from UC Irvine in Education. Not bad.

This was the point in my dating career where I was still really shy about flirting and marketing myself as a dateable woman. So I did the only thing I could think of.

I waited until we left, and I told Susan that I thought he was cute. As only my fifteen-year old side could.

Susan said she would talk to him.

After a few days, I heard from Susan — she had given Stu my number (this was around the time when texting was still a pain, and guys actually called girls), and he was going to call me. He did, and we chatted. We agreed to a date night in Newport Beach that Friday.

I picked out my cutest casual dress (I learned the error of my ways from last time) and my cutest flip flops, and drove the hour (with minimal traffic) to Stu's house. He was wearing cargo shorts, a button down collared shirt, and flip flops. He asked if I wanted to walk to the Spaghetti Factory for dinner. I said sure, so off we went. Along the way, he told me about how both of his parents were successful — his dad worked for the hospital at UCSD, and his mom was a professor. He was extremely close with his family, and had grown up in an affluent community in San Diego. Stu was short for Stuart, and it was his first year teaching math.

We went to The Spaghetti Factory, and conversation was easy. We talked a lot about work. At the end, he paid for dinner and we walked back to his place. Surprisingly, no one was home. We sat on the couch and chatted, and of course, we ended up making out.

His kisses were everything I dreamed about, and more. After what felt like an hour of kissing, he asked me to stay the night. I declined. He asked again, and I declined again. It was at this point that I decided to leave. I didn't want to feel pressured to do anything I wasn't ready for. He walked me to my car, and of course we spent another ten minutes making out against my car, where he proceeded to ask me again if I would stay the night. I told him no once more, but was able to make plans to see him the next weekend up near me.

For our second date, he came to my house on a Saturday. We went to lunch at a Mexican food restaurant. Again, he paid. At the end of the date, he came back to my house and we talked shop (teachers struggle to NOT talk about their jobs, and when you put two math teachers together, it's a guarantee that they're going to talk about work). In one of my less-proud dating moments, I created some graphic organizers for him out of some paper I had in my room — something we called "foldables" in my math department. We kissed for a bit, and then he left, foldables in hand, with an agreement to call me. He said he had a bike ride the next day, but totally wanted to hang out with me in the afternoon.

I waited for his call. And waited.

And waited.
For like...two whole hours.
Alright, I'm not a very patient person. And I liked this guy so much, and wanted to spend time with him. So I did what I thought was right. I called him. Twice. And left messages both times. Within the span of an hour and a half.
Eventually he texted me back later that evening. The gist of the text was that he was hanging out with his boys, and the bike ride took all day. I texted back that was okay, but did he want to hang out later in the week? He said he'd have to let me know. I should have taken the hint right then, but I was not very attuned at the time.

Of course, I needed to get Susan's opinion on the whole thing. After she had talked to him at work that Monday, she called me to give me the scoop.

Apparently I lived "too far."

She told me he was used to having things handed to him on a silver platter, so he wasn't willing to work for something. She told me he probably wasn't going to text me again.

And it's true. He didn't. But that's okay. He just wasn't that into me anyway.

## BLAME IT ON THE ALCOHOL

*Let's face it, I don't make my best dating decisions when I've been drinking. But they always seem like a good idea at the time... at least they're entertaining.*

# 12

# John

He was supposed to be a one-night stand. Why couldn't he just stay that way?

I met him at a club in Manhattan Beach in my early twenties. He seemed cute, so I asked him to come home with me.

His dick was giant. GIANT. It was some of the most painful sex of my life — back-of-the-cervix punching sex. I wasn't exactly thrilled, but he was nice enough so I let him stay the night.

In the morning, he was trying to decide how he was going to get home — turns out he lived about 35 miles from where we were clubbing the night before. I offered to take him home, if he wanted.

"Really? You'd do that? That's really nice." Yeah, back in the day, I was a really nice person. You know, before I became jaded and blasé. Or you could say it was before I knew how to draw boundaries. Whatever, two sides of the same coin.

I drove him back to his place, figuring I'd never see him again. He thanked me for the ride, and I headed back home.

No big deal.

Later on that week, I received a friend request on MySpace. (Yes, this was back in the MySpace days. Don't judge me.) It was John — he had also messaged me saying he was glad he had found me (I had told him my full name the night he came home with me, and the name stuck with him, apparently). He asked for my number, and asked if I was interested in getting together.

Why can't they just leave well enough alone? Stay in your lane, bud.

Fine, I'll give it a shot.

I gave him my number, and he called me (this is also pre-texting, people. We're practically in the Stone Age). He decided he wanted to take me out for breakfast that weekend. I agreed to let him.

He showed up to my apartment, and I drove us to IHOP. The restaurant was packed, so he asked if I wanted to take it to go. I said sure, so we sat and waited for our food to be packaged to go.

As we sat in the lobby among the grandmas and families, I started thinking about how we had met. And I got really curious.

"Do you always sleep with women and then try to date them? It seems kind of backwards."

He turned to look at me, wide-eyed. "Are you always so blunt? And loud?!? Everyone can hear you!"

The answer to both questions, of course, is yes. Of course I'm loud. And of course I'm blunt. I told him as much.

He just shook his head. "No, I'm not normally like this. But you seem really cool, so I thought we could hang out."

Fine. We got our food to go, then sat on the couch at my place. My roommate was home (yes, back when I lived with a roommate) so we all watched *Wedding Crashers* together while eating breakfast. I wasn't really that interested in him — he was making very little effort to get to know me. I also wasn't thrilled with the idea of having our date be breakfast and a movie at my apartment.

When the movie was over I told him I had a bunch of work to do — which was 100% true. I was in my first year of teaching, and usually my Sundays were filled with lesson planning, grading, and prepping myself for the week ahead.

"Can't we just have sex before I go?" he pleaded with me.

I was so not in the mood. He had done little to get to know me, and I wasn't really that interested in him anyways. Without my beer goggles I was not interested him. "No, I have a lot of work to do." Plus, he lived entirely too far away to turn into a fuckbuddy.

I thanked him for breakfast, and he got in his car and left.

And I never heard from him again.

# 13
# The Science Teacher

After 7 years at my first school, dealing with a lot of administrative bullshit and feeling undervalued as a teacher, I searched for a job elsewhere. I wound up at a small school down the street from my previous employer. I was excited to have a fresh start at a job where I didn't have history with anyone at the school, and there would be no awkward glances from men I'd previously hooked up with.

One summer day before school started at my new job, I visited the principal to pick up some textbooks and chat about classroom expectations. One of my new coworkers came in and introduced himself as "George, the asshole." I was slightly taken aback by that statement, and by the fact that the top of his head almost hit the frame of the door (I found out later he was 6'9). As the principal and George chatted, I sat quietly and thumbed through the physics textbook on the desk. I would be teaching physics that year for the first time. Another person appeared at the doorway — this guy was a lot shorter, about 5'8, and had the look of a science teacher. You know the type I'm talking about — pale, thick-rimmed glasses, wrinkled t-shirt, cargo shorts and hiking boots with tall socks. He had a shaved head, but it appeared to be a preventative measure since he was clearly going bald.

"Stephen," the principal pointed gestured towards me, interrupting her conversation with the alleged asshole, "this is Desirée. She's going to be the new physics and pre-calculus teacher." The principal turned back to her conversation and left Stephen to give me the third degree.

"Oh, is this your first teaching job?"

"No, actually, I taught at SHS before this."

"What did you teach?"

"AVID and Calculus."

"Wait," his face had the look of someone who was trying to fit a puzzle together. "You taught Math and AVID at SHS....and your name's Desirée?" As he finished his sentence, he had obviously completed the puzzle in his head.

"Yeah," I replied inquisitively, obviously missing something.

"We met at Bar Melody!"

I glance nervously at my soon-to-be coworkers to see if they'd caught wind of this conversation. Fortunately, they were still chatting. I have no recognition of this man whatsoever, and so I try to cover up by replying, "Oh, anytime I've been to Bar Melody, I'm pretty drunk."

"You live on Glasgow, right?" Now I'm starting to get a little worried. Do I know this dude? And please, GOD, don't tell me I've made out with him. I peer out of the corner of my eye at my boss and the asshole, but they haven't stopped talking about Algebra, fortunately. Stephen continues to just lay it all out there, "Yeah, you live in Westchester. We met at Bar Melody, and we chatted about a student that had transferred from my school to SHS."

Finally, somewhere in the back of my mind, it's there. A brief flicker of recognition. Damn. I HAVE been out with this guy before. It all starts to come back...math major, from New Jersey, kind of weird. Lived in my neighborhood, although I'm not 100% sure where, because I was *not* going to let this weirdo know my address. He seemed like one of those guys that would show up at your house, march his way in, and not get this hint when it was time to leave. I sit there, dumbfounded that he would bring this up in front of my new boss and coworker. Fortunately, the Algebra talk is still flowing. My mind begins to race as I try to remember how the date ended. I begin a conversation with myself. Was I nice? I know I'd had a few cocktails.....oh Sweet Jesus, DID I make out with him? I doubt it...I may have been drunk but I vaguely remember that I didn't enjoy chatting with him all that much. He was awkward, that part is obvious to me even now.

Stephen continues to talk. "It was about three years ago. I think I still have your number in my phone!" He pulls a gigantic phone out of his pocket that looks like it was one iteration from the Zach Morris phone, and begins to scroll through his address book.

"Oh!" I exclaim so loudly that the Algebra fiends stop their conversation. I'm a mixture of embarrassed, shocked, and humiliated. Thankfully, as far as I can tell, no one has heard our conversation (and by conversation, of course, I mean Stephen blabbing his mouth about my business). I jump up from the table, grab my books and head towards the door where Stephen is blocking the door frame. Please, just let me *out*.

"Desirée, do you need anything else? The librarian can check out any other textbooks you might need," the principal tells me, apparently oblivious to my flushed face. I can't look at anyone in the room right now. It registers in my brain that she hasn't heard any of the conversation, and she hasn't yet realized my flustered state. I relax a little.

"No, thanks, I've got everything I need!" I make a mad dash for the door and practically run Stephen over in the process. "I'll see you next week!"

I don't even glance back as I rush towards the parking lot and collapse into the car. I sit there. As I wait, my brain begins to remember small details of the date. It's still kind of fuzzy, with that vodka-induced haze mixed with three years of terrible dates. I run through a kind of checklist in my brain of what I seem to recall.

Smart. Educated. Teacher, so a big heart. But kind of an ass.... maybe the New Jersey side of things? Or it could have just been his awkwardness. He seemed to be lacking a certain set of social graces that the rest of us seem to have. Not one of those things I can put my finger on, just where you know something's not quite right. We chatted only about work, and nothing else. He taught Chemistry. I just wasn't interested in him, I remember that much.

Typical online date. I couldn't remember what website I'd met him on — it was either Craigslist, or Match.com. There was no way I was going to ask him which one. Hell, I was going to do my best job to stay away from him at all costs....which seemed like it was going to be difficult on a campus of 30 teachers.

So much for starting a new job where I hadn't dated anyone!

# 14

# Kid Rock

One summer in my early 20's I was bored. It was my first truly free season since I was 16 — no work, no school, nothing to do.

But I need goals.

I spent a lot of time thinking about what I wanted to do with my summer, and finally it hit me: I want to visit twenty new bars.

Look, it sounds like a lot, but it's really not. In my early twenties, I could drink 3-4 drinks a night without a hangover. I did the math: if each of these drinks is at a different bar, once a week, then I could hit 12-16 bars in one month. Twenty bars in a summer seemed doable. I didn't know many bars in my area, so I wanted to explore. And I love a good list, so why not keep track while I'm at it?

I decided to check out a bar that I'd been meaning to check for a while: The Zebra Room.

I pulled into the parking lot and walked in at 1 pm on a Friday afternoon (remember, nothing to do for a whole summer. Don't judge me).

It took a moment for my eyes to adjust from the sunshine-filled day to the dimly lit room. The bar smelled of stale beer and dishwater. As I stood in the doorway, the bartender must have taken note of a new patron in the bar.

"Well, you're new!" I heard him exclaim. By then, my eyes had adjusted and I could see that, including myself, there were four customers in the bar. Clearly I was the only one who was not a regular.

One of the guys at the bar wore a backwards hat. He had a blond ponytail, a goatee and wore long jean shorts with a white t-shirt. He looked a little like Kid Rock.

I kind of thought he was cute. (Okay, now you can judge me.) As I sat at the bar and ordered my drink, he started a conversation with me.

He was in construction, and had moved here from Virginia to help his sister with her kids. I could tell he had a kind soul. He didn't seem to be much in the brains department, but he was sweet. When he asked for my number, I gave it to him. I wasn't sure if we were just going to be friends, or something more, but I figured it wouldn't hurt to have a nice guy in my life.

My friend Kendra picked me up from the bar, and we told Kid Rock we were heading to another bar, back then called Big John's. I wondered if he would come join us, but didn't ask.

When Kendra and I got to Big John's we realized we were the only women in the place. We each ordered a drink, and caught up on what had happened for both of us that day. Kendra was mid-story, when the bartender interrupted.

"Which one of you is Desirée?"

Kendra and I looked at each other nervously. "That's me," I replied.

"You have a phone call," she replied as she handed me the receiver. I hadn't even heard the phone ring. And who gets a phone call at a bar? Who even knows I'm here?

"Hello?"

"Hey gorgeous!" I heard Kid Rock's voice on the other end of the line.

"What the hell??" I covered the receiver and mouthed to Kendra that it was Kid Rock.

"I just wanted to see what you were up to."

"Clearly you know what I'm up to — you called me at a bar!"

"Oh yeah. Well, be safe, and we'll hang out soon." I heard the phone click. I handed the receiver back to the bartender.

"Well, that's a first!" I told Kendra. I just got a phone call at the bar!

Kid Rock and I texted throughout the rest of the week, and we decided to meet up for drinks that Thursday. We met at another dive bar in the area — this one allowed smoking inside.

Turns out Kid Rock liked to smoke cigarettes. Yuck. As we conversed throughout the evening, I realized he was so sweet. But so, so dumb. We finished our drinks, then he took me to a bar with a live band. Throughout the evening, he was a perfect gentleman, but we didn't have much to converse about. Or, that is to say, he didn't have much to say on any particular subject. He did, however, know how to dance and that is a total turn-on for me. He gracefully guided me across the dance floor.

I tried to picture a future with him: could I be with someone who didn't match my intellect, but was extremely sweet?

Another downside was that he smoked cigarettes. I hated kissing someone who tasted like an ashtray.

At the end of the evening he walked me outside. As we stood in the parking lot, he leaned in to kiss me.

It wasn't great. There was something about the way his tongue darted in and out too quickly that just wasn't something I liked. I even tried to slow down, to control the kiss, which usually works, but he just wasn't taking the hint. When we finally finished the kiss he pulled back, sighed deeply, and told me I'm a great kisser.

Like I haven't heard that one before.

We agreed we would keep in touch. He mentioned wanting to do dinner sometime next week — his roommate worked at Chili's, and he could get a discount.

Rant: *Why do you have to go and say something like that? Keep the discount thing to yourself! Just say you want to take me to Chili's or something.*

We decided to go to dinner the next week. I tried my best to make conversation with him, but I felt like I just kept losing him. We were not even remotely interested in the same things. I loved the theatre; he was interested in NASCAR. I enjoyed Pub Trivia; he wanted to play darts or pool. I enjoyed reading books; he would rather watch the movie. He wanted to take me to Chili's for dinner; I'd rather eat literally anywhere else.

We were not on the same level at all. Don't get me wrong; he treated me really, really well. But I just couldn't see a future with him. He wasn't tied to LA anyways — he kept saying how expensive it was, and how he wanted to go back to Virginia. We ended the date on amicable terms, and even went out as friends once or twice after that, but I never heard from him again after that.

# 15

# **Mason**

I spent a lot of Friday nights in my twenties hanging out at The Schooner, a bar in the South Bay. I was a regular, and as such, I got to know the bartender really well. She started a bar softball team, so she gathered up her closest friends and managed to make the most motley crew of softball players ever.

Now, I'm not sure how this happened, but I ended up on the softball team. I am not a team sport kind of person: it gives me anxiety. But, somehow I got talked into it. And I managed to date and/or sleep with all of the single men on the team.

So maybe that makes me a team player?

Somehow, one of the people I ended up exchanging numbers with was Mason. Mason was a former military guy who had been wounded in combat, so he received veteran's benefits and didn't have to work. At this point I was friendly with everyone on the team, so I didn't think anything of it when he asked me to go for drinks at a nice local bar one weekday afternoon in the summer.

We sat outside on the patio at the bar and he opened up to me about his life. I chatted to him about my life, and we had a rather friendly date. We managed to tease each other a bit — you know, the kind where you're being a touch mean to the person, but not in a hurtful way. Clearly we were being flirty.

At the end of the date he kissed me, and I guess I wasn't that surprised. I was fine with it. I tried to see myself being with him in something long-term, but I wasn't sure.

We saw each other a few times on and off after that. Mostly, he would come over when he was drunk, and we would fool around for a while. We never actually had sex, but we would get off. He would be super sweet one minute, and then say something super asshole-ish the next. I could never read him. He told me some intimate personal details about his life that he said almost no one else knew about. But, he would never pull the trigger on us truly dating. No one on the team knew that we were seeing each other.

One evening, after I'd had a couple of drinks, I texted him to come over. He told me he would be there soon.

Well, soon ended up being two hours later. I was pissed, and tired, and I just wanted to go to bed.

We fooled around for a bit, and he went down on me, and made sure that I came. We took a break, in which time I was on the verge of sleep. Suddenly, he asked me to go down on him. I said that I was tired, that I would do it next time.

He threw a fit. I would swear he was a three-year-old. He leaped out of bed, called me selfish and said all kinds of things about how he always goes down on me, and I can't return the favor as he put his clothes on to walk out the door.

I stood there in silence. No one has ever called me selfish in bed before. I am always extremely giving (besides, it's always easier for the man to cum than the woman!). I was too tired to argue, and just let him walk out the door. If he had been so upset about our arrangement, why hadn't he ever just said so in the first place?

He stormed out of the house, and I didn't see him for a while since softball season was over. I was on Facebook not too long after the incident, and he had commented on a mutual friend's post — when I clicked on his profile, he had unfriended me! First time that had ever happened to me.

The next time I saw him, he ignored me altogether — didn't say hi, no eye contact, pretended I didn't even exist. It hurt my feelings, but I tried to keep the perspective that maybe he was interested in me and just didn't know how to handle a relationship emotionally. He seemed like the type.

I see him comment on friend's statuses on Facebook every once in a while, but from what I can tell he's moved to Florida, so I guess I don't need to worry about running into him any time soon.

# 16
# **Luis**

I walked back to my car in the rain, ashamed. I could still taste his dick in my mouth. This night had not gone the way I had predicted. I played back the evening in my mind as the water soaked through my coat.

Luis asked me to text him when I had parked my car — apparently because his parents were home asleep. It was 11:30pm when I had arrived, and he answered the door in red silk pajamas, hugging his muscles in all the right places. His ankle was wrapped, just as he said it would be since he had injured it the day before playing soccer. He hobbled to his room, and excused the mess. He lie back down on the bed and grabbed the remote, asking me what I wanted to watch. I sat down next to him and told him that whatever he wanted was fine with me.

Luis and his friend were sitting at the bar when I walked up on a Sunday night. My favorite bartender was working, and I was really trying to get up the nerve to give him my number.

"Is this seat taken?" I asked Luis. He turned, looked me up and down, and answered, "Of course not."

I sat, and he struck up a conversation with me. He was significantly younger than me — 6 years, in fact. He was a tremendous flirt, and very confident. He told me he loved to play soccer, and was currently attending the local community college. He lived at home with his parents and was only 22. I told him I was a teacher, and he spouted off the typical comments.

"Wow, if you were my teacher I certainly would have had trouble paying attention in your class. Were you ever attracted to any of your students?"

The answer, as always, is no. Never. Not in a million years. And no, none of your teachers were ever attracted to you. Stop projecting.

I glanced at the bartender, wondering if I was going to find some way to sneak him my number. I supposed not, since Luis had started flirting with me. I thought it best to abandon mission and focus on the task at hand.

At the end of the evening I excused myself. Luis asked if we could exchange numbers, and I agreed. We texted over the next few days. On a Friday night, he asked me to come over to his place.

And that's how I found myself sitting on his bed watching TV next to a man in red silk pajamas.

We watched TV in silence for twenty minutes before he made his move. He pulled me back on the bed next to him, nuzzling his nose into my neck until I turned to face him. Then he kissed me. It wasn't a sweet and innocent kiss; it was a kissed filled with desire, with passion and need. I could tell that it wasn't that he needed me, necessarily — he needed sex. I just happened to be the closest person nearby to satisfy that need. I too, however, was filled with longing. I knew this wasn't a formal "date," but I was hoping we would both end the night satisfied.

Eventually, my shirt and bra came off, and he kissed my breasts — more for his own pleasure than my own. He slid off his pajama pants and guided my hand down to his dick. It was large and hard. I stroked it a few times.

"Put your mouth on it," he breathed heavily into my ear. He laid back on the bed as I made my way down to his crotch, kissing his stomach and inner thighs on the way down.

I begin to go to work, listening to his whimpers and moans as my mouth filled. My jaw begins to tire, and I think about giving up until I hear the magic words, "I'm about to cum."

He cums in my mouth. I slow down my strokes until he empties completely. I pull away, and reach back up to kiss him.

He won't kiss me. Not only that, he won't really touch me. He's clearly done with me.

How selfish. An immature lover. Every man knows that you take care of your woman first — the man is going to get his no matter what.

I feel small. Embarrassed. Ashamed. Why did I bother going over there? I regretted my decision.

I was watching a terrible TV show once (*Bored to Death*. Don't bother, it's not very good) where a woman asked the man, "Are you a man or a boy?" He asked what the difference was. She said the most profound and true statement I have ever heard: "With a man you feel like you're being taken and you like it. And with a boy you feel like they're stealing something from you and you don't like it."

This boy had stolen my dignity. And I let him.

"Thanks for coming over," he said as he walked me to the door. I stepped out into the cold night, and began the two-block walk to my car. As I got to the sidewalk it began to rain, as if the sky understood the pain that I was experiencing in that moment. I've done the "walk of shame" before, but this truly felt shameful.

I got in my car, and drove home. I wrapped myself in a blanket and tried to forget what had happened. I did, eventually. It's one of those moments that sucks when you're in it, and then you realize that no one makes you feel a certain way — it's your feelings and yours alone. You control your reaction to the situation. I decided then that no one would make me feel small again. I would either not put myself in a situation where I would feel ashamed, or I would make sure to get out of a situation before I could feel that way. And that's a choice that I have, every day, because I am a strong woman.

And, for the record, that bartender? I did give him my number. He never called or texted. The next time I saw him at the bar he was with his lady-friend and child whom I was not aware of, so I'm glad he never called!

# 17
# Al

I met Al on Match.com. I don't remember much about him, except one key phrase that came out of our date: "hang and bang."

Don't worry, I didn't take on that title.

Al and I met up at a little Mexican food spot in Venice. He decided we were going to drink an entire pitcher of margaritas, with no food except the complimentary chips and salsa.

Sure, get your date liquored up.

We chatted, and I remember the conversation feeling easy. He seemed like a pretty good guy, I suppose. After drinking an entire pitcher of cocktails, we decided to go for a walk on the beach to sober up so we could both drive home.

As we walked along the beach, I finally got up the nerve to ask him, "So, what are you looking for?"

Ah, the unavoidable question. The one that should probably be asked before you ever even go out. Because, God knows, you want to make sure you're both on the same page about what you're looking for. It's pretty painful when you realize that you're looking for your soulmate, someone to marry, and he's looking for a one-night-stand. At this point, I'm looking for someone to date, someone to spend my time with, someone who respects me, listens to me, and wants to see me.

"I'm looking for someone I can hang out at the house with, and bang every once in a while."

Classy.

"So, you're looking for a 'hang and bang'?" I reply, thinking my name for it is pretty clever. I guess in today's nomenclature, we would call it "Netflix and Chill."

"Yeah, I guess that is what I'm looking for. I'm really busy and I don't want to be tied down. Is that something you're interested in?"

Now, keep in mind, before you read my response, this is back before I realized I had options, that I could say no, that I could have standards and respect for myself. That I could find someone who would appreciate me for all of the beautiful gifts I had to offer.

"Yeah, I think I could handle that."

Really, past me?! *Really?* That's okay?! That's how you want to be treated? That's not respect for yourself! That's not what you are looking for! You're not on the same page at all!

"Cool," he says, and kisses me as he grabs my ass.

Totally respectful. Right.

He walks me to my car after we've both sobered up. I drive off. He texts me a few days later, with the ever-thoughtful **hey.**

We chatted a few times back and forth, but never actually made plans to see each other again. We fell out of contact. I'm sure he found a girl that was much more forth-coming with the hanging and banging, so he didn't need to make the moves on me. Fine by me.

Update: I was out one night with some girlfriends about five years later, drinking and having a good time, when I saw him in a bar. He recognized me, and we hung out a bit. He was super grabby, and kept putting his arm around me. This was just as I was beginning to get my sense of what is okay for my personal space, and what's not. I kept trying to shrug him off, but wasn't being as direct with him as I could have been.

At some point, we all decide to go for pizza. As we get in line, Al grabs my arm and tries to talk me into leaving with him. I try to pull my arm away, and I say I'm not going to leave with him, but he grips my arm tighter. Alarm bells go off in my head.

I yell at him to leave me alone. I use my other arm to pry his hand off my arm, and I tell him to lose my number. He looks pissed, but makes the smart choice to leave before he can cause even more of a scene. And I never spoke to him again.

# 18
# BMW

Kendra and I went out one night to a bar to watch the Lakers in Game 7 at a local bar in Manhattan Beach. The bar was packed, and since the Lakers won, everyone in the bar was celebrating. Somehow in the celebratory melee I was chatted up by a beautiful 6'4 man named BMW. He was half Black, half Japanese, in his forties and absolutely gorgeous. We chatted throughout the night, and ended up drunkenly exchanging numbers.

The following weekend, BMW asked to see me — he wanted to grab drinks together. I suggested a bar close to my place. When we met up, I realized how bad my beer goggles were when I met BMW.

BMW worked for BMW, in their corporate offices in Los Angeles. And he wouldn't shut up about his job. All he wanted to talk about was cars. The more he talked, the more I realized he had nothing to say. I tried to overlook that since he was treating me so nicely. Maybe I could deal with dumb for a while? I deserved someone nice, at least...

BMW actually ended up coming out to a bar with me to have dinner with my Godparents. Fantastic first date, right? He seemed fine with it, and my Godfather is a little bit of a gearhead, so the two of them got along well.

After that date, BMW and I agreed to see each other again. He asked me out for dinner on a Sunday night — he actually wanted me to meet him in Hermosa Beach.

When I arrived, it turns out he had been partying all day with his friends — he was hammered. Apparently not an unusual occurrence for him, I learned. He got us a cab to a sushi place, and didn't understand that I didn't want to drink anything. He couldn't fathom that I wasn't drinking. Clearly someone enjoyed their partying. There was no way I was going to party on a Sunday night. I was a responsible adult and had work the next day. He kept trying to encourage me to drink, to get on his level. I politely declined.

BMW and I met one more time, at another bar. Once again, he talked about BMWs. Once again, he proceeded to get drunk. I felt like this game was getting very old, very fast. I already knew this wasn't going anywhere.

However, I had needs.

I proceeded to get him back to my place. We began to fool around, and eventually he pulled out his dick. It was the tiniest penis I had ever seen. Like, my whole mouth fit around it without any use of hands. Like, when we had sex, I had to stop myself from asking out loud if it was in. When he finally finished (because I certainly didn't) he commented that the sex was amazing.

Yawn.

I can't. Dumb, tiny penis, and drinks too much? This is not Mr. Right. This is not even Mr. Right Now.

Fortunately, our texts just sort of petered and died out after that. I didn't much have to do anything to end it. I was pretty certain he was only drunk texting me anyways.

We never spoke again.

## LOGISTICS: TIPS AND TRICKS FOR ONLINE DATING

*For those of you who've been in the game a while, please note my rookie mistakes. If you're hoping to get into the online dating game, do as I say, not as I do. I promise other people have had better luck than I have!*

# 19

# Hot Cop (aka Never Recycle)

I met Hot Cop through Match.com. He was 5'8, Asian, and a cop for LAUSD. For our first date, we met for coffee at a Starbucks in a shopping plaza. After coffee, we walked around Best Buy and looked through the music section. He was kind of shy, and was clearly following my lead. He was fine: nothing spectacular, kind of blah, but not an asshole. It was enough to warrant a second date, I supposed.

He wanted to take me to an Angels baseball game for our second date. I'm not necessarily an Angels fan (I look way better in blue than I do in red, so I'm definitely a Dodgers fan), but I had never been to Angels Stadium so I thought it would be fun.

During the game, they started to play Journey's "Don't Stop Believing" as part of a sing-a-long. Now, even if you don't love the song, you have to sing along, right? He was super serious and clearly didn't want to ruin his tough guy demeanor. He refused to sing along. I thought this might be a deal breaker — I wasn't much interested in someone who couldn't be a goofball, at least a little bit of the time. I'm a huge goofball.

I had a therapy session the week after our second date, so my therapist asked me how it was going with Hot Cop.

"Fine, except...he's boring!"

"I dated a boring guy like that once. He was *so boring,*" she told me. She then said I should continue to date him. I think she was hoping that he would grow on me and that I would end up with him. It was true: there was nothing fundamentally wrong with him. He treated me really well.

We continued to text daily, and he decided he wanted to take me to Disneyland for our third date. We were supposed to go on Saturday, and he had agreed to text me on Thursday night to confirm plans.

Thursday night came and went, without a single text from Hot Cop. That seemed a little off. I panicked a little at the thought of him abandoning me. He was so good about following through when he said he would. And it never feels good to think I'm being rejected. I tried not to have a complete meltdown about him not texting me.

Finally, after hours and hours of agony, my phone buzzed Friday afternoon.

**Hi**

Fucking really?! That's what you're going to lead with? I tried to hide my disdain.

The next text came through.

**This is Hot Cop's partner. Hot Cop had emergency surgery on Thursday night, so he wanted you to know he is okay. He'll give you a call later. He's still recovering.**

What? Surgery? What happened? I felt like a complete asshole. I had been selfish and hadn't even considered that he might have an emergency. Okay, time to take a step back and remember that other people matter too, Little Miss Selfish. Later that evening, I received another text from Hot Cop. He didn't want to talk about what happened, and he didn't think we could go to Disneyland on Saturday, but he still wanted to see me. He asked me if I was free on Sunday instead. I told him I was, so he asked if he could come over and then we could grab lunch. **Are you sure you're going to be up for it by Sunday?** I asked him. He said he would.

Sunday finally rolled around, and he showed up to my door with his arm in a sling.

"What happened?!?" I cried. I resisted the urge to mother the shit out of him. I am a natural caretaker, so I wanted to do everything I could for him. It's a habit I'm trying to reign in. I don't need to mother everyone all of the time.

"I got shot," he responded, with a sheepish chuckle. I gasped. He proceeded to tell me how after his shift at the school, the LAPD asked him to patrol for them for a bit. He ended up chasing a stolen car, and the guy hopped out and ended up shooting him. "If the bullet went two inches to the right, I would have to have major surgery to repair bone. Right now I just have to wear this sling and then they want me to do physical therapy. I'm just going to skip it though." He seemed to downplay his injury. He was supposed to do a triathlon in a few months, and he was still planning on doing the swim. He was going to have his doctor friend sign off on his physical therapy so he could go back to work.

"I don't think that's a good idea," I told him. He brushed off my concern, and again decided to play tough guy. I wasn't thrilled at the idea that this guy wanted to skip doctor's orders.

We went to dinner and had no more discussion about it. A few weeks went by, and we had a date planned. He canceled the date about an hour before we were supposed to meet up, because something came up at work. I couldn't get past the idea of constantly being worried about his well-being at work, plus I don't do well with canceling. Partnered with the idea that overall he was boring, I decided to end it. We still remained Facebook friends and on friendly terms.

Once, I thought I saw him working at the Rose Bowl during a UCLA football game, so I texted him to ask. It wasn't him, but it seemed to re-spark interest. He told me that he had moved to Colorado, but his parents still lived in Pasadena. We messaged back and forth a few times, and found our way to Facebook Messenger. He stated that he wanted to take me out on a date. I could see that his location said he was still in Colorado, so I called him on it. He stated that he was coming back that weekend, and wanted to take me out. I reluctantly agreed. Maybe I just needed to go with it. Maybe he would be different. Maybe I would feel differently about him. I was willing to give it another shot.

The day of our date, I messaged him on Facebook to say hello, he messaged me back. We were supposed to meet in just a few hours. Weirdly, his location still said he was in Colorado.

**How come it still says you're in Colorado?** I asked him.

Suddenly, it said he was offline. I couldn't send him any more messages. He had blocked me!

Weird. Clearly, this date wasn't going to happen. Why did he get so skittish all of a sudden? Had he ever really planned to go out with me again? Was he setting me up? Note to self: never recycle. I gave him up for a reason in the first place; there's no reason to go back.

I never heard from him again.

# 20

# Elijah
# (aka Value my Time)

I once went on a date with a guy from Match.com. I can't remember that much about him, other than that he had a child with the same name as his.

When we finally met up in Santa Monica, he didn't even take me out for coffee, a drink, or dinner.

Instead, we met at 3rd Street Promenade, and he asked if I wanted to walk around for a while. I agreed, thinking we would walk for a bit, and then grab coffee.

No, we walked.

For.

An.

Hour.

Look, I'm not one of those women who needs to have a man spend a bunch of money on me. And I realize that dating can get expensive. Even just for cocktails. But at least buy me a coffee. Show me I'm worth spending money on.

Instead, we walked around for an hour, and he even took a phone call in the middle of our date.

I don't need you to spend a bunch of money on me, but I do need you to pay attention to me. Show me that you value my time.

And he couldn't do either one of those things.

I can imagine he didn't much want to go on another date with me either. We left cordially, but I wasn't surprised or upset when I never heard from him again.

# 21

# The Custom
# (aka ALWAYS Talk to the Date!)

New rule: always, always, ALWAYS talk to the Internet date before you go out with him. Always. I cannot stress that enough. It doesn't have to be a long conversation, but just enough to know you can understand him!

I am what I call an "equal opportunity employer" — I don't discriminate against any of my dates based on religion, ethnicity or race. I *will*, however, discriminate based on age. I started teaching high school when I was 22. Some of my former students are only four years younger than me. I won't date anyone who is more than five years younger than me. Besides, men aren't as mature as women anyways, right? A guy who's younger than 26 doesn't typically know what he wants, may not have his career or housing situation in order, or isn't necessarily looking to get married, so I tend to stay away from those anyway.

As an equal opportunity employer, I find myself attracted to many different types of men. Guys often ask me what's my "type." I can't really ever answer that question. I've been on dates with men who identify as Latino, Black, Asian, Indian, Native American, White, and Other/Mixed Race.

On this particular occasion, an Indian man contacted me on Match.com. We chatted a bit online, and the conversation seemed to flow fairly well. After chatting on the app, we decided to meet up the next night. Fatal mistake: we set all of it up through the online dating messaging system.

We met at an outdoor pool bar close to my house on a weekday evening (I never give up weekend nights to go on a first meeting with someone from online — that's prime time!). The minute he opened his mouth, I couldn't help myself.

*Is he speaking English?*

You know how sometimes, once you realize someone is speaking in an accent, it takes you a minute to get past the accent and actually focus on what they're saying? Like your brain takes a minute to decipher the beauty of their language? Yeah, mine never quite got there. When he spoke, I had to focus all of my energy into deciphering what he was saying.

Apparently he'd been in the US for two years. He lived in a house with four other people, and worked for some cable TV company.

At no point during our date did he ask a single question about me. In fact, I hardly spoke. I'm not sure if he was nervous, or what, but he rambled on the entire date. All I did was sip my red wine. I was not interested in anything he had to say — he just kept talking about work or his roommates. He had no hobbies.

After my cocktail, I said it was getting late (it was 8:15pm) and I had to go home and lesson plan (I never do work at home).

He didn't message me, and I *definitely* didn't message him.

# 22
# Don't Do Any of This
# (aka I'm an Idiot a Lot of the Time)

One of my favorite date spots is this Cuban place down the street from my house. The food is good, the drinks are strong, and the prices can't be beat. I recently visited the restaurant, and recalled a date that I had there one evening. Now that I look back on this date, I'd like to run commentary on all of the mistakes I made.

I met the guy on Match.com. We chatted, I don't remember about what; it's inconsequential. I do remember he was an engineer, and had just bought a new Saturn. Somehow we decided that I was going to meet him at his house. (*Who does that??! I didn't even talk to this guy on the phone before we went out...this was before the previous story).* I met him at his house, he asked me to come inside, and he got something from his bedroom. *(I saw this dude's bedroom on a first date?!?! I had talked to this guy for probably not much more than an hour. This guy could have tried to sleep with me for all I know...or rape, even. Okay, maybe a bit extreme — but I've known people things like that have happened to.)* He drove us in his new car *(I got in the car with this guy? I bet I didn't even have cab fare in case something went wrong!)*, and he had to stop by the bank to get money.

Okay, here's my issue: it's tacky, just **tacky** to go to the bank on a date. And it's a waste of *my* time. That's shit that should be done ahead of time. Or just pay with a credit card. Alright, so it's not necessarily a red flag, but it is strike one.

We go to Havanamania, and dinner goes well. We have a few mojitos each. I'm enjoying myself, at least to the extent that I am sure I want to spend a bit more time with him. Dinner is fast coming to a close, and he pays the tab. He suggests going for a drive through Palos Verdes, the local hills (there are some romantic views, and some good make-out spots). I agree *(again, I put myself into this dangerous situation where, pessimistically, I could be assaulted in some manner. I know it's grim thinking, but I'm trying to be realistic).*

We get in the car, and we begin to cruise. As we come around the first curve, he guns it up to 60 mph. I realize he doesn't want to go for a romantic drive — he wants to test out his new car! He wants to see what it's capable of! I tense my fingers on the handhold of the door. As we zip through the first curve and into the second, I begin to realize what a bad idea this is. *(Really, genius? Now you think it's a bad idea? Especially after this guy has had a couple drinks and his judgment is impaired? Awesome call.)*

After about three minutes of crazy curves and savage switchbacks, I finally get up the nerve to tell him to slow down. He does, but only for a few curves, and then guns it back up. I begin to get really nervous. Eventually, I ask him just to take me back. I think I probably used the excuse of "it's getting late."

He dropped me off at my car. I think I was shaking too much to kiss him. I got in the car and decided that all of THAT was a bad idea.

I didn't see or hear from him again.

# 23

# Jeffrey
# (aka Never Dinner on a First Date)

I re-joined Match.com after a few years of teaching, when it became socially acceptable to do online dating.

One of the first guys I spoke with on there was a man named Jeffrey. We were both in our mid-twenties, and he lived in Hollywood. He was a comedy writer. His emails were witty and well put together. I couldn't wait to go on a date with him. I love to laugh, and a sense of humor is such a turn-on in my book, I knew I would really like him.

He let me choose the restaurant where we would have dinner, so I chose my favorite Italian place on the West Side. He arrived, and we were escorted to our table.

I started the conversation. I had read online that week that I should work to make my date feel comfortable, and in doing so, that would make me feel comfortable, and appear warm, open and approachable to my date.

"How was your day?"

"How was my day? That's a very interesting question," he replied, truly pondering his answer. He sat, deep in thought for what seemed to be a ridiculously long time.

He then replied with something boring. Something completely inane, and nothing I remember or care to even make up. Because it wasn't funny.

Nothing about the date was funny. He was kind of obnoxious, and couldn't relate to my students at all. He didn't understand my passion for mathematics.

And I was stuck at dinner with this guy.

Somehow I managed to make it through dinner. And it was at that point in time that I vowed to myself never to go to dinner with an online first date again. I didn't want to be stuck making conversation with someone I didn't like for an extended period of time. I decided then it would be a drink or a cup of coffee to start. And I've done a fairly good job of sticking with that rule ever since.

# 24
# Clyde
# (aka False Advertising Sucks)

Clyde was adorable in his photos. He had kind of a nerdy thing going on, with the thick-rimmed glasses, plaid button up shirt with suspenders, and button up suit jacket. He was stocky, and he claimed to be 5'9 on his profile.

When we met, however, his look was a different story. He was stocky, but closer to 5'6. He was a total Monet (c'mon, you have to know the *Clueless* quote: "From far away it's okay, but up close it's a big ol' mess.") He was cross-eyed, with a bad complexion. How much Photoshop was done on those photos? His pants were way too big — both in length and in the waist — and his shirt was way too tight. His breath smelled.

I call false advertising.

I may not be model-skinny, but at least I have truth in advertising. I provide up close facial photos as well as pictures that show my voluptuous body. I don't pretend to be anything that I'm not.

I wish I had had the nerve to Lemon Law him. (You know, like that episode of *How I Met Your Mother* where Barney wants to apply the car "Lemon Law" to dating? He wants to avoid spending time on a date when the date is obviously not going where he wants it to.)

Clyde and I had a happy hour drink, and then I called it quits. I think I said I had to run errands or something. I couldn't get out of there fast enough.

And I never heard from him again.

# 25

# Parking Lot
# (aka Don't Be Afraid to Say NO)

I met Parking Lot on OkCupid. He was a little more blue collar than I was used to: he was in a union and did electrical work for a living. I wasn't sure it was going to work out between the two of us from the start, but I thought I would give it a shot. Whatever I had been doing wasn't working, so I thought I'd change it up a bit.

For our first date, we had coffee in Santa Monica. Conversation seemed fine, so we proceeded to have dinner at a sushi place near by. As dinner came to a close and he walked me back to my car, he grabbed my hand and held it. It was nice. He kissed me in front of my car in the parking lot, but kept it very PG, which I appreciated. We agreed to go out on a second date.

Parking Lot picked me up from my house on our second date. He hugged and kissed me hello. The kiss seemed a bit long for a hello kiss, but I wasn't necessarily opposed, since I enjoy kissing. He drove us to a chain restaurant at the local mall for our meal.

Dinner was fine. The conversation wasn't anything amazing. He seemed nice enough. I was probably going to give him a third date, since there didn't seem to be anything glaringly wrong with him. I wasn't completely enthralled with our conversation, but I hoped maybe that would grow with time.

After dinner, we walked back to the car. Parking Lot put his arm around me, and I snuggled into him. It was nice, this physical intimacy. It had been a while since I had been close with anyone, and I was enjoying the closeness and bond we were building. As we approached the car, he turned to face me, and kissed me. It was a pleasant kiss. Tender, yet passionate. The passion intensified. We were standing under a street lamp in the mall parking lot. I was acutely aware of how public the situation was.

I suddenly felt his hand on my breast. I brushed it off, and we continued to kiss. He was pushing boundaries, but as long as he could respect the ones that I set, I would be okay with it.

Then it happened. He put his hand on my pussy. I pulled away.

"What the hell?!?" I was angry. I felt violated. How dare he try something like that? The trust we were building had been stripped away.

"What? You've been giving me mixed signals all night. You know you want it."

What kind of an answer is that? Mixed signals? Just because I show you interest doesn't mean I want you to stick your hand on my pussy in public! And brushing your hand off my bra was not an invitation for you to travel further south.

"Take me home. Now." He rolled his eyes.

"Fine." He clearly thought I was overreacting.

Side note: I can't believe I got in the car with him. I can't believe I let him take me home. I should have just walked/called a cab/called an Uber. I shouldn't have spent one more second with that man.

The ride home was silent. I was annoyed, and embarrassed. He was pissed off. He stopped the car in front of my apartment. I got out, and slammed the door. He sped off. I never heard from him again.

# 26

# The French Guy
# (aka Listening is Important)

I come across a lot of people who spend their time waiting to talk, instead of listening. It's like when I'm talking, you can see that they are eager for me to finish what I'm saying, just so they can talk about what they want to talk about. There is no shred of listening happening in the conversation.

Such is the case of the French Guy I met on Match.com. I don't even remember his name. I know he was older than me by about ten years, and he had been in the US for fifteen years or so. He smoked, which was on my "no" list, but I figured all of this list stuff hasn't helped me find the person I'm looking for, so I might as well open myself up to some things I hadn't considered before.

He decides that we should meet at a bar for our first date, on a Sunday afternoon, in the fall. Now, not sure if you've ever been to a bar on a Sunday afternoon before, but they're usually where football fans meet to watch their games. If I watched NFL football, I suppose I would know that. We'll just say that he gets a pass on not knowing, because he's from a foreign country.

We met for drinks, and practically had to yell to each other over the sound of cheering in the bar. I'm used to bar living, so it wasn't the end of the world. It's not exactly the situation I want for a first meeting, but it's fine.

Except that after about fifteen minutes, the conversation seemed to have turned into a pissing contest of who had been to which places. I was trying to find common ground between the two of us, but I felt like he was trying to one-up me at every turn.

Me: Have you been to this restaurant? It's my favorite...

Him: No. Have you been to this really expensive restaurant? I know the chef and eat there all the time.

Me: No, tell me about it. It sounds amazing. How did you discover it?

Him: *insert some pedantic story where it's obvious he just wants to talk and doesn't actually care if I'm listening.*

Him again: Have you traveled much?

Me: No, not really. I've been to London and Paris [this was a while ago], but that's it.

Him: Oh, well, I've been to *insert list of twenty countries here*

Me: Oh, that's so cool! Which one is your favorite?

Him: blah blah blah.

I know I was listening at the time. I just don't care enough to remember now. I just know that he wanted to hear himself talk.

After the date ended, we went our separate ways, and I never heard from him again.

# 27

# Racist
# (aka It's Worth It to Take
# Your Time to Weed Them Out)

He messaged me on Plenty of Fish (PoF) on a Friday. This was at the point where I was more interested in meeting than I was exchanging a thousand messages, so we decided to meet up the next day.

He was new to the area, so I found us a cool coffee shop halfway between us. From the text messages, I knew he was from Ohio, and had previously been in the military. I didn't know much else, but I was curious to see if there was any chemistry between us.

I'm big into chemistry. And scent. I have a very sensitive nose. If a man smells weird, or has a strange scent to me, I can't stand it. I always question whether or not I should be even doing online dating, since my primal instincts have a tendency to take over and decide whether I'm attracted or not.

I arrived early, and took a seat outside. I was wearing jeans, heels, and a cute top.

He came to meet me in flip flops, board shirts, a white under shirt and a hat. Already I'm disappointed.

We went inside to grab a coffee, and came back outside to have a seat in the beautiful California sunshine.

As we began to converse, I realized that he and I had fundamentally different views about the world.

He was definitely pro-gun. (I'm not necessarily anti-gun, but I have more views on the liberal end of the spectrum.)

He believed in being fiscally conservative (also not where I ally).

And he was racist as fuck.

I was speaking about my previous teaching job, where students from low-income communities were given access to college-preparatory materials so they had an equitable opportunity to attend college.

His response? "The only reason Black kids even go to college is for basketball."

No. Nonono. Fuck you, buddy. Your biased and uneducated views of America are so royally fucked, I have to educate you. Right now.

"How fucking dare you make a statement like that! That is the most racist thing I have heard in my life!" I proceeded to yell and berate him for a good five minutes about the inaccuracies of the statement that he had made, and how racist he was.

I announced to him that I was leaving. I can imagine at this point he was glad that I was taking off. I stormed off to my car, fuming angrily all the way.

I plopped into my car, huffing and puffing from anger. I was still irate at him, and the idea that there are people in this country who actually believe this statement to be true.

I drove off in a rush. I couldn't get out of there fast enough. Fuck that guy.

And I never heard from him again.

# 28

# Amir
# (aka It's Okay to Date
# Multiple People at Once)

Another lovely PoF date took place between myself and the amazing Amir. Amir was half Persian, and half Guatemalan, and 100% gorgeous. He was 26 (at the time I was 30) and still lived at home with his parents. We made plans to grab coffee after he got back from a weekend in Vegas.

He stood me up.

I texted him when we were supposed to meet, and said that I was at the coffee shop, and he texted me back with something along the lines of "oh my god I completely forgot! I'm so sorry! Will you let me make it up to you?"

I said fine, and he promised me he would meet me the next evening at Starbucks, and that he wouldn't forget.

He made good on his word, and didn't disappoint. He was sweet, but a little bit stupid. He was hot, but didn't realize that he was hot, which is the best kind — he wasn't smug or arrogant.

After coffee, we agreed on a second date. He picked out a cute sushi place for us to go to with one of those conveyor belts that goes through the whole restaurant. I had a good time — we talked, and laughed, and after lunch was over we walked to the 99 Cent Store that was in the plaza. It was a hot day, and he commented something about coming over to his house and using the pool. I politely declined, and we continued into the store.

We spent almost an hour in there, looking at random stuff, commenting to one another, making conversation. Three more times during our time in the store he hinted about me putting on a swimsuit and coming over to lay by the pool. All three times I told him no. It wasn't about going to the pool — this guy was trying to see me in as little clothing as possible.

Finally we ended the date. We kissed in the parking lot for a quick second (it was the middle of the day, and I am not big on public displays of affection), and we agreed to go out again.

Two days later he messaged me to go out again. I said yes. Somehow we got on the conversation about online dating and how Plenty of Fish was working out. I shared that I assumed the men I was dating were always seeing multiple people, until there was a conversation otherwise, and that I was the same. I likened online dating to buying a car: you are testing driving multiple cars to narrow it down to one car. Once you've driven that car multiple times, and you're familiar with it, that's when you decide to buy it.

Apparently our views differed. He stated that I should only be talking to and dating one person at a time. That once I began a conversation with a man, I should only be talking to that man, and that man alone.

So the minute a man messages me, I'm supposed to date only that person, even though I've never met them? That defeats the purpose of dating! You date to get to know someone! I can't automatically be in a relationship with someone I've never met! I argued over text.

Well, your [yes, he used the incorrect form of "you're"] obviously looking for a quick hook up and I'm clearly not looking for that, so this isn't going to work out. He replied. He basically called me a slut for going on dates with multiple people!

Never in my life have I come across someone who thinks that monogamous dating begins from the first message.

I never heard from him again.

## BAD IDEA

*Why oh why did I go out with him?*

# 29
# The Raven

When I lived in Westchester in my mid-twenties, I used to work out at the Bally's in Inglewood. I had a personal trainer named Ollie. When I was working out with Ollie once, his friend interrupted us to chat with Ollie. His friend was handsome — tall, beautiful chocolate skin with shoulder-length dreadlocks. I stuck out my hand and introduced myself. Ollie introduced the man to me as "The Raven."

"Hi, I'm The Raven," he responded back. This man just decided his name would be an animal, with a definite article? Not just "Raven" but *The* Raven. As we chatted, I learned this was his boxing name — he had been an Olympic boxer in his country a few years before. He was definitely older than me (in his late forties, I would guess), with eyes that peered into my soul when he looked at me. Somehow we flirted enough during my workout for him to ask for my number. He gave me his business card and sure enough, it had his name on it — "The Raven."

We ended up going out to dinner at one of my favorite Cuban spots. Conversation was fine — we chatted about his life in his country, his boxing career, and my teaching career. Suddenly, the conversation took a weird turn.

"So, would you consider yourself a freak?" he inquired. I was taken aback. How the fuck do I answer something like that? It's a first date and I'm not quite ready to reveal my freaky side. I need to have some sense of trust first. I feel like the freak question is more of a fourth date question. I giggled uncomfortably, then tried to recover with a coy smile. I replied that I'd rather save that for a later conversation.

He wouldn't let it go. "Yeah, I bet you're a freak. I'm definitely a freak." He then went into detail about the kinds of things he liked in bed, including some weird shit that made my skin crawl. I got the feeling he wasn't so much interested in dating me as he was in fucking me.

At that point, I had mostly checked out of the date. I wasn't attracted to a man who wasn't interested in getting to know me as a person. Finally, dinner ended and I rushed to get out of there as fast as possible. Of course, he tried to ram his tongue down my throat at the end of the date (some men just can't take a hint as to when a woman isn't interested), and I had to do my best to push him off me. I got in my car and sped away as fast as possible, trying to remind myself that I'm worth getting to know, worthy of a man who wants to take his time and get to know me. I don't need to feel objectified and uncomfortable with any man at dinner.

Fortunately I only saw him at the gym once after that, and I managed to avoid all contact with him. I moved shortly after and changed gyms. I never saw him again.

# 30
# Nathan

I met Nathan through Craigslist. He responded to an ad that I posted looking for a date. As a first date he took me out to dinner at a super nice restaurant on the Hermosa Beach pier.

I knew a bit about him before we went on our date: he was 27, as was I, and he had a son. He was living in Palos Verdes, an extremely nice area with giant homes.

When we met for dinner, he was very cute, and super sweet.

As we continued the evening though, I realized that this man was in a heap of drama that I didn't want to be a part of.

Yes, he lived in Palos Verdes, but that was only part time. The rest of the time he lived in San Francisco.

With his wife. Well, they were separated. But he was splitting his time up there for work because of his son. They were still living in the same house, though. Just sleeping in separate bedrooms.

"How long have you been separated?" I inquired.

"Two weeks."

Two fucking weeks. Wow.

Wow.

Talk about getting right back on the horse. He wastes no time, huh? Man, that is a whole boat-load of trouble I am not willing to get into. So disappointing, because he seems like such a great guy. But that is too much drama and emotional baggage that hasn't been processed yet, and I was not at a place to deal with or wait around for someone like that to get their shit together.

He paid for dinner, and I thanked him for a lovely evening, and went home.

I never heard from him again.

# 31

# Steven

Steven had just moved back from Germany. He had moved there to be with his girlfriend, and things hadn't worked out, so he had moved back about two weeks ago. I took another sip of margarita while I listened to his story. I didn't think he would be ready to date again so soon, but everyone is different and I figured he knew himself better than I did.

He had just moved into an apartment not too far from the Hermosa Beach Pier where we were enjoying drinks. He asked me if I wanted to go back to his apartment. I said yes, since I wasn't quite ready to drive home yet. We walked back to his place — what an amazing view of the water! If I was more superficial, I would have continued dating him just for his apartment, but I don't have the ability to be fake like that. He lived on the top floor of a building right on the strand, and his entire living room was one giant window. He also had a rooftop deck that was perfect for barbequing and watching the sunset.

We sat on his couch and he played guitar for me. I fell instantly in love: his voice was beautiful, and I'm a sucker for a musician. At one point he leaned over and kissed me. I was thrilled. I thought I saw a future with this man.

(That moment where you're blinded by what's happening: he's only been broken up with his girlfriend of two years for like 0.5 seconds. It's his first time being single in a hot second. He's invited me over to his place during our first date. Sometimes I don't know how to read a friends-with-benefits situation when I see one.)

Eventually I tell him I need to come up for air. I pry him off of me, put my shirt back on, and ask him to drive me back to my car. I'm not ready yet to sleep with him, I know that much. I'm not ready to let any part of him near my pants. He drives me back to my car, all the while professing his sincere like for me, telling me how amazing I am and how he can't wait to see me again.

I kiss him goodbye, and we agree to see each other again later in the week. He tells me that the following week he's trying out for American Idol, so he needs to be on his best behavior all week.

He comes over to pick me up later in the week. We sit on the couch before we head out for whatever he has planned for us. He reaches over to give me a kiss, and then immediately grabs my boob.

I push his hand away. Jesus, buddy, it's the middle of the day, we're sitting in my living room, and you've only seen me for less than 10 minutes. I push his hand away, and he tries to replace it almost immediately. I push his hand away again. I pull away. "Stop." I say to him.

"What? It's all in fun."

"I know, but I'm not ready for that yet."

"You know, you're going to have to open up to me at some point in time. You can't stay closed off forever."

I'm sorry, what? You're making it sound as if I'm staying emotionally closed off to you, when really I'm just not ready to give myself to you physically. And don't try to manipulate me into sleeping with you. That's not fun for anyone involved.

I tell him I'll open up to him when I feel safe to open up to him. I can tell I'll need to be closed off to him just a bit longer. I don't feel safe. I don't feel like I can trust him with my heart or my body. I don't think he's respecting me in the way I want to be respected.

We go out for a walk and come back, and again, he wants to go for it, and not respect my space or listen when I tell him no. He tries to use the line again that I need to open up. I tell him he needs to go, that he's not respecting me. The only fight he puts up is that he just wants to be with me, because I'm "so gorgeous." I'm not falling for that. He's just trying to sleep with me, and I'm not ready to sleep with him.

I never hear from him again.

# 32
# Cock and Bull

I met a guy from Match.com. We decided to have lunch on a Sunday at the Cock and Bull, a small British bar in Venice.

As we met and chatted, conversation flowed easily. I wasn't necessarily that attracted to him — there seemed to be some chemistry missing — but I thought maybe that was something that could grow.

At the end of the date, we said our goodbyes. It's always the most awkward part. Do you try to set up a second date? Do you even ask? Do you just avoid it and do it by text message later on? Because what if the other person isn't interested in a second date? Do you risk the rejection right then? Or what if you're not interested, and he tries to ask for a second date, you say no, and he flips out? (It's happened. It's been known to happen. Some guys don't handle rejection well.)

In my present-day life, I have been trying to be much more honest, brave, and vulnerable in all aspects of my life, including dating. If I'm interested in a guy, I tell him at the end of the date that I want a second date. I'll tell him that I want to see him again. I have to be brave to be vulnerable, but it helps me to be my most authentic self, and to never have regrets about not asking for what I want in life.

So, we said our goodbyes, our "nice meeting you's" and went our separate ways.

I thought about him the rest of the day Sunday.

And the next day.

You know, the feelings where you just want to know if he likes you back. The thought that you're desired.

I received a text from him on Tuesday.

**Hey, I had fun the other day. Interested in being friends with benefits?**

Boy, if I had a dollar for every time a guy asked me to be friends with benefits. I'd have enough money to buy a lifetime supply of batteries for my vibrator.

I thought about it for a second. I really did. Because sometimes you just need to be sexually satisfied.

And sometimes you just want to be respected as a person. And often times, for me, there is not a lot of overlap in those two circles.

I texted him back a quick **No thanks!**

His response? **If you change your mind, I'm interested.**

Gee, thanks. Glad you want to fuck me, but don't want to date me.

I never heard from him again.

# 33

# Mark

"So, I need you at my wedding because we're hiring a karaoke band!" proclaimed my friend Cindy into the phone.

"Wait...Derek PROPOSED!? You're getting MARRIED?!?! Of COURSE I'll be there!" I exclaimed with sheer excitement. "And you know I'll be the first one on the mic!"

"Great!" she said. "The wedding is in ninety days. We must be crazy, but it was the only time in the next year and a half that our schedules seemed to line up!"

I told her I'd be there, and hung up the phone.

As we chatted about the wedding in the days that followed, she told me she wanted to give me fair warning: Mark would be there.

*Mark?* I thought to myself. *Do I know a Mark?*

And then it all came back to me.

I met Mark two years earlier through Cindy at karaoke night at a local bar. He seemed nice enough. Mark was bald, black, short and sort of pudgy. He asserted right away that he thought I was attractive, and wanted to take me out sometime in the near future. I agreed. After a few cocktails and a drunk rendition of "Don't Stop Believing" by Journey, he asked for my number.

He called me the next day, and asked me to dinner. I agreed, and he picked me up.

And took me to Denny's.

Now, Mark is well over 30 years old. He also has a well-paying job, and dresses nice. Why does a grown-ass man feel the need to take a woman to Denny's on a date? I won't usually step foot into a Denny's unless I've had quite a few cocktails, and nothing else is open. (If you're keeping score, this is the second time I've been taken to Denny's on a date.)

We sit and begin to chat. He tells me how Denny's is his favorite restaurant. (What is with these guys? No taste in restaurants whatsoever? Where are your taste buds? Do you have a stomach of steel?)

He then begins to tell me about how well he treats women when he dates them. About how he will buy them Louis Vuitton purses. Then he tells me about the last girl he dated, and how he bought her multiple Louis Vuitton purses, and she was so happy about it.

*If you can afford Louis Vuitton, why am I at Denny's?*

I sit and listen patiently. I decide this dude is just not for me. I don't need Louis Vuitton purses, I need someone who is going to carry on a good conversation, and not talk about his exes the entire date. He takes me back to my house. We hugged goodbye. He kind of texted me a few times after that, but it just sort of fizzled out.

Fast forward two years: I'm at Cindy's wedding, where the only people I know are my friend Courtney and her boyfriend KC. We're sitting at our table, closest to the bar (note to self: thank Cindy for the fantastic seats!), and I spot Mark next to the bar. He is texting, and looks up the minute I notice him. He glances at me, and a look of recognition washes over his face. He smiles, and saunters over to my table.

"We went to high school together, right?"

I am flabbergasted. He doesn't remember me? Come on, I'm amazing. How can he not remember that we went on one date together two years ago? Oh...because I didn't remember either until Cindy reminded me. I've had enough wine at this point that I truly believe I can say whatever I want.

"No, we went on a date together a few years ago."

"Oh." He looks confused for a minute as he reaches into the recesses of his memory to try to figure out my name, and where we went.

"Yeah, you took me to Denny's," I tell him. This obviously isn't helping — he's probably taken many girls to Denny's.

He smiles and pretends to know who I am. "Yeah, I remember. Tell me your name again?" We chitchat for a few minutes after I re-introduce myself, and he proceeds to ask for my number, because he can't remember why we stopped seeing each other in the first place.

Good to know I'm still hot enough for him.

I tell him no thanks, I'm not really interested in dating right now. In reality, I'm just not interested in dating *him*. He says he understands, and we go our separate ways.

I sing "Love Shack" with the karaoke band and enjoy the rest of my evening.

# 34

# Q

Alright, I'll admit it. Sometimes I make bad choices when it comes to men. As if this entire book isn't evidence of that statement.

I met Q on OkCupid. He seemed nice enough from his profile. We decided to meet for coffee. The first strike should have been that he sent me the address for the wrong Starbucks. I get it: there is one on every other corner, so it can be a challenge to get to the right one sometimes.

When we managed to find each other and actually meet, he was wearing sweatpants. SWEATPANTS. I was in a sundress and wedges, and he rolled up in his house clothes. I tried to cut him a little slack, and take into consideration the fact that he had his foot in a boot, but I'm not sure that warranted sweatpants. Maybe that should have been strike 2? Conversation on our first date seemed normal, although he did ask me, "Have you ever been with a Black man?" (He was Black.) I told him I had, and he said he'd never been with a white girl before. I thought nothing of it, but it apparently should have been strike 3.

For our second date we met at a Peruvian restaurant. He spent the entire date telling me about how he had never slept with a White girl, and he kept telling me he was really interested in sleeping with me. He kept trying to ask me questions about what it would be like to sleep with me.

"So...do you like to be on top? Do you like to give blow jobs? What's your favorite position?" I tried to laugh off the questions, but I felt uncomfortable. I began to get the sense that he wasn't actually interested in me as a person, but more as an object, a conquest, a box (pun intended) that he could check off his list. By the time the bill came I felt completely objectified, and ran out of there as fast as I could.

He texted me once to find out if I wanted to have dinner at his place.

I couldn't say no fast enough. I never heard from him again.

# 35
# Ugo

He messaged me on OkCupid. He lived in the Valley, and worked for a company that packaged plastic ware for a restaurant. After chatting a while, somehow we got on the subject of wine. He had never been wine tasting before. I mentioned that there was a great bar in Culver City that did wine tasting — they had twenty different wines available to sample. We discussed the idea of wine tasting for quite some time. I was excited to show him how to taste wine — the color and structure of the wine, the scent of the nose, the taste on your palate, the finish.

We agreed to go on a date— I met him at the wine bar, excited to do some tastings with him. I couldn't wait to share my knowledge about wine. The bar had bottles of wine in aerators scattered about the room, so one could mingle about and get a taste of wine from each of the aerators.

The server brought us food menus, with a wine menu on the back. As we sat there looking at the menu, he asked if we wanted to order a bottle of wine.

What the fuck? I thought the whole point was to try a bunch of different wines? We had discussed the idea endlessly. That was why we were here.

I stared at him. "I thought we were supposed to do some wine tasting?"

"Well, I just think it'll be better to get a bottle of wine. You should pick it, since you know so much about wine."

Had he forgotten everything we had talked about before? I was already completely turned off to this man. Why didn't he want to follow through on what we had agreed to?

I ordered us a bottle of wine (a nice full-bodied red), and we proceed to drink it. As we chatted, I just wasn't interested in anything he had to say. I can't deal with anyone who doesn't follow through with things they say they're going to do.

I'm sure there were other reasons for not wanting to date him as well, but this is the one that sticks out in my mind the most.

We left, and I never heard from him again.

# 36

# James? ...Or maybe Corey?

Alright, admittedly I have no idea what this guy's name is. He's actually kind of forgettable, except for a photo he sent me after our date.

I know what you're thinking — no, it's actually **not** a dick pic. (Okay, or maybe that's just what I think of when someone mentions an online date and a photo.)

We matched on Tinder. Yup, so you already know I'm winning. He lived close to where I work, so put that in the plus column. (Yay geographically desirable!) He's a nurse (a man with a career!? Yes please!) and owns his own house (in LA, that is a feat. For all I knew, this fool was straight up *rich*). I waited to find out what the catch was — why is this guy single?

He arranged a date for us to meet at a local deli in my neighborhood. Apparently it was some place that he often went with his family. He was a local, and had gone to high school in the area.

I noticed the first minus right away: his hair was thinning, and he was short. Okay, okay, I'm being petty, I get it, but I love wearing high heels. Like, *love*. This guy stated that he was 5'8 in his profile, and that certainly was not the case. I happened to be wearing flats that day: daytime first meetings do not require heels, so gold flats it is! We were at perfect eye level, and I'm 5'5. Alright, I can move past that if everything else seems great.

As we sit for lunch, I can already tell that he's nervous. And shy. Neither of those are in my wheelhouse. I'm ridiculously outgoing, and I don't do nervous. Well, unless I have to speak in front of about a thousand people. *That* makes me really nervous. But, for a first date, I'm clearly old hat and don't get nervous anymore. In fact, I hardly even get excited about a first meeting. (How sad, right?) Part of the reason I don't get nervous anymore is because I read some great advice somewhere — when you are nervous, pretend it's your job to help the other person feel comfortable. This is often why I choose some place that I am familiar with (hello, home court advantage) so I feel at least somewhat comfortable, and can focus my energy on what questions to ask that might put him at ease. That way, I tend to forget when I actually get nervous, because my attention is on him.

I go through my usual barrage of questions — what's your favorite movie? Where is the last place you went on vacation? What do you like to do when you're not working? As we chatted, I found out his dad actually owned the house, and he was just allowed to live there rent free (free ride, huh? Must be nice...) and that he collected weapons.

Yup, you read that right. *Weapons.* Like, Medieval weaponry. A mace and a sword and a scythe, oh my.

I'm not exactly a fan, but it's still not necessarily a deal breaker. Although, I am pretty weirded out by it. He then said he actually kept his collection in his living room. On the living room wall.

Huh.

So, that's the first thing I'm going to see when I walk into your house? A ton of weapons on the wall? Meh. That's not really something I want to see. That also says something about your personality, that you'd have weapons on the wall as a way to greet guests into your home. I'm more of a fan of photos of friends and artwork, but to each their own, I suppose.

As he continues to drone on about his weapons, I have a disappointed and annoyed look on my face. It's clear that I am not amused by this idea, and that he should stop all talking about this at once. (By the way, I'm totally that meme that says it's not my mouth that is going to get me in trouble, but my face. I can't hide any of my emotions: they all show on my visage.) I finally attempt to change the subject, and am thoroughly annoyed as he continues to bring the conversation back to the weapons.

We finish our lunch, he pays (plus!) and we go our separate ways.

When I get home, I get a text message from him.

And then a picture message.

Of the fucking wall. The fucking weapons. There must be twelve or so weapons on his living room wall! I don't respond. I can't bring myself to do it. I'm infuriated.

Look, I don't ask for a whole lot when it comes to dating. There are three things that I am looking for in someone I date: I want a man who makes me feel safe, a man who respects me, and a man who listens to me when I talk. This man didn't make me feel safe — in fact, I wasn't sure if suddenly he was going to bring a weapon on one of our dates to murder me. I also feel like he didn't respect me since he kept talking about something that so obviously annoyed me. (Although, to be fair, I never said the weapons bothered me, so I guess I can't expect that he can actually read facial expressions, but I guess I'll give him the benefit of the doubt.)

And we never talked again.

# WE'RE STILL FACEBOOK FRIENDS

*Not all of my dates have been tragic and ridiculous. Some of them have actually been decent, and we've remained friends to this day. Yes, they know they're in the book. The names have been changed to protect the innocent.*

# 37
# BevMo!

"Let's just go out for one drink." Famous last words, right?

Kendra and I went wine tasting at our local BevMo! on a Saturday morning. At Beverages and More, known locally as BevMo!, they have a small area in the back of the store when you can taste a couple of wines for five cents.

Yup, you heard me. Five cents.

So, Kendra and I met at BevMo! for a wine-tasting adventure around noon on a Saturday. When we walked up to the counter, the guy who was working was a total flirt. He was about 6'3, shaved head, and beautiful blue eyes. As Kendra and I drank our wine, I absolutely enjoyed being my snarky self and exchanging glances with this handsome stranger. Besides, anyone who pours me wine can't be all bad, right?

After about an hour, Kendra and I headed out to have a drink at the restaurant across the street. I was asking her if I should just backtrack and leave him my number. I decided not to do it. I was too nervous. We headed to the bar, but I couldn't stop thinking about BevMo!. I wondered if I should go back in and give him my number after we were done at the bar.

No, that looks desperate. The moment has passed. I'll just have to wait until I go back into BevMo!. How did I even know he liked me anyways? He could just be a big flirt. Was he even interested? If he was interested, wouldn't he have asked for my number? Maybe not, since it would be weird for him to do that while working, even if he was interested. He was probably trying to be professional.

Kendra and I then headed to another bar, in a somewhat shadier neighborhood. This place looks like it was someone's home that they turned into a bar. It was called Fantastic Bar. I'll tell you right now, it's not fantastic at all. It's the kind of place where everyone who goes is a regular, and they can recognize right away if you've never been there before. The place smells like cigarettes because people still smoke inside, even though smoking in bars hasn't been legal in California since the 1990's. The bar is always sort of dark, and when someone opens the door everyone at the bar squints when looking into the light.

It's the perfect place to day drink. They have games you can play while you're drinking, so Kendra and I belly up to the bar with a game of Scattergories. We end up making friends with the two young guys in the bar, and become Facebook friends with Brandon. Kendra gives her number to the other one (they ended up dating for a while, but that's a story for another book). I was beginning to have heartburn from drinking wine all day, but I decided to push through it. I left Kendra and ended up meeting friends for dinner, something we had planned two months in advance.

I show up to dinner, and my heartburn is really bad now. I decide all I need to do is eat a little bit of bread. That'll calm my stomach. The minute I put the bread in my mouth, I am in severe pain. My stomach aches. I have to take deep breaths to try to get through the pain. This is more than heartburn. I excuse myself, and tell the girls I'm not feeling well. I head home, and make myself throw up. I feel slightly better, so I decide to go to bed.

Somewhere around 3 am, I get up. I'm feeling sort of thirsty, so I take a sip of water. The pain in my stomach immediately flares up. Am I dying? I'm dying. I need to go to the emergency room. I wake up my roommate, and she drives me to the closest hospital. We wait. I am admitted to the hospital at 5 am on Sunday morning. I have gallstones and need to have my gallbladder out. Some of the gallstones have escaped into my pancreas, causing my severe stomach pain. They need to wait for my pancreas to stop being enflamed before they can operate. Probably Monday.

I have the surgery, and am home recovering for the week. I return to work the following week.

A month after my surgery, Kendra asks me to meet her and Brandon back at Fantastic Bar. I am less than thrilled at the idea, but it seems better than sitting on the couch. I am enjoying a drink with Kendra and Brandon, when suddenly I hear a voice behind me.

"What, I pour you some wine, and you can't even say hi?"

I turn around. It's BevMo!! He's at the same bar as me, a month later. He clearly remembers me. We chat for a few minutes, and he says he wants to ask for my number, but doesn't want to get in anyone's way. He looks over at Brandon.

"Oh, Brandon? He's just a friend!" I tell him. BevMo! seems surprised, then asks for my number.

He texts me, and we go for coffee the following weekend. We sit outside, and he seems super relaxed in his khaki shorts and t-shirt with vans. As we sit over coffee, he tells me he used to work at a winery, used to own a house, and was previously engaged. He was originally from the area, and was currently selling weed, but just to his friends, to supplement his income.

"Is that a deal breaker?" he inquires. Well, it's not exactly a selling point. I tell him I'm not really a fan. I'm too much of a rule follower to feel comfortable with something that is so illegal. I'm unsure at this point where this date is going. I paid for my own coffee, and he has seemed so relaxed, like he's not really that interested in me. He suggests we see a movie.

"I don't really like watching movies. It's hard to get to know someone in a dark theater," I explain.

"Okay, do you have some suggestions for things we could do?" He asks me. I suggest frozen yogurt since the new Yogurtland just opened down the street. He agrees, and drives us in his giant truck over to Yogurtland. In the car he's playing Mickey Avalon. He apologizes for the lyrics. I begin to sing along to one of the songs, and tell him I love Mickey Avalon. He is thoroughly impressed. When the CD ends he changes it to Sublime. This seems to fit the stereotype of what kind of music I envision he might listen to.

We enjoy our frozen yogurt, then he drops me back at my car. I've liked hanging out with him. I wonder if he'll try to kiss me. It is still light out when he drops me off, and we're in the mall parking lot. Guess not.

He agrees to come over later that week for some wine. He brings over a bottle of red wine and hands me a rose he's snipped from his neighbor's yard. It's the thought that counts, right? At least it smells nice.

We drink wine and chit chat. The movie I put on becomes background noise as we continue our conversation. I am intrigued by this man who seems to know so much. He admits to me that he has stopped selling weed, because he knows I don't like it. I am impressed by this maneuver. At some point, he makes fun of me because my mouth is stained purple from drinking wine. He starts to sing the lyrics of a song I don't recognize. I stare at him, quizzically.

"You don't know that song?" I shake my head. He types something into his phone, and a song I've never heard comes on. He begins to sing along.

*How I long to hold her tenderly*
*How I long to hold her close to me*
*Maybe someday she will change her mind*
*And let me taste her lips of wine*
*Lips of wine woah,*
*Lips of wine in the morning*

He stops singing, and the song continues to play. He looks at me. I'm sitting on the kitchen counter, and he is standing in front of me. He kisses me, softly, sweetly, tenderly. I am taken aback and pleasantly surprised. I can still hear the song playing in the background, taste the wine on his breath, feel his hand on the small of my back. I can feel the ball of his tongue ring against my tongue. I had forgotten for a second that he had one. He pulls away. I am breathless. He looks at me.

"I really want to spend the night, but I don't think it's a good idea yet," he admits to me. I tell him that I'm not ready for that anyways, that he needs to stay at his place tonight. He agrees. It is as this point that I know he truly likes me. Any man who isn't actually trying to get in my pants right away is really trying not to blow it. He surprises me at every turn.

I send him off with a sweet kiss goodnight.

Over the next few weeks, we spend more time together. I pop into BevMo! to say hi and get a bottle of wine for a party I'm attending. He visits me at a coffee shop while I'm grading papers and brings me a frozen yogurt from Yogurtland. He invites me over for dinner one night, and makes me orange chicken while we watch a movie. I end up sleeping over that night because I don't feel like driving after a few glasses of wine. We mess around a bit, but don't have sex. I'll tell you what, though. That tongue ring really does feel good on my clit! He walks me to my car in the morning and kisses me goodbye.

One afternoon we meet at Fantastic Bar for a drink, and somehow we talk about my dating history. I tell him that I tend to go on dates with multiple people, and that I don't assume a couple is monogamous until there's been a conversation about it. The "DTR" — Define the Relationship has to happen at some point so that both parties are clear on where they stand. He makes some comment about how I get around. I turn to look at him, somewhat offended, and then he tells me he's quoting song lyrics by TuPac. That afternoon we joke about a variety of songs — I tell him I love the Beatles. He makes some joke about me being a teacher, and him having a teacher fetish. Like every man I've ever known. He doesn't take it too far, though, like other men seem to do.

During one of our dates he brings me a CD that he has made me. On it are a bunch of songs we have talked about while we've seen each other. It includes the TuPac/Digital Underground Song "I Get Around," a Mickey Avalon song, a Beatles Song, "Lost Without U" by Robin Thicke, "Teach U a Lesson" by Robin Thicke (a song about getting with a teacher) and "Lips of Wine" by Dennis Brown. How thoughtful that he included every song we'd talked about. I am impressed, since no one has ever made me a "mixed tape" before. I listen to it on repeat in my car.

One night while I'm out, he calls me. He's in Lancaster, about 1.5 hours from LA. His grandmother has passed away, and he's out there for the funeral. I listen while he talks about what his experience is like being with his family, celebrating the life of his grandmother. I feel his pain. I tell him that my grandmother died four years previous, and I understand what he's going through, that he will heal, and he will never forget her. He seems comforted by my words, tells me he's glad I'm there for him. I tell him of course, and that he can call me any time. He says he'll be back the next evening, that he wants to see me. I agree, and tell him I can't wait to see him.

He comes by my place the next evening. He looks tired, and emotionally exhausted. I'm not actually sure he's in any mental state to hang out with me. He tells me about the funeral, about crying with his family. I listen, and my heart breaks for him. Thank God he doesn't start to cry then, because if he does I know

I will cry too. He says he wants to go check out tattoo shops, to get a tattoo that represents his grandmother. I tell him that's a great idea. He says he wants to check them out right now, and will I go with him? Right now? I ask. Right now, he says. It's 9:30 on a Sunday night.

I say okay. We hop in the car, and he drives to a local tattoo shop. We spend almost our entire time together at this tattoo shop, and he spends the whole time talking to tattoo artist about what kind of design he wants. I'm bored. This is before I understand that I can ask for what I want on a date — I should have told him no, it wasn't okay for me to go with him, no, if we are going to hang out I get all of his attention, and he should have gone home to get sleep. We should both be the best versions of ourselves in those early dates. There is plenty of time in our futures to half show up. I am trying to be a supportive lady-friend, but it's actually not part of my job description — mostly because there has been no job created yet. He leaves that night, and I am frustrated. I bring it up the next day, and we talk it out, and he understands that he wasn't being his best self, and that he appreciates me being there for him.

At some point I ask BevMo! to come with me to my brother's college graduation party. My parents won't be there, but my aunt, and my Godparents will. It's a big deal, and to that point I had never taken anyone to meet a part of my family before. We weren't exclusive, but I was willing to let this man meet my family. I look at him with my family and wonder if I could see myself with my family for the rest of my life. I try to picture what that might look like. I can't quite see it — but is that something you can actually see? Can you see it if you think it's the right person? I'm not sure. We drive home, and I am impressed with this man, and how he handled himself among the bat-shit-crazy that is my family.

One day out of the blue he asks me if I like Pitbull. He's performing in concert in downtown LA. BevMo! has gotten tickets for the following Saturday, and asks me if I'd like to go.

I agree, saying it'll be a fun date. He eludes to sleeping together that night for the first time.

The week of the concert, he tells me he's moving the morning after the concert. Since his grandmother passed away, his grandfather is really lonely, and BevMo! can get a job at the BevMo! store in Palmdale — he's moving in with his grandpa. There's somehow an unspoken agreement that it means the end for the two of us.

He picks me up, and we head to the concert. We have a great time together. I am kind of sad that our time together is going to end, but I also feel like it's the right decision for us to be done after this evening. As he drives me home, he's hinting at staying the night, at sleeping together. I tell him I can't, I'm still not ready. He seems upset, but also seems to understand. We hug for a while, and we are both sad to see the night end. He kisses me goodbye, lovingly, sweetly, passionately. I am sad, and relieved at the same time. I care a lot about him, but I am afraid to fall in love with him — he is not everything that I am looking for, not all of the things that I need from a man, and I know if I let myself, I could fall for someone who is not right for me, and it would turn into a toxic relationship.

And, of course, I don't remember this fact two years later. BevMo! and I were still Facebook friends, and I put out feelers for someone to accompany me to the Jay-Z and Kanye West concert in Downtown LA. He volunteers, and I think to myself that it might be fun. I remember all of the little romantic things he did for me when we dated (and I don't remember all the stupid annoying shit — revisionist's history is amazing, isn't it?) so I tell him sure.

We meet for dinner at an upscale steak restaurant near the concert. He brings an amazing bottle of wine, and we enjoy a romantic dinner together. I remember that feeling of being with him, that he looks at me like I'm magic, and as the night goes on I think that maybe, just maybe, I would like to date him.

We have a fun evening together at the concert, and at the end of the night he walks me to my car. He leaned in to kiss me, and I let it happen.

In therapy that week, I lamented to my therapist that I wasn't sure what was happening, and I was tired of going on multiple first dates. I just wanted to be monogamous with someone. She encouraged me to pretend I was monogamous, in a relationship, with BevMo!. "If you were, what would you do?" I told her I would go see him that weekend. She said I should call him and tell him I wanted to see him.

I drove out to Palmdale, not once, but two weekends in a row. I met his roommate, a Spanish-speaking man from Guatemala. I also met Bevmo!'s mom one weekend that I'm there. He acts like it's no big deal for me to meet his mom. (For the record, in this whole book, he's the only man I've dated whose mom I've ever met.) We actually had sex for the first time the night I met his mom. She was also staying in his house. It felt a little bit naughty in a fun way. However, he was a selfish lover — never even tried to make me cum.

The next morning I drove home. I was a bit upset that he was such a selfish lover after I had been so giving — of my body and my emotions. I went home and we texted a few times over the next few days, but nothing much came of it.

Later that week he texted me.

**Chupa me verga.**

**What?!** I replied back?

**My roommate has been teaching me Spanish. He told me to send that to you.**

I was pissed. After I'd given myself to him sexually, he tells me to suck his dick?! Fucking disrespectful. And you thought that it was a good idea to send that to a girl that you're dating, who's already sucked your dick and you haven't gone down on her at all? C'mon bro. Not cool. Think for a second, buddy. Know your audience.

I don't text him back for a while.

**Are you mad?**

Ha. If you have to ask, don't you think you already know the answer to that question?

**I just think it's rude to send me something like that.**

**Can't you take a joke?** No, apparently I can't. Sorry.

That ends what we have for a little while. (Yes, I get that I'm a commitment-phobe. Let it go.)

I end up seeing him two years later, and we exchange numbers, because I just can't seem to learn from my mistakes.

We text back and forth for a while, and then he starts in with some weird shit.

**Do you think you're smarter than me?**

How do I respond to that? Yes. Wait, that seems rude. I try a diversion tactic instead.

**Where did that come from?**

**You're just so smart, I wonder if it intimidates men sometimes. You're a catch though. I was going to ask you to marry me.**

Oh good, the diversion tactic works...wait did he just use the M-word?! What the hell? We were never even that serious, how is he going to say he wanted to marry me?

I contemplate saying yes for a half a second. At least it will end my dating misery. Then I snap to my senses. I would have to live in Palmdale. No thanks.

He continues with the text messages.

**Dating is hard out here, especially at our age. Women are a mess or have a ton of kids.**

Ah, so you're in the same boat that I am. Yes, dating still sucks, and by 35 everyone has all kinds of baggage. I try to be positive, and at the same time let him down easily.

**You'll find someone! Don't give up!**

We chat a bit more, but it's clear it's not going anywhere. We're each others' last resort option.

I haven't heard from him in a while, although we are Facebook friends. I'm not sure I'll ever actually see him again.

# 38
# Tank

During the Summer of Twenty Bars, out of boredom I posted an ad on Craigslist to ask if there were any guys who wanted to show me any new bars and help me in my quest.

Yes, I said Craigslist. This was before the days that online dating was the norm. Craigslist was the best way I could get multiple responses. Plus, they were always entertaining.

I opened one guy's response, and laughed out loud. He included a photo of himself in a shirt and tie, in an office conference room, covered in Post-its. The wall behind him was also tiled with Post-its. This guy clearly has personality. Put that one in the yes pile.

Another guy sent me a headshot of himself. He was not just hot, but *hawt*. Clearly a model.

Now, I said again, this was in my early twenties. Of course I picked the hot guy over Mr. Personality. Because I still didn't know any better.

Hot guy and I exchanged numbers, and we texted back and forth a bit, and then set up to meet the next day.

And then he stood me up. Ugh. Story of my life.

Alright, back up plan. Let's go with Mr. Personality.

We email back and forth a few times, then exchange numbers. His name was Tank, and the photo was a project for school — he got his degree in photography. How cool and artsy. Tank finally decides he wanted to show me some bars in Culver City. I couldn't wait, because I'd never been to any bars there — any bar we visited there could go directly on the list!

I let him pick me up.

From my house.

No, seriously.

I thought this was a good idea. I had never met him before, and I thought it would be a good idea to let him to pick me up from my house and take me out for drinks.

Good thing he turned out to be a nice guy, and not a fucking stalker ass creep.

Note to self: don't do *that* again! Meet the dude out in public. Seriously.

He picked me up, and drove me to Culver City. We stopped at a bar called Rae's (now Big Foot West, for all my CC folks) — it was a dive. There were a wide variety of age groups — from college-aged kids to old timers.

We each ordered a well drink — him, a whiskey coke, me a vodka soda. As we sipped our cocktails conversation flowed easily. He was from Oklahoma, and came to LA to try to make it in acting. He was currently driving for a limousine company, and was doing photography on the side. Not bad, not great.

After we finished our drinks, he asked if I wanted to add another bar to my list. I told him of course I did! Let's add as many as we can!

He took me to a bar I'd wanted to go to forever, called Saints and Sinners. The interior was dark and sexy. As we took a seat at the bar the bartender slammed a shot, lit a match, and blew the shot out over the flame, making it look like she was breathing fire. Rad.

He bought me a drink, and we chatted some more.

We talked about what brought him out to LA, where he was from, and how I got to where I was in my life. I could tell he was a genuinely sweet guy. As the night went on, and we had another cocktail, I knew I wanted to see him again.

As we walked back to the car, and he held the door open for me (chivalry: found mostly in LA-transplants), he leaned over to kiss me. And it was nice.

As he drove me home, we talked about a second date. Sure, I'm into it.

For our second date, he took me to a Mediterranean restaurant down the street from his house.

For our third date, he made me dinner in his adorable apartment he shared with his female roommate. Also on our third date he shared that he was over $150,000 in debt. Yikes.

I have a thing about money. I grew up super poor, and money was always an issue in my household, so I vowed to myself as an adult that I would always have a steady job so that I would never have to experience that. $150,000 in debt is a lot of money. I freaked out a little. He sounded financially irresponsible, so I kind of pulled back a bit.

He invited me to a 4th of July party that he and his roommates were hosting. I decided to attend — and meet all of his friends. That's a big step. I'm not one to usually meet all of a guy's friends. I don't really want to share the person I'm dating at first — I like a lot of attention on me.

During the party, we all sat in Tank's bedroom. Only then did everyone comment that he had a stack of books next to his bed. One of them, Mystery's book *The Pickup Artist*, sat on his nightstand. Everyone laughed at him for owning the book, and admitting to reading it. I felt sort of sorry for him.

Alright, if you were lucky enough to avoid VH1 in the early 2000s, then you were missed the ridiculous debacle that was Mystery. His show *The Pickup Artist* was lovingly referred to in our household as "Who Wants to be a Douchebag?" Mystery (yes, that's his name) would take these super awkward twenty-something virgins and teach them how to hit on girls. But not in a classy way that felt respectful towards women. No, he would take them to strip clubs to get them to try to take a stripper home, or talk about "negging" the girl — come up with a way to put her down that makes her more attracted to you. Mystery's book was a way for men to learn the art of picking up women.

Unfortunately, anyone that I had known that read the book was not a success before or after.

I suppose most would find it endearing that he owned a book like that. I just added it to the annoying list.

If you can't tell, I'm easily bored.

Eventually, Tank quit his job as a limo driver. This was at the beginning of the recession though, and so suddenly he was unemployed and contemplating what he was going to do with his life. Maybe he was going to go back to his home state and work for his dad. Again, this set off my monetary stability alarm bells. Not a fan.

Once, not too long after that, he ended up house-sitting for some friends nearby. He invited me over to go swimming. I went, but reluctantly. (At this point in time, my self esteem was still really low, and I thought I was too fat to wear a bathing suit, so I didn't want anyone to see me in anything skin-tight that would show off my curves. Thank God I now appreciate and love my curves.)

I ended up going over, but felt uncomfortable the whole time. We fooled around a bit, but he could tell I just wasn't into it.

The next time I saw him, it was clear to both of us that it was over. Awkward silences and a general feeling of not having a great time on both ends. We remained Facebook friends, and would comment on each others' posts, but no real interactions. Until later.

As Facebook friends, we reconnected when I posted that I was going to New York for spring break seven years after we dated. He was living in New Jersey, and decided he would tour Rockefeller Center with me, and then we would grab dinner afterwards. I wasn't sure where we stood: was he going to try to hook up with me? Were we meeting up as friends? Was he dating anyone? I couldn't really tell from his Facebook. All these unanswered questions made me anxious as I saw him for the first time since we had dated.

We met up at a restaurant for happy hour before our tour. As we got a drink and chatted, he asked me to catch him up on what I'd been up to. I told him about the guy I had dated most recently, and then I asked him if he was dating anyone.

"Yeah, we just started dating..."

"Oh? Cool! How'd you meet her?"

"Well, see, there's a Facebook support group for people with herpes..." my face grew pale as I stared at him, wide-eyed. He could see the terror growing on my face. "Oh...no, this was after you...she cheated on me and gave me herpes."

"Oh." I breathed a sigh of relief. Okay, good to know that he's seeing someone. And that he has herpes. Definitely not hitting that.

We finish our drinks and start the tour at Rockefeller Center. There were about 10 people in the group, and our tour guide takes us around the outside of the multiple buildings that make up the center. The guide stops in front of a round metal plaque in the floor. As she continues to speak about the history of the plaque, Tank leans over to me and whispers in my ear.

"You know, I was considering getting down on one knee and proposing to you, just to see everyone's reaction," he chuckles.

I turn to look at him. What the fuck? Awkward! I had forgotten that he has a weird sense of humor. "Not funny," I tell him.

"No, it would be hilarious!" he argues. "Imagine! We'd totally make these tourists' day!"

Yeah, I'm a little uptight about things like that. Not down.

We finish the tour, and then we grab a quick dinner on the way back to where I was staying in Brooklyn. I enjoyed being in the presence of someone who treated me nicely, even if neither of us was romantically interested. He dropped me back off in Brooklyn, and we promised to keep in touch.

We would chat everyone once in a while on Facebook. I noticed that he had moved to Oklahoma, and that he was no longer with his girlfriend. Two years after our New York "date" he posted on Facebook that he was expecting a child with his girlfriend. I commented "Congrats!"

He messaged me to thank me for my comment, and to tell me it meant a lot. I told him he was welcome — of course I was happy for him.

And I was. Of course, deep inside I was insanely jealous. Not because I want a kid. Not because I want to be with him. But because he had *someone*. And I'm still single. I felt that twinge of jealousy. And by God, it hurts. It's hard to feel that dual feeling — the one that says *I'm happy for you* and *I am going to die alone* — at the same time.

A few months after our message exchange, he messages me again, asking me to call him because he needs a favor.

I wonder what he needs. I'm not in a space where I can talk. I'm out to dinner with some girlfriends.

I text him. **I'm out and can't talk — what's up?**

**Can you get me a copy of the *LA Times* with today's date on it?**

I wondered why he could possibly want something like that. I checked his Facebook. Ah, yes, the baby was born today. He wants a newspaper to commemorate his son's birth.

That's a weird request. Ask a woman you used to date for a newspaper on the day your son is born.

But, I'm nice. I comply. I get him a newspaper. He insists that he's moving back to LA, and that he and his significant other want to have me over for dinner. I tell him sure, sounds great!

As of the writing of this story, I still have the newspaper on my desk.

But I will say, the photos of his son are really fucking cute.

And I'm still single.

# 39
# Deaf Mark

Early in my Craigslist days — around 2004, I believe, one man who sent me a picture and message was Mark. He included photos of himself with a giant grin. I could tell he was a lot of fun. He was from Compton, had gone to Cal State Northridge for college, and was working for the city of Los Angeles.

We exchanged messages back and forth a couple of times, and we decided to talk on AOL Instant messenger. Texting was in its early phases, and he was the only person I knew of that had a Sidekick (Jesus, remember those?). It was much easier to communicate through AOL Instant Messenger at the time, so we chatted back and forth a few times. Turns out he was always near where I was — we frequented the same places.

One day, a few weeks into our virtual conversations — Valentine's Day, and the day after my birthday, coincidentally — he messaged that he was at the Starbucks down the street from my house. He wanted to meet me. And he had a gift for me. He just sort of sprung it on me suddenly. I happened to be free, so I messaged him that I would be there in ten minutes.

And then he dropped the bombshell:

**Oh yeah, by the way, I'm deaf.**

That's the last message I received from him before I left the house.

I guess I'm grateful he told me before I went to meet him. That would be a bigger shock, not realizing that the person I was about to go on a date with is deaf.

I had the five minute drive to Starbucks to process this information — which, it turns out, is not enough time to process something like that.

When I approached him in Starbucks, I was nervous. Would I be able to understand him? Would he be able to understand me? I don't know sign language, so would I be able to communicate with him? How was this going to work?

He was 6'2, and holding a giant teddy bear. I smiled, and he smiled back. I realized how much non-verbal communication is possible. A lot can be shared without words. He handed me the teddy bear, and said hello in a scratchy, throaty voice. It was the voice of someone who is hard of hearing.

Oh good, he can speak. I thought to myself. At least this will be easier.

He told me he reads lips as well. Okay, so he'll understand me, I thought to myself. Maybe this could work. He's pretty adorable.

He began to tell me about his day, his life, his interests. He didn't leave much room for me to talk about myself. When I did talk about myself, he would think he had the gist of what I was saying, and then take off talking about something. I had to pull him back from going off on whatever tangent he was on, and repeat myself, making sure he was looking directly at my mouth when he did it. I talked about how I took French in high school and almost majored in it, how I was a teacher, and how I loved to go out dancing.

I wasn't sure how I felt about him, so I figured I would give it a second date. I want to feel listened to — would he make me feel that way?

He showed up to pick me up for our second date, and this time he brought me a letter he had written. He told me to read it later.

We headed out to dinner at a local sports bar so he could watch some sporting event on TV while we were having dinner.

Great, so now not only is he not hearing me, he's not looking at me either? Awesome. Dinner was silent. He was enjoying the game, though.

At the end of dinner he dropped me back off at my apartment. I opened the letter he had written me. It was typed, and in French. I knew he didn't speak French, so he had clearly used a translation program to write the letter. It was difficult to read because it had been translated word for word rather than as whole phrases or with correct grammar, but it was essentially a love letter. He was clearly interested in me, and wanted to prove it with this letter.

I still wasn't sure where I stood with him, so I decided to give it one more date. This time, he brought his best friend, who was visiting from San Francisco, so that I could meet him.

The minute I met Kent, I instantly liked him. He was flirty, and we got along really well. We had witty banter back and forth. While Kent and I bantered, Mark sat silently staring off into space.

I knew I had to break it off with Mark. This thing with Kent felt so easy, so effortless. My time with Mark felt so forced, so full of effort.

I messaged Mark that evening to say that I didn't think it was going to work out between the two of us, that we just weren't compatible.

Mark and I still stay in contact to this day. We've said hi to each other on a variety of dating apps, and we remain Facebook friends. He has done amazing things with his life: he's been an advocate for deaf rights, run a couple of marathons, and has become a staple in the LA running community. I wish him the best and hope that he finds the woman he is looking for. I know she's out there for him!

# 40

# SummerSex

I used to keep a blog on Xanga in college and during my first year of teaching. Before the Facebook craze, most of my friends and I used Xanga to keep in contact with one another. On Xanga, I could see who was following my blog, and I could read the pages of those people that I was following. Since I lived in the LA area I was also a part of the LA "Metro" and could search public Xanga blogs — people that lived in my area.

At the time, I was dealing with some disordered eating, and I came across a girl who used to write about her journey with bulimia and was obsessed with her weight. She would literally weigh herself three times a day, and record everything that went into and came out of her mouth. I used to read her stuff obsessively, and wonder if I could do what she was doing. I would compare my weight to hers, my food to her food, and I wondered if what she was doing would actually work with my body, and if it was something that I could sustain. (Oh, I do not miss being in my early twenties!)

My Xanga consisted mostly of funny things my students said, shit I cried about after talking to my self-centered, alcoholic mother, and my inability to find a man. I also wrote about an ex, since this was right around the time I met him and we began our relationship, but that's another story for another book.

Once, in my search of the LA Metro, I came across "SummerSex" — a guy who lived in the same city that I did, and wrote about his sexual encounters. The profile picture was displayed in such a way that I couldn't see the guy's face, just a part of it. It was all very mysterious. I, of course, wondered if there was some sort of way I could end up dating him.

As I continued to read his material over a period of weeks, I became disappointed in the girls he had slept with. They were selfish — he always seemed willing to go down on them, but none of them ever reciprocated the favor. His stories were always from the past, and he always eluded to the fact that he was short, fat, and lacking self-confidence. I wondered how true that was.

At some point, I decided to contact him, and we began to chat. It turned out he didn't live very far from me, and was in a band, but wouldn't tell me where he performed. He wouldn't even tell any of his friends where he sang, because he didn't want them to come see him since he'd become too embarrassed to sing. I shared with him that I had a passion for music, just as he had, and I told him that the school that I worked at was hosting a "Battle of the Bands." Somehow I decided it was a good idea to invite this complete stranger, this man who's complete photo I had never even seen, to my house to pick me up and take me to the Battle of the Bands so he could hear my students play. He claimed it would be a date, but I told him I probably was not interested in a date, and just wanted to see how it went.

For the record: this was one of the first times that I did this (but unfortunately not one of the last) and I was lucky. SummerSex was NOT a serial killer, nor was he a pathological liar, or a rapist, but he damn well could have been.

When he picked me up in his truck, he was just as short and fat as he had claimed. But so was I. We were like two peas in a pod. Except he was the self-deprecating pea. The one that put himself down every chance he got. The one that kept harping on the fact that I was adamant that this was not a date. The angry pea that was upset that I had declared we were just going to be friends. I'm probably making him sound worse than he actually was, but he was that guy that makes you say, "No, you really *are* a nice person, and I really *do* want to hang out with you! You're *not* an asshole — where did you get that idea from?"

So we headed to my school and talked through the Battle of the Bands contest. We had a great time. Afterwards, he dropped me off, and we both blogged about how much fun we had. We decided we were going to go out again in the near future.

One Friday night, I wanted to go out for drinks. I put on the only outfit I would wear when going out at that time: a slutty schoolgirl skirt and a white blouse, half unbuttoned. SummerSex picked me up from my house and drove me to a bar close to his house. We drank the night away, including beer and shots. We were drunk, and I was happy. I was comfortable; I felt like I had found a true friend. Someone who was from my tribe.

After the bar closed, he drove us to Norms to get a bite to eat. For some reason, he was feeling gentlemanly and wanted to open my door for me. I waited patiently in the car, the alcohol warming me on a cool fall night, making my thoughts a little unclear. As he opened the door and I got out of the car, he hugged me.

When he let go, he looked extremely embarrassed.

"What's wrong?" I asked, with a concerned look on my face.

"I can't believe I just grabbed your ass!"

I tried to recall back to not ten seconds before, but the alcohol impeded any hope of storing anything in my short or long term memory.

"It's fine," I slurred. And really, it was. I didn't feel threatened or harassed that he had grabbed my ass. I actually thought it was kind of cute.

We had our late night drunk food at Norms, then he drove me home, apologizing the entire way about grabbing my ass.

Even to this day, he still brings it up when we get together. We've been friends for over ten years...we've even spent a few orphan holidays together when we didn't feel like hanging out with our families. He's someone who I know will always be in my life.

Sometimes you just have to bond over discussing sexual encounters.

# 41
## JC

I met JC on Match.com. He was a math major at UCLA and a few years younger than me. It was obvious from his photos he was a typical math major — a big bushy head of hair, terrible dresser, and a big nerd. In some ways I'm attracted to this, since I'm also a big nerd. We began to send messages back and forth, and eventually exchanged numbers. He texted me to set up our first date — a movie.

A movie is a terrible first date idea. There's no opportunity to have a conversation and see if there's any chemistry. I'm not sure he's thought this all the way through. I suggested that we meet for a drink at the bar inside the theater beforehand so we can chat and hang out. He agrees.

We decide to see *Burn After Reading* — if you haven't seen it, it's got George Clooney, Brad Pitt and John Malkovich in it.

We meet at the bar, and he's obviously nervous. He's sweating bullets, and orders a scotch, neat. I enjoy my vodka soda as we talk. He tells me about his job with computers. I am completely fascinated because it totally plays into my dorky side, and means that he is smarter than me, which is hot. We finish our cocktails and head into the theater.

The movie begins, and it's pretty funny. George Clooney's character is an online dating whore. At one point in the movie, he goes on a date with Frances McDormand's character. They meet up in a bar for a drink. At this point I sort of elbow JC as if to say "look familiar?"

The next scene has George Clooney and Frances McDormand watching a movie together and laughing. JC and I look at each other and giggle. It's us on screen! The next flash is them having dinner together. I think to myself that it's a possibility. We could grab a bite after this, if he suggests it.

As we continue to watch in the next minute, the actors end up back at George Clooney's apartment, and he invites her to the basement where he has a device he's ordered from a "gentleman's magazine" that is some sort of rocking chair with a dildo attached. I stare at the screen, wide-eyed, my hands gripping the arms of the chair. Please, God, don't let JC make a joke about this part!

The next scene flashes to Clooney, on top of McDormand, mid-thrust, and then into full climax. I am mortified, my eyes glued to the screen. JC can't think this is how our date's going to end, can he?

*Can he?*

I slink into my seat. I just want to crawl in a hole and die. I sit through the rest of the movie without so much as a look at JC.

When the movie finishes, he looks at me and remarks something about the social commentary that the movie is trying to portray. I just nod, thinking that it was just another weird movie with John Malkovich. I tell him it's getting late, and I should probably head home. He walks me to my car, we hug, and say goodnight.

The next day he texts me, and asks me for another date. The way I see it, he's smart, sweet, and kind of funny, so why not? I say yes. He lets me choose where we'll have lunch — I decide on a Mexican restaurant not too far from my house.

Lunch is fun — we chat, and he is somewhat socially awkward, but funny. I wonder if he's just nervous. It's really the first time we've had a chance to spend some time getting to know each other better. He's kind of subdued, and isn't very aggressive during our date: at the end of the date, he doesn't go in for a kiss. I think it's odd, by our second date, but I can kind of handle it. I'm certain by the time we get to the third date he'll kiss me. He friend requests me on Facebook, and I accept.

A few days later he texts me to tell me that he's got tickets to Halloween Horror Nights at Universal Studios and is supposed to meet friends there. He asks me if I want to go. I agree, thinking it might be kind of a fun group to hang out with. It's my first time at Halloween Horror Night. He gives me the option of what to do first. I figure the tram is probably the least scary ride there is — I mean, how much can they do to you when you're sitting on a tram, right?

WRONG. So wrong.

They make you get off the tram. You have to get out and walk. Through a zombified area. Through a dark, tree-laden forest crawling with characters who are just aching to jump out and scare you. Of course, JC takes this opportunity to put his arm around me, so that we can awkwardly walk through this area together.

Great. It's at this point I realize that I think he's a great friend, but I'm just not that into him. Dammit.

After surviving the scariest tram ride of my life, we meet up with his friends. Oh. They're a couple. We ride two rides with them, and ditch them after a bit. I begin to get tired, and after surviving so many scares, we decide to call it a night. We walk back to the car, and he drives me home. He parks the car in my driveway, and I give him a hug. He kisses my neck.

But not in one of those "I want to smoochie-smoochie with you in the car" kind of neck kisses. This was more of a "I think I want to kiss your cheek, or maybe even your lips, but I missed and landed on your neck," kind of kisses. I pull away slightly, and he just looks at me. I can see in his eyes that he has every intention of kissing me, but he doesn't pull the trigger.

I move away completely, thank him for a lovely evening, and get out of the car.

The next day, he sends me an email. He tells me about how he *wanted* to kiss me last night, but he's kind of shy. He tells me that any time I want to take the reins, he'd be happy to let me.

What? Alright, I'll admit, I don't always like to play into traditional gender roles, but in some instances, I think I like it. And in the case of being kissed, I *know* I want the guy to take the lead. I don't want to be the aggressor. I want to be the receiver. This guy isn't aggressive enough for my taste.

I email him back to say I've had a great time, but I don't think it's going to work out. We remain Facebook friends even to this day, although I don't think we've spoken since.

## WHAT WAS I THINKING?

*Most of the time I'm a smart woman, but sometimes I question my decisions.*

# 42

# Carl

This is one of the few stories that makes me feel like a complete asshole. Most dates I can justify blaming the guy's idiocy for the whole thing not working out. In this case, I know the whole thing is my fault.

Look, nice guys always complain that girls don't want them — girls end up friend-zoning the guy. And it's true — for a while. Especially in your early twenties. Here's my theory on that: as teens, we are learning to push boundaries and take risks. Somewhere in there comes that idea of dating the "bad boy": the one that smokes, drinks, and does illegal things. The one that we, as women, know we can fix. The one that brings us close enough to risk-taking, but keeps it at an arm's distance so we feel just boundary-pushing enough.

The nice guy, on the other hand, is too "safe" when we're in our teens and early twenties. We as women haven't experienced enough heartache, disaster, and pain to realize that *the nice guy is the one you should marry.*

One of my best friends my senior year of college was MrKnight. He still is one of my best friends to this day and will end up being the "mister of honor" at my wedding. He's a nerd in the truest definition of the word: he plays video games (I used to spend hours at his house waiting for him to finish his World of Warcraft missions just so we could get lunch), was obsessed with *Star Wars* before being obsessed with *Star Wars* was cool, and his first tattoo was of the auryn from *Never Ending Story*. I love this man with all my heart.

MrKnight used to throw parties in college, and would invite all of his gamer friends, as well as his high school friends. One of his high school friends invited Carl, a classmate from photography school.

Now, I'll start this by saying when I met Carl, he was slightly intoxicated. You know, in the way that every college student is "slightly intoxicated" at a college party. And by slightly, I mean very. Although, to be fair, I wasn't exactly sober myself. Carl was downstairs in MrKnight's bedroom, sitting on his bed when I walked into the room. There were two other people sitting on the other side of the room, and they were all caught up in some deep conversation. I caught some snippet that involved religion, in the way that college kids often talk so definitively about what's right and wrong about religion.

At that moment, someone else in the room asked me what my religion was. I said that I wasn't really practicing, but that I had been baptized Episcopalian just to make my grandma happy when I was twelve years old.

"Wait, you're an Episcopalian too?!" Carl exclaimed as he hopped off the bed. "Will you marry me? My mom would be really happy if we got married."

"This is Carl, by the way," Mr. Knight explained.

I blushed. What am I supposed to say? My mom would be happy that I would be married, but I don't even know this guy. But if he's a friend of MrKnight's, I know he's got to be good people. I tried to think of a good response, but this was back when I didn't have much confidence when it came to talking to men.

"Geez, buy me dinner first," is what I wanted to say. It came out more as "uhhmmm uh whaaaat, I mean..."

I somehow recovered from my word fumble, and Carl and I started talking. He lived about 45 minutes from me — without traffic. Now, in LA terms, that kind of thing comes in a category all its own: GEOGRAPHICALLY UNDESIRABLE. Living so far is definitely a bad thing. He did, however, live about 15 minutes from my family, so at the time it seemed to make sense to try to go on a date with him.

Because he was a friend of a friend, we became MySpace friends (yup, that long ago), followed each other on Xanga (where both of our blogs were posted), and were messaging each other on AIM daily. We pretty much had our social media circles intertwined before we had even gone on a date.

When it came time for our date, I drove up to his apartment. He lived in a place with a few roommates, and it was cute. He told me I looked nice. I felt comfortable with Carl, and he was a good listener. He told me about some of his interests, which included photography and sending things to people in the mail. He told me about the website Post Secret, and even showed me photos online of some organization that he had sent cereal to.

Yes, I said cereal. He was into sending people unusual things in the mail, but I'll come back to that.

He drove us to dinner at TGI Fridays (I was 21. This is a totally acceptable date place when you are 21. Way better than Denny's.)

The waiter asks for our drink order. I order some ridiculous sugar-filled, hangover-inducing cocktail with a thousand mixers in it. Carl orders a water.

I stare at him. "How come you didn't order a drink?"

He sheepishly admits that he's not quite 21.

"How old are you?" I demand.

"Nineteen." He replies.

I am flabbergasted. These are my college years, where fun in my twenty-first year is dependent on how much alcohol we can consume, trying new cocktails, or just dipping our toes in bar culture. Also, pretending we have enough money to actually drink at bars, relying mostly on financial aid money to do so. I can't date someone who's nineteen! He just doesn't *get* me.

I'm already slightly turned off, but part of me tries to reason that I'm just being a bitch. He'll be twenty-one eventually. Besides, he's funny. And he makes me laugh! I push his age out of my mind, and decide to truly give it a shot.

We finish dinner (and I chose to only have the one drink. Look at me, drinking in moderation!) and he pays. HE pays! It's a financial aid miracle.

Okay, so if you're keeping track:

Plus: He's funny, he's in school, he paid for the date. He already wants to marry me, and thinks I'm gorgeous. He's nice. He's a good listener, and easy to talk to.

Minus: He's 19, and can't legally drink in a bar. And he's too nice. (I'm so fucked up.)

He drives us to the beach, and we take a walk at sunset. We walk, hand in hand, along the sand until we get to a small cliff with some rocks. We sit on the rocks, and finally, *finally*, he kisses me. It's a sweet kiss, the kind a nice guy gives. The kind of kiss that a respectful gentleman gives to a woman he cares about.

(The kind of kiss that a twenty-one year old with low self-esteem doesn't want. Where's the heat? Where's my groping? Aren't you going to try to grab my ass?)

As we walk hand in hand back to the car, we both decide we don't want the date to be over. Carl decides we need to have pie. He drives us to Marie Callendar's. We each get a slice, and we share. Carl then drives us back to his place. We share an appropriate kiss, and I get in my car and drive home.

We message (through AIM) a few times over the next few days, and then I suddenly get a card in the mail. As a nice and respectable gentleman, he had sent me a thank-you card for such a fantastic date.

Add *that* to the Plus column. Wow. How adorable and old-fashioned!

So what do I do? I post on my blog. Something vague enough that no one will know who it's addressed to, but specific enough that he will know it's directed at him. Basically I said he was not aggressive enough for me, and that we weren't going to date.

I sent a fucking break-up message. That everyone could read. *Really?!?!* Who does that? Twenty-one year old me is an asshole.

Fortunately, Carl is a sweet enough person to forgive my asshole-ish ways. He continues to be my friend, and even sent me a box of macaroni and cheese in the mail — he literally slapped a label on it and addressed it to me.

Look, I'm not saying that it's always completely appropriate to tell someone you don't want to date them to their face (sometimes it's just not safe. Don't believe me? See the *Shouting Match* chapter.), but it *is* appropriate to be direct and to the point with them. And private. It's not a conversation for everyone's eyes, and it's definitely not appropriate to share on social media. Basically, it's a good rule of thumb that I should break up with someone the way I would want to be broken up with.

# 43

# Mario

Back in my early days of dating, I was not very familiar with how a date was supposed to work.

I met Mario in my party days through my friend Jane. Jane and I used to go out for drinks, and she always brought along five or so friends, and they would bring a friend. Once, we ended up back at Mario's house at the end of the night. Mario and I seemed to vibe pretty well, so we exchanged numbers.

Mario invited me over for a date to his house.

Now, for those of you who are unaware, as I used to be: a first date at a man's house is not a date. It's a hook-up.

I assumed that since he wanted to see me, he was interested in dating me. Boy, was I wrong.

I dressed up in my cutest outfit: jeans, an adorable top, and a pair of heels. I knocked on the door.

He answered in sweats and a ratty t-shirt.

Should have been my first indication, but this is pre-"Netflix and Chill" and at this point in my life I am so inexperienced that I don't know the signs.

He offers me cold red wine from a glass jug. I accept. This is also before I become a wine snob, so I'm ok with drinking anything with alcohol in it. Ah, the good old college days.

We chat for a few minutes, and he turns on a movie. Somewhere in the middle of our conversation, it comes up that I am taking pole dancing fitness classes.

Hey, Past Desirée: don't bring that up on a first date. The dude is only going to think about one thing. Save that for when he knows you better. Future Desirée, take notes, will ya?

He gets an excited look on his face.

"You take pole dance classes?! Like, you're a stripper?"

"Well, no, not a stripper. I learned a little dance routine that we do that's kind of fun." I say shyly. I am so not ready to show this guy my routine, but I am also not confident enough to just tell him no. I *really* want him to like me, and that means I have to do whatever I can to make him happy.

(Note: this is NOT the way to approach dating. Or people in general, actually. Thank the Universe for therapy, and for helping me realize that no, in fact, I can absolutely say no, and if he is not ok with it, then I can just leave and it's not my job to make him happy. I get to be me, and do what makes me happy, and if he wants to be a part of that, then fine.)

"So, can I see the routine?"

I hesitate, and then, because I'm at this pathetic point in my life, I agree. In part, because when I dance, I am another person. I am confident, sexy, and powerful. I can have any man when I dance.

I ask him for some music. He asks what I'd like to hear. I hesitate for a moment (this is before I've figured out my sex anthem), and he puts on "Pony" by Ginuine.

Fine. That'll do just fine.

I saunter to the wall and face it. I put my hands against the wall, and begin to prance against it. I try to concentrate on the wall, but I can feel his eyes on me. As I spin myself around to face him, with my legs spread wide, me on my tiptoes, back against the wall with my hands running up and down my body, I catch his eye. My emotions waver between complete confidence and utter humiliation at the intimacy of this act with a total stranger. I feel a rush of adrenaline as my eyes close and my hands run up and down my body. Goddamn, I'm sexy.

And Mario thinks so too. As I pry my eyes open, I can see that look of lust on his face, in his eyes. (Never mind in his pants.)

I slide my way down the wall, onto my hands and knees. I do a few hip circles, flip my hair a few times, and slink my way over to him in the sexiest way I know how. I end up on my hands and knees in front of him, hip circling and running my hands up my stomach, to my breasts, and through my hair. I'm really into it now, and I close my eyes again. When I open my eyes to face

Mario, he is looking at me with such determination, such lust, it's almost scary.

(Only because at this point in my life, I haven't had enough experience to realize the power that I have over this man at this moment. Oh, no, that understanding comes much later.)

I stop as the song ends. He bursts into applause. I feel embarrassed. That dance was too personal, too soon. And I am not confident about my sexing abilities.

And then he kisses me. I feel on top of the world. He likes me! He really likes me! We make out on the couch for a few minutes, before he takes me to his bedroom.

I'm still convinced that he truly likes me and respects me. I'm sure he cares deeply about my hopes, dreams, and aspirations. Even though he hasn't asked about any of that.

I lie down on his bed, and he lies on top of me. We're kissing, and suddenly, somehow, I'm naked.

How did that happen?

He tries to finger me, but this is before I'm comfortable with anyone touching me, so I grab his hand to stop him.

"What?" he asks. "Is something wrong?"

I stammer to find the words, to explain that I'm a virgin, that I'm waiting to be in a relationship, to be with someone who cares about me. Unfortunately, all I can do instead is just kindly suggest that he doesn't do that anymore. I'm ashamed, and don't know how to share my feelings.

"You don't like it?" He looks hurt.

"No. I mean, yes, but...," I trail off. "I should go."

"Really?" he suddenly seems angry. "You're just going to get up and go, and leave me here like this?" He points to his dick.

"I'm sorry..."

"No, you're not, because if you were, you'd stay and finish this." He is clearly fuming.

"I just...I don't want to. I can't."

I put my clothes back on as quickly as possible, all the while he is giving me the death stare.

He stayed in the bedroom as I made my way to the door, and out into the living room. He didn't follow. I let myself out.

Clearly I was never going to hear from him again.

Now that I am ten years past this story, I can see the red flags clearly. Jesus, did I really think that was date? Sweat pants, stay at home, and strip tease? Please. This dude was looking for one thing. He clearly thought we were on the same page, so of course he's going to be pissed when I don't put out.

But then again, I don't have to put out if I don't want to put out. And my first date needs to be okay with that.

# 44

# Mr. Coffee

I met Mr. Coffee at my local Starbucks. I was hanging out there one afternoon during the summer, reading a book to pass the time. He approached me, asked what I was reading, and struck up a conversation. He told me he would love to take me out sometime in the upcoming weekend. I had to break his heart and tell him I was leaving the next morning to visit my best friend in Mammoth for a week. He insisted on taking me out to dinner that evening.

Who am I to turn down free dinner?

I agreed, told him my address (I must have been insane to let a complete stranger know where I live!), and he agreed to pick me up that evening.

He drove me to the Cheesecake Factory in Marina del Rey. Fairly fancy for a first date. Conversation in the car was casual. He drove a Chrysler, had a job, lived on his own, and wore a suit on our date. He was nice — he opened the car door for me, and obviously wanted to make sure I was well taken care of.

The waitress seated us for dinner, and we each ordered a cocktail from the gargantuan cocktail list that Cheesecake Factory has to offer. I ordered a steak salad, and he ordered pasta.

We sat, chatting, with the recessed lighting putting a spotlight directly in the center of our table. It was romantic — the two of us, in a beautiful restaurant on the water, both dressed to impress. Our food arrived, we chat through dinner and the waiter clears our plates away. I was walking on cloud nine. This guy seemed pretty great!

After dinner, we continued to chat, and at one point, he leaned in, as if he wanted to tell me a secret. I leaned in. I couldn't help but think how beautiful this moment was, how gorgeous the view was and what a lucky girl I was to be able to live in a city where I can experience these things. I looked into his eyes.

He stared intently into mine, and whispered seductively, "Your mustache is so sexy."

I paused. I replayed the words over in my head. Yes, he *really* did make a comment about my facial hair! I could only imagine the look on my face was a cross between confusion and shock.

"Wow, um, thanks, but I don't find my facial hair to be sexy." Of course, he had no idea that I'm self-conscious about my facial hair, as with most other things on my body. This one, however, is not because of my own nit-picking — my dad used to make fun of me for my mustache — which is truly invisible. It's blond. And matches the amount of hair on the rest of my face.

I confusingly thanked him and told him not to talk about my facial hair. He insisted that yes, it really *is* sexy. I insisted that he change the subject. I'm slightly weirded out.

He drove me back home, and walked me to my door. He told me he didn't want to kiss me goodnight, because he wanted to take things slowly. At the time, I thought that was a little weird. (Now, I actually completely respect that belief).

I got up the next morning and drove to Mammoth. I told my best friend Laura all about the date. She noted that he sounded promising, and I hesitantly agreed. Laura and I headed out to do some local shopping.

The day after our first date, I got a text from Mr. Coffee.

**I miss you.**

Alright, I tried not to panic. This dude has hung out with me for a total of an hour, and now he wants to tell me he misses me? I don't reply.

He then proceeded to call me six times within the course of the evening. He left me more voicemails where he told me how much he missed me, and how he couldn't wait until we're together again.

On the seventh phone call, I was so tired of hearing my phone ring, I picked it up and told him, very shortly, that I was on vacation, and that I would give him a call when I was good and ready.

Of course, I didn't call him again.


# 45
# Fifty

My friend Jenny and I went out for drinks one night to a fantastic dive bar in West LA. It's got amazing martinis that taste delicious and knock you on your ass. Jenny and I somehow wound up chatting with an older gentleman and his lady friend at the bar. We discovered that they were not actually a couple as we originally thought.

Through conversation I found out that he was twice my age. I was twenty-five. Fifty was...well, fifty years old. Jenny got the impression from the lady friend that the two were swingers. I tried to ignore that fact as Fifty and I flirted together. We exchanged numbers and decided to get together sometime in the near future.

He called me to set up a date. He informed me that his uncle, who lived close to me, was throwing a dinner party that weekend and Fifty wanted me to accompany him. I politely agreed. It would be a great way to get to know him, and see what he was all about.

He picked me up, and we rode to his uncle's house a couple of miles away.

Have you ever seen that episode of *The Office*, where Pam and Jim go to Michael and Jan's place for dinner, and they have to wait three hours for the Osso Bucco to cook? Pam and Jim sit around awkwardly waiting for the whole thing to be over. It was like that. We waited over two hours for dinner, and had to entertain ourselves in the meantime. I spoke with Fifty's uncle and uncle's wife, as well as the two other guests that were there. Party conversation included Venice Beach city council meetings. Yawn. Just what every twenty-five year old wants to talk about.

What am I doing here? How did I get myself into this mess? I am the youngest person here by at least twenty-five years. It's not like I can just fake my way out of it — I have no way home! Plus, I really liked Fifty. I didn't want to ruin things between the two of us.

Dinner was finally served around 9pm. We ate, said our goodbyes, and Fifty drove me back home.

When we got to my place, I invited him in. I'm not sure why — I knew I wasn't ready to sleep with him. I hate that stupid code that says that inviting a man in lets him know that you want to sleep with him. We made out in my living room for a few minutes, and eventually I kicked him out. I was tired, and so ready for bed.

We texted back and forth a few times after that. He was splitting his time between New York and LA, but his texts just sort of died off after a while. I didn't bother to rekindle things between the two of us.

I never heard from Fifty again.

# 46
# Legs

Ladies and Gentlemen, News Flash!

In my twenties I did not have very high self-esteem. This meant dating a lot of men who were not men I should have spent my time on. The following is a perfect example:

I was hanging out with some friends at a local tiki bar when I saw Legs. He was about 6 feet tall, stocky football player build with short blond hair. He had tattoos on his arms and legs. He was seated near the pool table when I spotted him with a male and female. I was instantly attracted and couldn't take my eyes off of him.

The way he joked around with the woman, I wondered if they were dating. I still continued to stare, though. There was some kind of animal magnetism that drew me to him. I honestly couldn't help myself. I knew it was going to be trouble too, since that woman would damn well kick my ass if she caught me looking at him.

My friends and I were seated at the bar, not too far from the pool tables, so there was a definite chance that he was going to come near us to ask the bartender for a drink. When he did, I noticed he grabbed a cane. He hobbled, placing each foot with care until he made his way to the bar.

Alright, I couldn't help myself. I mustered up the courage to talk to him. I didn't feel quite as vulnerable, since I figured he was with his girlfriend anyways. I was just having a friendly conversation with a fellow bar patron — right?

"Are you okay?!" I squeaked. I knew I was asking for trouble. I eyed the girl at the pool table. She hadn't even looked up from her game. I was truly asking an innocent question, but I knew I was playing with fire.

"Sky diving accident," he replied, and grinned flirtatiously.

"Okay, you're fucking with me," I replied. He responded that no, he had broken both of his legs skydiving about six months earlier, I could ask his friend. He pointed in the direction of the pool table.

Friend, eh?

"Wow, that's crazy," I tried my best to flirt with him. "How did it happen?"

He then told me about how his chute didn't open in time, so he came down too fast and broke both his legs. It was his four hundredth jump.

Someone was clearly an adrenaline junkie.

We proceeded to chat at the bar for a few minutes, and then he took me over and introduced me to his friends. I knew at that moment that I was safe — this girl definitely was not his girlfriend. I breathed a sigh of relief. I never want to be the girl who interferes in someone else's relationship.

Legs and I spent the entire rest of the night in our own little world, chatting away.

I learned a lot about him that night:

-He was 37 (I was 24. Okay, not the worst thing in the world. I've been out with men older than him).

-He lived in the Valley (geographically undesirable).

-He had a daughter (at 24, I was way too young and unprepared to become insta-mom).

-He wasn't working at the time (he was in construction, and because of his legs, he couldn't work).

-He couldn't wait to get back out there to jump out of another plane! (I am so anti-adrenaline, it's not even funny).

-He smokes cigarettes (I fucking hate the smell of them).

-He lived with his mom (we have a winner!).

-He had done time in jail (it was just, like, a little petty theft. No big deal, right?).

He seemed like the opposite of everything I was looking for in a partner. Of course 24-year-old me wanted to date him. So badly. What a bad boy! I just want to take care of him, poor thing! (Dude, how much tail do you think he pulled because of his legs? Women are suckers for that nurturing bit.)

We ended up exchanging numbers. I was excited that the guy I liked, liked me too. I felt powerful. I had made that happen. I hadn't sat around and waited for him to talk to me — I had gone out and gone after what I wanted.

Even if he wasn't what I needed.

For our first date we went for drinks at another bar. The conversation was fine — he wasn't brilliant, but I was too blinded by my desire to nurse him back to health to see that this wasn't a match made in heaven. After drinks, I told him I needed to stop by a friend's house party, and asked if he wanted to join me. He said sure, so we took a cab to my friend Steve's house.

Legs and I enjoyed a drink and each other's company at Steve's place. After about an hour, Steve pulled me aside.

"Dude, that guy is a loser. You can do so much better than that."

Could I? At the time, I didn't think I could. I thought I had to settle for someone who was interested in me. Or at least, seemed interested in me.

I respected Steve's opinion. He's an engineer for a major company, and as a good male friend, I trusted his moral compass. Maybe Legs was a loser. Maybe I could do better.

Legs and I took a cab back to my place, where he dropped me off before heading back to his mom's house (yes, his mom's house). Before he left, he kissed me goodbye. It was a kiss that tasted like an ashtray, and I knew I couldn't spend the rest of my life tasting that every time I kissed someone.

He left, and I was torn. On the one hand, I thought I really like this guy. Or, at least, I liked the idea of being with someone, and he seemed to fit the description of "someone." On the other hand, Steve said he was a loser, so...

After careful consideration, I decided to side with Steve's opinion. I find that when I'm blinded by my lust/passion/love/stupidity, I can trust my good friends to be 100% honest with me, even if it's not an opinion that I agree with. I know they have my best interests at heart, so I need to listen to them.

The next time Legs texted me to say that he wanted to hang out, I happened to be out of town, and told him so. I never heard from him again.

# 47
# Alex

In my first year of teaching, MySpace was extremely popular.

Somehow, I became friends on MySpace with Alex. Alex told me he was a waiter at a restaurant in Beverly Hills.

We agreed for our date to meet up at Sharkeez, a small local bar in Manhattan Beach. It was the Wednesday of Thanksgiving week, and I didn't have work. He came and met me for happy hour after he finished at work, and we enjoyed a few drinks and each other's company.

He was half Guatemalan and half German, with large brown eyes and a fantastic laugh. He had his tongue pierced, and had bleached tips (it may or may not have been past the time that it was appropriate to have bleached tips, but we're letting it go, okay?) He radiated a positive, party-boy vibe. You could tell just by looking at him that he was fun and outgoing.

We grabbed happy hour drinks. Happy hour drinks turned into late night drinks as we talked and laughed into the night. I enjoyed every second of being with Alex: he made me laugh, and made me feel like I was the most important person in the room. He looked at me with his big brown eyes, and I could tell he was listening to what I had to say, and that it was important.

At the end of the evening, I invited him to come home with me. I was 22 and thought the only way to get a man to stick around was to give myself to him physically. I thought this would make him respect me and want to be in a relationship with me. This is clearly before I realized that my value and my self-worth are not tied to sex, and that it's appropriate for a man to get to know me without sleeping with me.

I was at Sharkeez again for happy hour some years later, when a server delivered food to our table. I looked into his face, and after a second it finally registered: Alex. He was back!

He recognized me, and even remembered my name. We exchanged numbers, but nothing ever came of it. He worked at that Sharkeez for an extremely long time, and I would see him every time we would go after work — which was practically every Friday.

Every couple of times I would see him, he would end up hitting on me or texting me to see what I was doing after I was done hanging out with my friends. A few times he tried to come over late night, after he was off work. I always thought each time that he was still interested in dating me. I was too young and naive to realize that he was just looking for a fun little booty call. He seemed like such a genuine and fun guy, but I wanted to see what I wanted to see — he was interested in me for a relationship, right? I couldn't wrap my brain around the fact that someone could be interested in me as a person, and want to sleep with me, but not want a relationship with me.

I eventually found a better spot to happy hour and stopped all the foolishness with Alex. Since I was out of sight, I was also out of mind. I never heard from him again.

# 48
## MC

Alright, so sometimes I date out of convenience.

Somehow I arranged for MC to pick me up from the mechanic's where I dropped my car off for service on a Saturday morning. The mechanic said it was only going to be an hour and that they'd call me when it was finished. MC took me to the Starbucks nearby, where he shared with me that he was really hung over. Best foot forward, right?

He had driven 45 miles to get to me that morning, and wore his sunglasses the entire time. I never saw his eyes, through the entire date. Somehow we got on the subject of jail. I asked him if he'd ever been.

He hesitated. "Yes," he finally responded.

"Oh really? For what?"

"Umm....I don't want to say."

He wasn't going to tell me? What the hell did he go to jail for? Was it something stupid and embarrassing? Or was it something that was going to make me run away screaming? *Oh my God,* was it sexual assault? Domestic violence? I hope it was just some white collar crime. Cross my fingers that it was fraud. He wouldn't say anything else except that he was in jail for "a while," whatever that means...

I checked my phone. Damn, still no call from the mechanic. Please, let them call soon! It's already been an hour. I'm sure it'll just be another five minutes, right?

An hour turned into three. What the fuck?!!? Things got really uncomfortable really fast. We went to Marie Callendar's for pie, and it became clear that he was only keeping me company because the mechanic hadn't called yet. Eventually, he demanded that I call the mechanic. The mechanic said they had been backed up that morning, and they would be done in just a few minutes.

I have never seen someone move so quickly. As soon as I told MC that my car was going to be ready, he threw money on the table, jumped up from the booth, and rushed to the car, keeping ten paces in front of me the entire time. The minute I got in the car, he put the car in reverse and peeled out of the parking lot.

At least he stopped the car to let me out when we got to the mechanic.

# 49
# Shouting Match

Shortly after moving into my own apartment, I went back on the dating websites.

You see, I had taken a break from online dating to get away from the crazy guys, to get a different perspective and hopefully change my energy. I was hoping that this time around I would attract a different type of man.

Well...

Alright, I'll admit, this dating story is my fault. I shouldn't have tried to open up my dating horizons. When *inkandcuddles* sent me a message, I should have said no. But, I wanted to give him a chance. He had a ton of tattoos. (I'm not saying this is a bad thing. I'm not saying it's indicative of a specific type of person. But there appears to be a correlation in my experience between the number of tattoos a man has over the visible surface area of his body, and the depth (or lack thereof) of conversation that I'm able to have.) We'll call the tattoos red flag #1. He seemed nice enough through the website, so I gave him my number.

He texted me. And texted me. And if I didn't send a response back within five to ten minutes, he'd either re-text me or send me a question mark. Sometimes if I didn't comment on a statement he'd made, he'd assume that I didn't like the answer and wasn't interested. Hello, insecure. Red flag #2.

Not only that, but when I asked him what his three best qualities were, he responded with nice, motivated, and *smells good*. Smells good!? That's your best quality? What about smart? Sweet? Funny? Loyal? Honest? Any number of generic adjectives that could describe a potential mate! And you choose smells good? So does my body wash, but that doesn't mean I want to date it! Red flag #3.

Eventually, I have some free time (which is rare for me) after doing some work so I ask if he wants to meet me for a drink. He told me to text him my location, so I gave him a major intersection. I asked him to text me back when he had chosen a location. He proceeded to text me a bunch of texts about how excited he was to meet me and how he couldn't wait to meet me.

Me: **Did you text a location and I missed it?**

Ink: **No, I haven't picked one. I'm really excited to meet you.**

Ink: **You seem chill.**

Ink: **Have you started working yet?**

Ink: **Text me when you're finished working.**

About 20 minutes later:

Me: **Have you picked a location yet?**

Inked: **No, not yet.**

Red Flag #4. Dude. Pick a spot already. It's not rocket science. There's a giant mall near my house with four restaurants inside, there are two bars down the street from my house, and there's a row of restaurants on the other side of me.

Me: **Text me back with a place.**
Ink: **El Torito**
Me: **Ok, what time?**
Ink: **I'll text you when I leave here.**

I have no idea where "here" is, and that wasn't a time. He was being evasive with my questions. And it's not even like I was asking him about his marital status. Just pick a time, bro.

Me: **So what time do you think you'll be here?**
Him: **Like 4 or 4:30?**
Me: **Ok, let's make it 4:30.**

I'll admit, I'm a bit OCD about nailing down location and time. And I'll own up to it. I take full ownership of my crazy. And in my world, I need someone who can nail down a *time* and *location* for when to meet someone. I don't think it's too much to ask. Maybe for some people it is. Then again, those people are not for me. I'm going to call that Red Flag #5.

I live close enough that I could walk to the date. So I did just that. At 4:20 I got a text:

Ink: **Where are you?**
Me: **Walking. We said 4:30, right?**

(By the way, I'm always punctual)

Ink: **Yeah where are we going to meet? The bar? Parking lot?**
Me: **You choose. Where are you now?**
Ink: **My car lol**

He never texted me a location of where to meet, so I walked towards the entrance, figuring I could text him from the front door. As I crossed the parking lot, I heard "Yo!"

This is how you greet a woman? Red Flag #6.

He was dressed in a baseball cap, tank top, jeans and tennis shoes (hell, I'll take tank top over sweat pants any day. Some guy once asked me if he could dress comfortably on a date. I told him it wasn't going to work out between us. Seriously. Put your best foot forward.) He was also wearing a gold chain and a few rings, one of which was a double ring that covered his middle and ring finger. There was something engraved on the base of it that I couldn't quite read.

He walks me inside, sits at the bar, faces his chair toward me, and asks me what I want to drink. I tell him skinny margarita. He proceeds to order for me. Sometimes I find this adorable. In this case, I didn't. I already knew this wasn't going to go well.

I began to ask him the standard first date "getting to know you questions."

"So what do you do for fun?"

"Friends, movies, you know, whatever. I'm just really chill."

Hmm...not very communicative, are you, buddy?

"What do you do with your friends?"

"Just like, whatever. I'm chill. Whatever's fun."

"Ok, but what do you consider fun? Like, drinking? Bars? Popping molly? Museums?"

He suddenly looked upset. "Aye, don't try to put me in a box. I don't do molly. That shit is nasty. I don't understand why you're trying to investigate me!"

Has this dude never talked to a stranger before?!?! I'm trying to find common ground, trying to see if we're compatible. I shared that with him.

"Yeah, but you're trying to put me in a box! I'm just chill, I do whatever. I'll go to museums, go to bars, just whatever's fun!"

I informed him of an exhibit I went to at MOCA about graffiti art, and tried to share with him a recent project my students had done in the community to approve a mural on the wall of a local business. In the middle of telling my story, he interrupts and yells down to the bartender at the other end of the bar, "Can I get a shot of patron?"

Red flag #7, 8 and 9.

7. He interrupted me while I was talking, without apologizing.

8. He asked for a shot on a date at 4:30 in the afternoon.

9. He didn't ask if I wanted one.

We continued talking (and by we, I mean that he would speak, I'd try to share what was on my mind, and he would cut me off). At some point when chatting about online dating, he shared his online dating gems, which included:

"Yeah, I was fucking some girl, and she told me to choke her and that shit was a turn-off, so I got up and walked out without saying shit to her. That shit was nasty. She looked all shocked when I got up. I mean spanking is okay, but that choking shit means she's got issues."

"I like getting in fights at Dodger games. After we get kicked out, we try to wait for those fuckers in the parking lot after the game but security always makes us leave."

"I once went out with a girl who told me dudes from online dating sent her dick pics. I can't be with a girl like that, can't deal with that drama, so I dumped her ass."

I tried to explain him that a girl has no control over whether or not a guy from the Internet sends her dick pics. He didn't seem to get it. He got really defensive. I became frustrated, mostly because if a guy I actually liked (not this one, obviously) decided to dump me because some other asshole that I thought was a nice guy sexually harassed me with a dick pic, I'd be upset. I have no control over whether or not someone decides to send me a dick pic within 5 minutes of receiving my number (it's happened before, and now I'm much more cautious about giving out my number).

He asked me if I was upset that he kept cutting me off. I responded that I was, because what's important to me is being listened to, since I get ignored all day long in my job. He demanded that I not be upset.

Dude, don't tell me how I should feel.

I grew frustrated with our conversation, and at some point (after my second cocktail) I blurted out that I felt he and I were not compatible. He was extremely offended.

"I've been nothing but a gentleman to you! I was respectful! How can you say we're not compatible!?"

"Wait...were you feeling me?" I asked him, shocked that he would even think we were a good match.

"Yes!" he responded.

I couldn't believe it. This guy must come from a dysfunctional family to think that this much arguing was how a first date should go. I asked him if he wanted me to stay while he finished his drink (because at this point, what am I supposed to do? I'm too nice to just walk out, and dammit, I wish I wasn't...) He said I could stay if I wanted.

Of course now awkward silence ensues. I wrack my brain to come up with something to talk about. I ask about what his ring says.

He replies with an attitude, "It doesn't matter now, does it?"

"OKAY! That's it!" I cry out. "I'm leaving!" I hop out of my seat and begin to gather my things.

"Wait, I was just kidding!"

"I was just trying to be nice and continue a conversation so we don't have to sit in awkward silence, but obviously you just need to be a dick about it. I'm gonna go!" I storm out of the restaurant. He follows me.

"Wait! I get that you're loud, but I'm a private person. There was no reason for you to disrespect me in front of all those people!" he shouts when we're out of the restaurant. I turn around to face him.

"Oh, that wasn't loud! You want to see me get loud?!"

"I just don't understand! I was nothing but a gentleman towards you!" He is becoming more agitated as he stands there, facing me.

I thank him for the drink yet again and tell him that I'm just not interested. He then tries to convince me that I'm just going to continue to date assholes, that my dating expectations are unrealistic, and that he has a few other things he wants to say to me. I look at him quizzically, and decide that I don't need to listen to his speech.

I thank him again (in the least sarcastic tone I can muster) for the drink, and walk off.

"You're insane!" he howls as I walk away.

I begin the walk back to my apartment. He texts me.

Ink: **LMAO**
Ink: **You're fucking weird.**
Ink: **This is definitely a story I'm telling my friends.**

Well, Ink, this is definitely a story I'm telling the world. And my dating expectations are not unrealistic. I'll never settle.

I blocked his number and his profile.

# WHAT WAS <u>HE</u> THINKING?

*I'm a smart woman, but sometimes I question his decisions. Sometimes I'm not sure if men are from this planet.*

# 50
# Jackson

My friend Emily always puts together these big dinners with 10-12 people at a restaurant. She's got a healthy social network of friends. I've met some interesting characters through her dinners.

One evening, I was seated across from a black man with dreadlocks. He looked like he might be about five years younger than me, skinny build, probably about 5'10. As we began to converse over dinner I discovered he was a drummer for a band, and had traveled a lot with the band. He was currently working on a project as a drummer for a Michael Jackson cover band.

We flirted throughout the meal, and by the time we finished dinner Jackson and I had exchanged numbers. I wasn't sure exactly where this was going to go, but I was willing to give it a shot. Who am I to decide what the Universe has in store for me? Maybe he was my soulmate. I'd give it one date to decide.

We texted back and forth a few times. The texts were super platonic, and eventually he asked me out to lunch. He asked me to meet him at In-n-Out at 11 am on a Tuesday morning (it was summer time, so I wasn't working).

Alright, I love me some In-n-Out burger, don't get me wrong. But I'm not sure that's where I want to go on a first date. Maybe it's not a date? Maybe we're just doing lunch. I'll just roll with it and see what happens.

I show up in jeans, flats and a nice shirt. He is wearing a ratty t-shirt and jogger sweats. No effort into your dress? Okay, maybe it's not a date.

We stand in line to order, and like a gentleman, he lets me order first. I place my order, and the cashier asks, "Anything else?"

I look back at Jackson, wondering if he is going to order. I stare at him, and he stares back at me, and smiles. He makes no move. After a long, silent, awkward pause, I turn back around slowly. I am fuming.

"Nope, that's it."

She tells me my total. I turn around one more time, looking back at Jackson expectantly. He grins at me once again. I whip around, and hand the cashier my card.

I paid for my own meal. At fucking In-n-Out.

Okay, so confirmed. Not a date. I mean, if this were a date, he would have paid for my meal, right? It's not like we went to an expensive place. He decided on In-n-Out, for fuck's sake.

We grab a booth. I ask him what flavor of milkshake he got.

"Oh, chocolate and vanilla swirl, in honor of our date."

Assholesayswhat? Did he just say date? I must not have heard that correctly.

My brain is trying to process what has just happened. So, he thinks we're on a date, but he shows up to a fast food restaurant in sweat pants and then makes me pay for myself? How romantic.

I sit through my meal with him, and we chat about his projects. He talks about how he's going to be famous, that's his big aspiration, and how he likes to tour on the road a lot. Then he starts in on the teacher fetish.

"I wish my teachers were as hot as you."

Yeah, okay, that's nice.

"Are any of the kids 'Hot for Teacher'?"

Yes. Ew.

"So, have you ever had a crush on a student?"

No. Double ew.

"Man, when I was in school…"

Yes, please, tell me more about what a terrible student you were, about how you didn't understand anything, about how essentially you aren't motivated, didn't go to college, and never learned any of the mathematics I teach.

Yes, I'm bitter. This conversation happens more often than not. It makes me feel like you're not actually interested in me as a person, you're more fascinated with the idea of dating someone who is a teacher — you are living out some high school fantasy of yours where the thirty-something teacher may actually be interested in a seventeen-year-old child. Not in this lifetime, buddy. Barf.

We finish our food, and I'm a ready to be out of there. If I knew I was going to have to pay for my meal, I would have fought for something more impressive than In-n-Out.

He walks me to my car and gives me a brief hug goodbye. I get in my car and leave.

He tried to text me two weeks later to say hello, and to see if I wanted to go out again.

First of all, who waits two weeks? Clearly you're not that into me. Second of all, where are you going to take me this time? Jack in the Box? I'll pass.

I sent him a polite message to say that I just didn't think we were compatible, but thanks anyways, and good luck with the band stuff.

I never heard from him again.

# 51
# Guy #9

Kendra, Roommate, and I took the metro (almost unheard of in Los Angeles) to check out another friend's restaurant preview night. In order to sample the cocktails on the menu and stay safe, we decided to have a metro-venture.

After enjoying food and drinks at the new restaurant, we decided we wanted to enjoy a little more time downtown before heading back on the metro. Kendra had almost a bottle of wine, I'd had a few cocktails, and Roommate had two drinks — the most I'd ever seen her drink.

I'd noticed a lounge on the way from the metro station to the restaurant, so I suggested we stop there.

We stepped inside, and a woman in her forties immediately hounded us. "Are you here for speed dating?"

"No." I responded.

"Oh. Well, let us know if you'd like to do it! We start in ten minutes. We could really use some more women."

The three of us were all single. "How much is it?" Kendra inquired.

"Thirty five dollars each," the lady responded.

My friends and I looked at each other. What the fuck!?!?! Thirty five dollars?! This bitch must be crazy! We wanted to do it, but not at that price. Kendra said to wait it out — she figured eventually the woman would get desperate and let us do it for free. Roommate was a little nervous, but I told her it was kind of fun. I'd done it before, I told her, and you only had to talk to the guys for two minutes before someone rang a bell and they got up and you talked to someone else. Two minutes was no big deal. Totally manageable.

Kendra was right.

"Alright, don't tell anyone — especially my boss — but you can do it for free."

As soon as we were assigned to tables, I realized why she was so desperate for us to participate. Including the three of us, there were six girls. And nine guys. The organizer would have been screwed if we decided not to participate.

Roommate was at a table immediately to the left of me, and a few tables to my right was Kendra.

Guy #1 sat down. We chatted, and after what I'd thought was two minutes, I awaited the bell. It didn't ring. At least not two minutes in. I began to worry. How long was I going to have to entertain conversation with this guy? I began to grow impatient.

After six excruciating minutes, the bell finally rang, and the man moved from my table to Roommate's. I couldn't help but think he would get along with Roommate.

Let me give you the list of who I met that night:

Guy #1: Boring. Owns para-sailing company. Not my type.

Guys #2 and 3: forgettable.

Guy #4: speaks no English. Like, has been in the country eight weeks. Do you know how painful it is to have a conversation with a guy for six minutes who speaks no English? Really painful. I teach all day, I don't want to teach in my off time too.

Guy #5: I don't remember much about him, other than being completely embarrassed — Kendra (who's had 2 more glasses of wine) comes over to tell me how much I'm going to love Guy #9, who she's currently talking to, because he's so funny! I tell her to go back and sit down. I sneak a peak at her guy — he's cute! I can't wait to talk to him.

Guy #6: Lame.

Guy #7: He was alright. We talked a little about education. He had a daughter. About two minutes in, Kendra drunkenly stumbled over to tell me she didn't want to talk to her guy anymore. I glanced over at her table. No-English was sitting there, glancing back and forth between Kendra and I, looking like a lost puppy dog. He obviously is trying to make friends to practice his English, but he definitely bit off more than he could chew with speed dating. I look Kendra dead-seriously in the face, and sternly tell her to go sit back down. She's got two more people to go. Just sit there. #7 and I continue our conversation. I look over at Kendra, and she's looking around the room, avoiding eye contact with No-English, and definitely not talking to him. I roll my eyes. #7 comments that my friend is a little drunk. Thank you, Captain Obvious.

Guy #8: Fucking awkward. Oh good. Six minutes of my life I'll never get back.

Guy #9: Finally. FINALLY. Someone interesting. And cute! From Detroit, works in computer programming. Lives in my hometown! (Which, come to think of it, is kind of far. It's 45 miles from my house.) As we chat, I'm certain I'm going to mark "yes" to him on my sheet. He is definitely the only one. And I'm fairly certain he's going to mark "yes" to me as well, which means that the dating company will give each of us the other's email address.

We both mark "yes."

We email back and forth a few times, exchange numbers and set up a date.

We met at a wine bar, and ordered an appetizer to share and a glass of wine each. The conversation was good: we chatted about our lives, and how we'd gotten to where we were today. I could tell he was mildly socially awkward, but it was alright with me. He was gorgeous and very sweet. He told me about how he had two daughters that lived in Michigan, one of whom was 14. He was 37, and was doing contract work and occasionally traveling to San Diego to work for some company. At the end of the date, I commented that one of the times he was on his way to San Diego, he should stop by and we would go out on a second date. He said that sounded like fun, and would split up the three hour drive.

So, after a few weeks of texting (including drunken photos of him half-naked just out of the shower — which were, in a word, yummy), he told me he was heading to San Diego on Sunday night, so he'd love to come take me to dinner. I picked out a nice tapas bar on the beach and made a reservation. He came to the door and picked me up, and said hi to Roommate, since they'd already met.

As he walked me to his car and opened the door he cautioned me to be careful, because his car was full. I asked him why.

"Oh, because I'm moving to San Diego. Today was my last day in Thousand Oaks."

"What?!?" I was shocked, because in all of our texting, he never mentioned moving.

"Yeah, the moving truck picked up my stuff this morning and will deliver it tomorrow morning."

"Oh." I was surprised, and disappointed. This guy was already impossible enough to date 45 miles away, never mind trying to date him now that he'd be 100 miles away. San Diego is so far — he might as well be living in New York. Hell, most times, I won't even date a guy that lives in the Valley.

We enjoyed dinner together. On the way back to my house, the conversation took an interesting turn.

"It's too bad you're moving to San Diego! It's so far!"

"Well, you could move with me." I looked at him. I thought to myself how I'd only known him for a few weeks, but we'd really only been out twice. I decided to play along with this little scenario he proposed.

"Only if I don't have to work."

His response led me to believe he didn't understand that I was only joking, that I wasn't *truly* considering moving with this guy. He really believed I was contemplating his offer. "No, you don't have to work. I'll give you a salary so you can buy shoes, and all you have to do is fall in love with me."

I laughed nervously, realizing that he was serious. He truly intended for me to move with him if I wanted to! I kindly declined his offer, and got out of the car. This fool was crazy! There was no way I was going to move with him, nor was I going to continue a long distance relationship with him after two dates! I told him to have a safe drive, and he left.

We texted a few times after that, but it just kind of petered out. I've never heard from him again.

# 52

# Dominic

More than anything in the entire world, I just want to be listened to. I'm not a woman who talks excessively. I'm not a woman of many words; I choose my words carefully, and never talk more than I feel is necessary. I spend my day as a teacher being ignored by a portion of the class at any given time. I don't think it's too much to ask for the person I date to listen to me when I am speaking.

Maybe I'm setting the bar way too high though.

In my early twenties I met a man through Craigslist. His name was Dominic, and we became MySpace friends (yup, it was that long ago). We decided to meet for coffee.

We sat together over coffee and chatted about our favorites — movies, music, TV shows. I felt indifferent about him. I didn't necessarily like or dislike him. We'd been out for about thirty minutes, chatting, when he suddenly proposed an idea.

"Let's go get something to eat!"

I stated that I wasn't really hungry, but he insisted. "Come on, we'll go to TGI Fridays, it's right down the street." I repeated that I wasn't interested in eating, but once more he persisted. I reluctantly agreed, and we got into his car.

I know where the restaurant is — it's walking distance from my place, so I wasn't too worried about being in the car with him. If it all goes downhill, I can walk home.

He pulls out of the parking lot, and he turns onto the main road. He continues to speak, and finally he asks me a question. "So, what made you decide to be a teacher?"

I open my mouth to answer, to tell him about the tag-team duo of teachers in middle school who impacted my life, who saved me from a painful childhood, who inspired me to love learning.

"Well, I've always loved school, but I had two teachers who-"

He cuts me off. "Oh, I love this song!" He leans over, turns up the radio, and begins to sing along with the radio. I stop talking, figuring he'll quit singing soon enough, he'll apologize for interrupting me, and he'll ask me to continue. I mean, I get it — a good song is a good song. Right? I try to justify his behavior.

The song finally ends, and like some sort of kid with ADD, he starts with a new question, without acknowledging he's cut me off.

"So, what's the best trip you've ever been on?" I begin to answer, when he recognizes the next song on the radio. He turns it up again, belting out lyrics, drowning out my words. I'm forced to stop mid-sentence. My face is flushed with embarrassment and anger. I was trying to connect with my date, to be vulnerable with him, but he has proven that he is not worthy of my vulnerability. I immediately clam up.

After another minute of singing, he realizes that I am not talking. "Why'd you get so silent?"

We are pulling into the parking lot at TGI Fridays. "You cut me off and started singing!" I reply harshly. "TWICE!"

"Did I? I didn't mean to," he says, somewhat sheepishly.

I proceed to describe the events of the last five minutes to him. He looks surprised, as if he's finding out about it for the first time. As if it wasn't he who was just acting like an inconsiderate asshole.

"Sorry about that. Let's just go in and grab something to eat and forget about the whole thing." His apology feels hollow. I don't believe he actually means it, and I don't think he understands why it's a big deal. I am more angry now than I was before.

"No, I don't want to get anything to eat! You also didn't listen when I said I wasn't interested in getting food!"

"But it's just a little something to eat, it'll be fine. C'mon!" He opens the door like he's ready to get out. He is ignoring my feelings, putting himself first. I can't help but wonder, if this is his best first impression, what does the rest of his life look like?

"No, I want you to take me back to my car."

"You don't want to go eat?" Jesus, the guy *really* doesn't listen.

"NO!" I practically scream. I'm infuriated. If he's listening to me and hearing me just now, he thinks I'm insane. I am screaming about not wanting to get food. I'm sure I appear to be a lunatic since he hasn't understood from the get-go that I wasn't interested in eating in the first place.

"Wow, okay. I'll take you back. Sheesh." He gets back in the car, starts up the engine, and we head back out on the road. My car is only seven minutes away, but it feels like an eternity. The silence between us is heavy. I can feel the confusion emanating from his body.

I finally break the silence. "Look, all I want in my life is to be listened to. I felt like when you turned up the radio, you were ignoring what I had to say, and you made me feel like I wasn't important."

"I just really like that song!" he defended himself.

He missed the whole fucking point. He's not mature enough to realize the error of his ways. I'm over it.

He pulls up to my car. I get out, thank him for the coffee, and slam the door. He speeds off.

I never hear from him again.

# 53
# Mark

I met Mark on OkCupid. He was gorgeous. After our first coffee date, we decided we would see each other again soon.

The next day, he said that he wanted to see me after he got off work at midnight. I told him that was entirely too late for me to meet up with him. He told me in all seriousness to "just leave the door unlocked" for him, and he would find his way. I had known this guy for a total of an hour. There was zero percent chance I was going to leave the door unlocked for him. He can find his hookup elsewhere. Creep.

# 54
# Karaoke

Karaoke was half Asian, half White, and all kinds of nerdy: glasses, about 5'7, and self-deprecating in all the right ways. We met for coffee on our first date, and it was fine. I got to laugh what I thought was the appropriate amount, and I was intrigued by our conversation. I agreed on a second date. He picked me up, and we went for ramen in West LA. It was lunch time on a Saturday.

Again, our conversation fascinated me. He was kind of a goofball, and a few years younger than me — I was twenty-four, and he was twenty-two. He still had some childlike qualities about him. After lunch together, he wanted to karaoke.

It's daylight. On a Saturday. We're sober. What the fuck bar has karaoke?

He said he knew a spot, so we meandered to a strip mall. He walked right up to the door marked Karaoke, and marched right in. We were in a reception area, and Karaoke told the guy there were two of us, for two hours. The guy grabbed two microphones, and told us to follow him. He led us into a room with two couches, a table with some three ring binders on it, and a TV.

Our own private karaoke room. I am too sober for this shit. I am not emotionally prepared to sing for two hours in front of a stranger. I do not have my list of songs prepared. I mean, don't get me wrong, I love to karaoke, but I need some time to mentally talk myself into it first.

I sat on the couch, and he immediately typed in a song. I heard Michelle Branch pipe through the speakers. He started to sing in a high-pitched voice.

Not a turn on.

Obviously he's done this before. I tried to ignore him as I flipped through the book to find my song.

"Stand Up" by Ludacris. They have it! Yesssss.

I managed to make it through the song without looking at him, trying not to acknowledge that there's anyone else in the room to listen to me. This is a level of intimacy I am not ready for. There is some intimacy involved with singing to another person. There was no way I was going to look him in the eye.

I spent most of the rest of the time looking through the book, trying to ignore his terrible singing. His poor attempt at "U And Dat" by E-40 made my skin crawl. He also sang Miley's Cyrus's "Wrecking Ball." I think it was around this point that I couldn't contain my laughter. This is one of the more ridiculous dates I've ever been on. I didn't respect him. Plus, he was paying more attention to the microphone than he was to me. He just wanted someone to be in the room with him, to take up some singing space while he looked through the book for a new song to sing.

When our time was up, I thanked him for the laughs (mostly *at* him, not *with* him), and said goodbye. We went our separate ways. I never heard from him again.

# 55
# The Lawyer

Know what's romantic on a second date? Walking by a murder house.

I met The Lawyer through an online dating site. On our first date, we had dinner at a Mexican food restaurant in Westchester. He commented on my lack of jewelry, and said that most women he's been out with before wear a lot of jewelry. He found it odd that I don't wear any rings, and when I pointed out the eleven earrings shared between my ears, he didn't really seem that impressed.

He was great on paper — good upbringing, from the East Coast, went to some prestigious college, and then an even more prestigious law school. He practiced law for a large firm in LA, dressed well, and was extremely nice.

The problem? He was boring.

He only talked about law. I felt like he didn't have any hobbies. Nothing that we could share, no common interests. I don't remember much about our conversations leading up to our first date, other than the fact that I felt like I really *needed* to like him, since he was successful and had his shit together, much more so than any other guy that I'd ever been on a date with. When I met him, I *really, truly tried* to like him. I was determined to date him since he seemed so perfect when I described him to my friends before we'd even met.

I didn't *dis*like him. I just didn't want to make out with him. (Side rant: *isn't that always the case? It's either you want to fuck the shit out of the guy the minute you meet him, and he probably doesn't have a car, or a job, and is kind of an ass but works out twice a day and looks super hot or he's a super sweet guy, kind of boring, with a career, college education, and owns his own house...and you just want to be friends with him. I'm waiting for my overlap. I think they're few and far between. At least for me. If*

*you've had other luck…let me know where you meet these guys!*)
But, since I felt like I *had* to like him, I decided to give it a second
date.

He lived in Brentwood, so we met at a Chinese restaurant
near his apartment. Conversation through dinner was adequate,
but not compelling. After dinner, he asked if I wanted to go for
a walk. He seemed excited. I begrudgingly said yes. I had worn
sitting heels, not walking heels.

And so we walked the streets of Brentwood. In sexy heels
that were a little too high (seriously…who *walks* in LA anyways?!)
I tried my best to keep from wincing in pain with every step that
I took. As we walked, he talked more about lawyering, and I
just listened. As we came down Bundy Drive he pointed to an
apartment on the opposite side of the street.

"That's where Nicole Brown Simpson was murdered!" he
exclaimed with, what I considered, slightly too much excitement.
And of course, on a second date with someone from the Internet,
I get a little leery of what this dude is saying.

"Seriously?" I mutter, incredulous that this dude mentions
this on a date. Does he know how this looks? I've spent a total of
two hours of my life with The Lawyer. For all I know, that could
be his plan for me later in the evening. Besides that point, if he's
not planning on killing me, does he think this is romantic?

"Yeah, that's where OJ killed Nicole! Obviously they
repainted, and someone else lives there now, but that's where it
happened!" he responds, not realizing that my query wasn't out
of disbelief at his statement, but at his nerve.

I stared at him. "You know, it's getting late. I need to get
home. I have to be at work early tomorrow." I turned around and
headed back to my car.

Somewhere along the way, he picked up on body language
clues. The date ended with the obligatory hug, and no talk of
"that was fun, we should do it again!"

We both knew that was the end of that.

# 56
# Two Choices

Through Craigslist I went on a date with Two Choices. He was handsome. Half Black, half Native American, he had played football at ASU for a while before he tore up his knees and decided to take some time off. He lived in West Covina, a city that, on a good day in LA, took 45 minutes to get to.

We met for coffee in Redondo Beach and chatted for a bit. After coffee, we took a romantic walk on the beach. We held hands. He wasn't the brightest bulb in the box, but he was sweet, and super hot. We made out on the beach for a bit. When the date was over, he walked me back to my car, and I decided I wanted to see him again.

In the coming weeks, we chatted on the phone a few times, and texted back and forth as well, he on his Sidekick, me on my Motorola Razr. We were certainly nothing serious, and we hadn't slept together. Hell, he hadn't even touched my breasts.

One night in December, maybe two months since we'd been talking, I attended a Christmas party for the dance studio where I was taking classes. I had a few cocktails. My grandpa had passed away about a week before, and I was still in mourning. I, in my infinite wisdom, invited over Two Choices. I needed attention, and I certainly did not need an empty bed.

The following incident explains how Two Choices obtained his nickname.

I invited Two Choices over around midnight on Friday night. Of course, coming from West Covina, the drive takes 45 minutes. And of course, he needs to shower and do God-knows-what before he can come over. So by the time he calls me to let me know he's arrived around 2 am, I'd fallen asleep. I wake up when he calls, walk the straight pathway from my bedroom through the living room to the front door, and tell him to park in my driveway.

At the time, I was living with Roommate in a two bedroom duplex. We were the front house, and there was a long driveway that connected the front house to the back house, where another tenant lived. She parked in the driveway next to the back house. When Two Choices pulled up, there was no street parking, so I told him he'd be fine if he parked in the driveway. "If the neighbor needs to get out, she'll honk and we can just move the car. No big deal," I told Two Choices.

After he parked in the driveway, we walked in the front door, through the living room, and directly into my room. Next door to my room, a bit further down the hall, was Roommate's room. She had her door closed over, but not completely shut. As I shut the door to my bedroom, I told him that Roommate was asleep in the next room, so we needed to keep it down. I told him I just wanted to go to sleep. He seemed ok with that.

Of course, that turned into some heavy making out. Just some PG-13 making out though; everything was above the belt. It was 3 am, and I was emotionally and physically exhausted. I just didn't want to sleep alone. I fell asleep in his arms, contented with the fact that I wasn't alone.

Early in the morning, I was awakened to the sound of a car honking its horn. Over. And over. And over. Incessantly. I was trying to piece together the reasons why someone would be honking their horn so much as I slowly drifted out of my dream state. Then I realized.

"Two Choices!" I exclaimed. "Get up! You need to move your car!" I shook him wildly, realizing that the woman in the back house was trying to leave her house, and his car was blocking the driveway. Two Choices grumbled, opening his eyes. Moving like molasses, he slowly struggled to put his pants on as our neighbor continued to lay on the horn.

"Hurry up," I urged him. After what felt like fifteen minutes, he stumbled out of my room, back through the living room, out the front door to his car. He backed down the driveway, and into a spot on the street. The minute the driveway was free, our neighbor zoomed onto the street and sped off, running the stop sign at the corner.

I waited for Two Choices to finish parking the car, and he lumbered back towards the house.

He walked into the house in front of me. Through the front door. Through the living room. Skipping right past my room...

And opened Roommate's half-closed door before I even realized where he was going.

"Where the hell are you going?" I hissed, and followed up behind him just in time to see Roommate sit straight up in bed, and wonder who the fuck was in her bedroom.

"I'm so sorry!" I exclaimed to Roommate, and grabbed him by the back of his shirt and dragged him back to my room. "What the hell? My room is the first door!"

"Sorry...this house is confusing," he mumbled. I ran back to Roommate's room, and apologized again. I closed her door once more, but it was obvious that the shock of seeing a total stranger in the room provided the equivalent of two cups of coffee, and she wasn't getting back to bed any time soon.

Two Choices and I cuddled for a bit, and eventually I kicked him out with the excuse that I had so much to do on that Saturday morning. After he left, I apologized to Roommate once again, and she asked me how he ended up in her room. I told her I wasn't sure.

"I know he's not very smart, but really, he had *two* choices for which bedroom to choose. And he chose the wrong one." She and I laughed about that for a long time.

I didn't talk to him much after he left that day. I realized I wasn't that interested in him, he wasn't too bright, and he lived so far, it wasn't going to work out. We texted a few times, but I just wasn't interested in texting him back. One Tuesday around

10:30 am, my Razr dinged to notify me that I had gotten a picture message from Two Choices. I opened my phone.

And was shocked by what I saw. He had texted me a picture of his dick. Completely unwarranted. I hadn't even seen the real thing, why would I want a picture of it? It was 10:30 on a Tuesday morning! I was so surprised that I began to push buttons on my phone to try to make it go away...and accidentally discovered a menu that showed me the details of the message. I could see who the message was from.

And who he had sent it to.

He had sent a picture of his dick to me. And three other numbers.

A MASS TEXT?!?! I was MASS TEXTED a dick pic?! Who does that?! How LAZY do you have to be? I mean, I don't hate the game by any means. I have been known to have my player-player days back in the day. But for God's sake, if you're going to send inappropriate photos to your lovers, at least have the decency to do it one person at a time.

# 57
# Eric

I met Eric through OkCupid. He seemed adorable: was into anime, comics, etc. I sometimes like my guys really nerdy, so I thought he might be great. He seemed bright from reading his profile, which included the words "esoteric." Okay, smarty pants.

Our first two dates went really well. I had a great time talking to him, even if he was a little bit on the strange side. He paid for coffee for our first date, and for a drink at a bar for our second date.

On our third date, however, things went a bit differently. It was about two weeks after our first date and it was Valentine's Day, which is, of course, a weird time to go out on a date with someone you just started dating. It's also one of the busiest and most expensive days of the year to go on a date.

He wants to pick me up and take me to dinner at a restaurant in Little Tokyo. Alright, fine. At this time, I wasn't a big ramen fan, but I guess he didn't really care much about that idea since he wanted to take me to an extremely popular ramen shop. We arrived at 7 pm on a school night.

As he parked the car, I asked if he had made a reservation. He said no. This place doesn't take reservations.

Hmmm...alright.

We walk toward the restaurant, and the line is out the door. Down the block. Around the corner. There are people everywhere waiting to get into this place. He inquires about the wait. Two hours.

TWO HOURS?! Again, it's a school night. I worked all day, and my last meal was lunch at 11:30 am. You must be joking. He puts our name in for a table, although I politely mention that I am starving now and am not sure I can wait two hours for a table. We walk around for a while, and I am HANGRY: Hungry and Angry combined. I can't believe he wanted to take me out on Valentine's Day, but then not make a dinner reservation. This place is madness.

I finally politely mention that I cannot wait two hours to eat, and could we please find somewhere else to eat instead? He looks at me, sort of rolls his eyes and spits out "fine" in huff.

We end up at another ramen shop. The conversation at dinner suddenly feels strained. I think he's upset that he didn't get his ramen. I'm feeling more revived now that there's something in my stomach.

We get to the end of the meal, and the check arrives.

"Normally on the third date, I make the girl pay." I stare at him. Did he just say that out loud? "But, since it's Valentine's Day, I'll pick up the check."

You were going to make me pay?! The first two dates we went for coffee and one drink. Today we had a meal. You were going to make me pay for the meal? And what do you mean, *make* the girl pay? I am all for equality, and I will gladly pay, but it should be out of kindness, not out of obligation. And it should be a fair trade as well, not coffee versus an entire meal.

I sarcastically remarked that it was kind of him to pick up the tab on such an occasion. He smiled, not realizing or maybe choosing to ignore my tone. We walked back to the car, and he leaned in for a kiss.

I have never swerved so hard in my life.

I thanked him for dinner, and asked if he would kindly take me home. He looked taken aback, like his generosity at dinner warranted him earning a kiss from me.

Nope-ity nope McNope Nope. I don't owe you anything. We rode back in silence, except for the sound of The Gorrillaz on the radio.

He dropped me off at my house, didn't even get out to walk me to the door, and sped off as soon as I closed the door.

Needless to say, I didn't hear from him again.

# 58
# Patrick

I met Patrick on OkCupid. He was geographically undesirable, but he was a biology teacher so I thought we would at least have some common interests when it came to values about education.

He rode his motorcycle to meet me for coffee on a Saturday morning, and he brought his grading with him in case I didn't show up. Glad to know I'm not the only one that gets stood up on dates.

The date was pretty bland. He didn't have much of a personality. I wondered how he did as a teacher. I spent most of the date thinking about his classroom management style. Real romantic.

The date ended, and I didn't hear from him again, which was fine with me.

A year later, he found me on OkCupid and messaged me: **I can't believe it's been a year since we went on a date! How have you been? Are you still teaching?**

Hm. That seems like a weird thing to celebrate. Why would you send me that? Fine I'll play along.

**Yes, I'm still teaching. How about you?**

He never messaged me back.

Okay fine.

About six months after that a girlfriend and I went to a Match.com mixer. We spent the evening avoiding the awkward men who tried to start conversations with us, including one guy who said, "You know, you can't just use the bathroom excuse every time you want to get away from me."

It's a mystery to me why you're still single, sir.

At one point I spotted Patrick. I avoided saying hello, since we had only met once. There was no reason to spark up a conversation. He eventually approached me though.

"Hi! Remember we went on a date once?"

"Yes, Patrick, I remember you. How's teaching?" He looked shocked once I said his name. Ah, he thought I didn't remember.

"It's good. Tell me your name again?"

Why the fuck would you approach me if you didn't remember my name? What the hell. We exchanged niceties, and he left abruptly.

"Wow, I can see why you two didn't work out," my friend whispered as he walked away.

I rolled my eyes. This event was a bust.

I never heard from him again.

# 59
# The Singer

At one point in my dating career I began to think that I must be attracted to the wrong kinds of men. I decided I should attempt dating someone who went against the type of guy I was normally attracted to.

The Singer messaged me on PoF to tell me how beautiful I was. He mentioned he was a computer engineer by day, and had songs published on iTunes. He had a degree in computer information systems and a Masters in music.

He was also a bit larger than the guys I usually date — he must have been about 350 pounds. I am not a tiny person myself so I try not to discriminate based on size, but he is not someone I would normally find myself attracted to. I decided to give it a shot — maybe his personality would win me over.

When we finally got to the stage of meeting The Singer picked an extremely fancy restaurant in Long Beach. He wanted to do dinner. This struck me as a surprise since I normally do coffee or a drink as a first date option — I don't want to be stuck sitting for an hour with someone who I'm not interested in.

The restaurant he chose was right on the water: a girlfriend and I had gone there for happy hour once, and it seemed expensive to me even during those discounted hours. But, if that's what he wanted to do, I was not one to argue.

I arrived on time, hoping I would be the first one there. Apparently he was so excited to meet me he had arrived fifteen minutes earlier to make sure to be there when I showed up. He was 6'1 and looked somewhat menacing, but when he opened his mouth to say hello he was soft-spoken. I was impressed with his punctuality and dress — he was obviously working to impress me.

We chatted throughout dinner — I had to lean in to hear him over the din of the restaurant. I, on the other hand, was my loud boisterous self. I'm sure the people across the restaurant had no trouble hearing me. By the time we got to the end of the date I hadn't quite decided on my feelings about him — he hadn't thoroughly annoyed me enough to give him up completely, but I also wasn't enthralled with him. Usually, in those cases, I give those guys three dates, just so I can be sure. After he paid for dinner, he walked me to my car, gave me a brief hug goodbye, and left. He then texted me later that evening to tell me he had a wonderful time, and that he wanted to see me again. I told him that sounded great.

He texted me the next day to say good morning. He was thinking of me at work. I replied that he was sweet, and we chatted throughout the day over text. He texted me every morning to say good morning, every night to say good night, and just throughout the day to say hello. I began to notice after a few days that there wasn't any substance to his texts — it was always the same set of texts day after day.

Eventually he asked me out on a second date. He arranged for us to go a beautiful restaurant in Long Beach on the 13th floor. When I told a friend where he was taking me, she said that her friend had her wedding reception there — this place was beautiful and expensive. I told him it would be fine if I met him there, but he insisted on picking me up. He lived in Long Beach, but was pleased to drive the 30 minutes to my place, pick me up and drive right back down to Long Beach.

When we arrived at the restaurant, the host escorted us to a corner window — we had a view of both the city and the ocean. This was extremely fancy for a second date (a first official date since I often don't count the initial meeting as a "date" — it's more of a "meet and greet.") The waiter told us that a famous basketball player had eaten at the restaurant the evening before. The Singer was impressed. I didn't much care; I'm not a huge sports fan.

Dinner was fairly quiet. He was still soft-spoken, and didn't have a lot to add to the conversation. I'm not really one to divulge information without being asked, so we sat in long silences for a chunk of the date. It didn't quite feel uncomfortable, though. My mind still wasn't made up about him. He seemed extremely sweet and had gone through a lot of effort to make this date happen. Maybe he was just shy. A lot of people take time to open up. It's worth it to me to go on a third date with him. After dinner he drove me home. When we pulled up to the house, he got out of the car to open my door for me. I thought for sure he was going to try to kiss me, and I still wasn't sure how I felt about it. I was numb. He walked me to the front door, and gave me a hug, then turned around and walked back to his car. No kiss after the second date? Weird, but clearly he is trying to get to know me before he makes this relationship sexual. Chivalry isn't dead, after all.

As we texted throughout the weekend, he told me he wrote another song, and he was excited for me to listen to it. He asked for my email, and emailed me the file. I opened the track and was serenaded by an R&B love song entitled, "God Sent You to Me." I listened to the beat the first time. It was sort of generic. There was nothing about it that screamed #1 hit. I also wasn't that impressed with his voice. I began to think that he and I weren't a forever thing: if I couldn't support someone's dream because I didn't think he was that talented, this wasn't going to be a long-term relationship. I listened to the song again. Maybe it would be better the second time? The lyrics jumped out at me the second time. He was professing his love for a woman who had just walked into his life.

Wait.

It couldn't...

There's no way he...

Is he talking about *me* in this song?

He made it seem so important that I should listen to it.

Shit.

Don't panic. Maybe it means nothing. Maybe it's not about me. Right? Right. I'm just going to ignore it and hope it goes away.

I agree to a third date.

Somewhere between the second and third date we begin to follow each other on Instagram. I don't think anything of it — I follow lots of people on social media.

He picks me up for our third date, and I ask him where we are going.

"Beverly Hills," he replies. He tells me we have reservations at a restaurant there.

He pulls up to the valet, and they open the door for me. I hopped onto the sidewalk, and The Singer holds the door for me as we enter the restaurant. He approaches the host stand, and gives his name. "Oh, yes! Right this way, Mr. Singer!" She seems to know who he is, like she had taken the reservation. Or he had made special requests. She walks us to our table.

It's covered in rose petals.

I panic. What have I gotten myself into?

This is one of those restaurants where you would have an anniversary dinner, or maybe a romantic birthday. This is not some place to take a third date.

Am I just panicking because I think I'm not worthy of such nice behavior? Is my self-esteem so low that I really just think I don't deserve to be treated this way? I'm trying to wrap my head around this place. I try to embrace the generosity. I try to convince myself that he just has a different love language than I do: I'm all about quality time. He is clearly about acts of service, or gifts. I've been working on trying to accept other love languages, so I try to talk myself into being okay with this romantic gesture.

He tells me to order wine, if that's what I want.

If he insists. I get a glass of red. He is clearly going to let me make all of the choices. The server asks if we are celebrating something exciting this evening. I look around at the tables nearby. One couple is celebrating an anniversary, and has the same rose petals on the table that we do. Another larger table is celebrating a birthday. I shake my head, embarrassed. I order an appetizer that looks good. We each order our entrees. I get up to use the Ladies room, and run into a girl from the birthday table.

"Is it your anniversary?" she inquires.

"Nope, third date!" I respond. I am trying to accept the niceness this man is giving me. I deserve this. I'm not begging him for it. He's offering. I'm not gold digging. I'm genuinely trying to decide if I like him. I don't need to feel guilty or uncomfortable. Right?

Right.

"Wow, he's a keeper!" she exclaims. She's clearly surprised that a guy would bring a woman here on a third date. I'm still surprised myself.

We finish our entrees, and the waiter walks over with two champagne glasses. "And we've got a special dessert for the two of you."

I look at The Singer. He's grinning from ear to ear. He's been hiding this. So this is what the hostess knew about. The waiter brings back a bottle of champagne. He disappears again, and reappears with a small cake. It's chocolate, heart-shaped, with a candle and rose on top.

I feel dizzy. I'm trying to figure out if it's from the wine, or because I'm overwhelmed. I take a few bites of the cake. He eats the rest.

He pays for the check, and we head to valet. I thank him for dinner, and tell him it was really nice. I feel like I've made up my mind at this point. It's all too much. If I was another person, I would take advantage of his generosity and make him take me out multiple times. But I'm not. I can't lead someone on if I'm not interested. The conversation between us is lacking. There is no substance. I know I need to break it off with him, but I can't do it after a fancy night like this. I decide I'll wait a few days to break it off. I cross my fingers that he doesn't try to kiss me at the end of this date.

He drives me back to my place, walks me to the door. The date ends, yet again, with a hug. He turns around, walks back to his car, and drives off.

He texts me again the next day, the same "good morning" I've gotten used to. I text him back, replying with my usual "good morning." I head to yoga with my friend H. H is fit, and kind of hot. He's got amazing muscles and can arm balance like nobody's business. After yoga, H and I head to brunch. We sit outside at a cafe, listening to music and enjoying brunch in the sunshine. I post a photo on Instagram of H and our meal.

I get an immediate text from The Singer. **Hey, what are you up to?** You follow me on Instagram. You know damn well what I'm up to. Are you that insecure? You're bothered by me being out with another man? Come on. It's been three dates. I ignore his text, deciding to text him later. I need to end this.

I arrive at work the next day, and my coworker presents me flowers to say job well done for organizing a field trip for 120 students. I post a photo to Instagram to thank my coworker for the flowers.

The singer texts me his usual mid-day texts. I respond, knowing that I have got to end this. I decide tomorrow will be the day. I can compose a well thought-out text message to end this. Yes, text message. It's been three dates, and I don't want to agree to a fourth date to break up with him, because who knows what he'll plan.

I head to work the next day, and proceed through my day as usual. At lunch, the office calls me.

"There are flowers here for you in the office."

What. The. What.

I walk to the office, and at the front desk there is a giant floral arrangement. There is a card attached.

"You are sunshine in what was once a cloudy life."

I can't.

The breakup text is definitely happening when I get home.

I never told him the name of the school where I worked. His stalker skills were good enough for him to Google my name and have flowers delivered. I deduced that he had probably seen my Instagram post and wanted to one-up the flowers I had posted the day before. Now, I have to walk across campus, during lunch in front of all of my students with a giant bouquet of flowers. I try to hide behind the bouquet as I avoid shouts of, "Oh, Miss, who sent you the flowers!? Oh, you're so lucky! Someone LOVES you!"

Yeah, kid. That's the problem.

About thirty minutes later, I receive a text.

**How's your day?**

He knows full well that I've received those flowers by now. He was waiting for me to text him to say thank you. He's got another thing coming.

When I get home that evening, I compose the nicest text message I can think of.

**Thank you for the flowers, but I think they deserve to go to someone who can appreciate them more than I can. I'm not that girl. I just don't think it's going to work out between us. I wish you the best of luck.**

There. That's the end of it. I breathe a sign of relief. It's over.

He sends me a response text.

**It has been a privilege getting to know you. Whoever you end up with is a lucky man.**

Such a sweet sentiment, but just not the right guy for me.

He still emails me every once in a while to say Merry Christmas, Happy New Year, or Happy Teacher Appreciation Day. I think he's trying to see if somehow I'll change my mind about him at some point.

I recently had a conversation with a girlfriend about him. Would my feelings about the flowers have been different if I really liked him? Would I have thought it was sweet that he had sent flowers to my work? Or that he took me to such amazing restaurants? Maybe. But I think it still would have been a red flag that he was so stalker-ish and obsessive about my Instagram. I think at some point if we had dated that whole situation would have come to a head over something or someone. I do wish him all the happiness and self-confidence in the world, and I hope he finds a woman who can appreciate all of his generosity.

# 60
# **Jay**

PoF has this weird feature where you can send someone a voice message instead of a typed message. I've never started with this as an option, but that's mostly because most people wouldn't send their voice to a complete stranger whom they've never contacted. It's like talking in voicemails, repeatedly.

Jay's messages started as the usual texts: **Hi, how are you?**

I responded in the usual manner: **I'm fine, how are you?**

And suddenly, this weird icon appeared on my page.

I listened to a man's voice asking me some rather innocent questions. I was taken aback.

I was not ready for this man to hear my voice. Plus, I don't like talking on the phone. Especially plus, I hate leaving a voicemail. I ramble on way too long, and then feel like a moron talking out loud into thin air. I thrive on the non-verbal cues I can see from someone who's listening to me — the slight nod of the head, a raise of the eyebrows, a smile — that communicates to me that someone is engaged. I don't get any of that with a voice message.

I texted back a response to his question. We continued in this manner a few times, until eventually he cornered me into trying to voice message him.

I sat, alone, in my room, speaking into my phone with no one listening to me. And I felt like a complete moron.

It was also different than all of the other interactions that I had had on PoF, so it kind of caught my attention. Alright, Jay, I see your game, sir. Well played.

He inquired what I was up to, and I told him I was in the process of moving from my roommate's house into my own apartment. I also noted that I was having issues with my low back, which was making the move impossibly difficult.

Then, this man, who I have never met before, offered up the nicest thing I have ever heard in my entire life through this awkward voice message.

"Well, if you want, I can help you move. It's not a big deal."

Hallelujah! Bless you, Jay! I am never one to ask for help, but if you offer, I am certainly going to take it!

So, for our first date, Jay helped me move. He showed up to the house I was moving from, ready to help me with boxes. I was wearing yoga pants (okay, I at least had to show off my ass, right?), no make up, and my hair was a mess. I stooped a little when I walked since my low back was in pain. It was not one of my finer moments, nor was it one where I should have been on a date. But I will take help when it is offered.

He moved boxes from the house into my car so I could drive over to the new apartment. When he put boxes into his own car, I got a little nervous. I had to be ready to let those boxes go if he somehow decided he didn't follow me to the apartment. I didn't know how far I could trust this guy — I mean, I get that he's offered to help me move, but I wasn't sure if he was actually going to follow through on the moving. Maybe he was just going to take my stuff and drive away, never to be heard from again.

I watched his headlights in my rear view mirror for the entire twenty minute drive to my new apartment. He parked, and met me at my car. He made sure I didn't have to lift a finger. A total gentleman.

After all the boxes had been moved, we sat on my apartment floor amid the pile of boxes and had a real conversation. Turns out, this man was newly transformed.

Jay had a day job in an office, and until recently, had been severely overweight. After losing 80 pounds, with more to go, he had decided to get back into dating. He was a salsa singer on the weekends, and recently began coaching others on their weight loss journey. I was intrigued.

And also jealous.

I've been overweight my entire life. For the longest time (probably up until about ten years ago) I hated my body. Loathed. Really thought no one would ever want to sleep with me or even be interested in me. After hundreds of hours of therapy, and a lot of self-reflection, growth, and understanding about the pressures I was putting on myself, I learned to accept my body. I still struggle with being a single woman dating in Los Angeles, a city built on model/actress looks, but I still manage to maintain what I think is a healthy outlook on my body.

Jay talked a lot about his weight loss journey and his new-found passion for helping people with their weight loss. It was inspiring. Maybe eventually I could get into his program and lose some weight! I was looking for someone who could bring out my best self — maybe he was it!

He asked me out for coffee later that week, and I agreed. I could definitely see him again. We both agreed that this was the most interesting first date in history — who goes on a date to help someone move?

When we met for coffee, I realized his transformation was still very new to Jay. The conversations about his weight loss and the weight loss of the people he was working with took up a lot of space in our conversation. He kept talking about what he was going to do when he reached his 100 pound weight-loss mark — and that wasn't even his final goal. My jealousy of his situation reared its ugly head. I wanted to lose weight. I also wanted to talk about something other than him and his weight loss, but that seemed to be the focus of his entire life. I decided to give it one more date.

On our third date, I took him to one of my favorite small cafeteria-style restaurants in Manhattan Beach. We each ended up with a delicious salad for dinner. As I asked how his day was, he began to fill the space with talk of one of the women he was coaching. He couldn't understand why she couldn't just stick to the program, and why she was deciding to go off track and...

I zoned out. While I appreciated the journey that this man had taken, and what he had accomplished, I couldn't do this. He needed to be more comfortable in his current skin. I couldn't handle the constant bombardment of the transformation of his body. Maybe it's fucked up, but I don't want to hear about it constantly as we're getting to know each other. I want to know about the multiple layers that make up Jay — but all he can give me is the same layer, over and over.

As we left dinner, we walked back to his car in silence. I'm sure at this point he could sense my annoyance. Unfortunately, I don't have the ability to hide my feelings very well. I blamed my mood on being tired, and he dropped me off.

The next day, he texted me. I made up some excuse about me not seeing us work out, and I bid him good luck in his search.

Two years later, I was swiping through Tinder when I came across his profile. I decided to swipe right, just for the hell of it. We matched, and he messaged me almost immediately.

He wanted to exchange numbers and catch up. I gave him my number, wondering if now he was able to uncover some of his layers since he had lived in his new body for a while. We texted a few times, and he said he would call me the next evening around 8 pm.

And he did. I didn't pick up the phone, because who calls in this day and age? He left a voicemail in which he reminded me that he remembered a lot about me: "I know you like it when people do what they say they're going to do, so I made sure to call you." Yes, you're right. I do like it when people keep their word. That's a basic social contract. It's not just a tenet of dating, it's a life skill. Am I going crazy? This is something other people require, right?

I texted him to let him know I got his message. I never heard from him again.

## TRAVEL DATES

*I like to think to myself that I'm not confined living in my current city. Maybe my soulmate lives elsewhere. That's why, whenever I travel, I have a tendency to meet and go on dates with men — either accidentally (happenstance meeting) or on purpose (I'm looking at you, Tinder). At the end, you'll find a list of some of my proudest (or maybe least proud?) Vegas stories. Because what happens in Vegas is sometimes too good to stay in Vegas....*

# 61
# Minneapolis

During one of my summer vacations, I went to visit my friend Jen in Minneapolis. I stayed at her house, and we had a fantastic time: we talked, drank, traveled north to see her family, and partied a little bit. Two nights before I was set to go back to California, she and I decided to dress up and go out to a fancy dinner.

We had a cocktail before our dinner at a restaurant across the street, and the waiter told us how stunning we looked. I had on a purple one-shoulder dress, tall black strappy stilettos, and bright red lipstick. I looked *hot*. We walked across the street to a delicious dinner, and then Jen took me to an amazing bar on the 27th floor called Prohibition. The cocktails were delicious and Jen and I talked and giggled in a booth on our own. All of a sudden, three men of what appeared to be Indian descent appeared at our booth. They sat down and proceeded to tell us how attractive we were. They bought us a round of drinks. Jen entertained two of them, and the cutest one began to chat me up. His name was ....well, we'll call him Switzerland. He was in Minneapolis for work at the Mayo Clinic, but had been living in Switzerland for the last few years. We chatted about teaching, about his job, and about places we had traveled to. At one point, our whole crew decided to change to another bar and the guys proceeded to buy us another drink. Switzerland asked for my email address and said that he wanted to see me the next night, and I agreed. It would be my last night in Minneapolis, so why not go on a date?

The next day he emailed me to ask me where to meet him. I gave him my location, a quiet bar that Jen recommended. She sat with me as we waited for him to show up. I had a cocktail while I waited. I was nervous. I wasn't sure what my expectation was — if things worked out, would we date over seas? Would he fly me out to come see him? Would I fly out and stay with him? What if things worked out? Would I move to Switzerland? Would his job ever allow him to move back? (I have a tendency to get ahead of myself. I think about these things a lot, before I even get to the first date. Sometimes they have a tendency to trip me up when I like a guy. And by sometimes, I mean every time.)

As he greeted me, I couldn't help but think that he was much cuter and had a better personality when I was drunk (isn't that often the way it goes?!) but I thought I might still have a fun time with him. He had made reservations for us, so we said our goodbyes to Jen and I hopped in the car he had borrowed from his friend. He drove us to the restaurant and we sat and ate dinner. Conversation was fine — nothing that really made me love or dislike him. (I was rather impressed with the restaurant though!) We enjoyed more cocktails at dinner.

Afterwards he took me to a bar and we looked out over the Minneapolis skyline. The view was spectacular. We had a few more cocktails. At this point, I'm drunk. I'm not sure if he is, but I know I am. And I'm enjoying being out, on vacation, with a guy. However, I'm beginning to get tired. I ask him to drive me home.

We pull up to the house, and he kisses me. I enjoy it just enough, but not so much that I really want it to go any further. However, in my drunkenness I think everything seems like a good idea. He asks to come in, and I say okay. Jen had given me the green light to bring him home if I wanted to, and I knew she was already in bed. As we enter the house, we sit on the couch and he leans over to kiss me. Then he's on top of me. He tries to pull my pants off. I stop him, and ask him for a break. We stop for a second, and then he immediately jumps back into it, and tries to pull my pants down again. I hesitate, not wanting to seem like a prude. Then I come to my senses, and realize I'm not okay with this, and push him off. I tell him it's late, and he should go. He looked at me, and said "really?" (something about expecting me to sleep with him...about how I'm sending him home before he's gotten his...) I can't bring myself to argue with him anymore, and I usher him out the door.

As is expected, I never talk to him again.

# 62
# New York

I have met many men through online dating, but I have only met one through Instagram.

Through doing yoga for eleven years, I have formed a variety of yoga friendships, which have turned into following yoga teachers on Instagram. One friend I follow, KO, was doing a yoga challenge, and planned to give away a prize to anyone who participated in the yoga challenge.

Somehow, Michael found this challenge, and starting following KO. KO followed back. Michael was really into fitness. His posts and videos were all about his workouts — arm balances, inversions, weight lifting, etc. Around New Year's, he posted about the gym being crowded in January. KO and I often joked about this exact thing, so she tagged me in a comment on his post.

I started following his page. He was freaking hot, and obviously strong. He also worked with a special needs adult, so I knew he had a good heart.

He started following me as well.

Somehow I figured out that he lived in New York.

For Spring Break that year I decided to go to New York to stay with my friend Lauren. I messaged him on IG to ask if he wanted to meet.

He said sure.

Well, wasn't I excited. Meeting up with a hot guy for lunch in New York?! What could possibly be better?

We exchanged numbers, and he eventually called me to find out what my plans were.

"Well, I'm going to the Met, and to Central Park, and I'm going to meet a friend in Harlem for drinks."

"That sounds like a fun trip!" he replies.

"Actually, that's just my plan for tomorrow."

"Oh, wow. You like to be busy!" He then asked if he could join me at the Met tomorrow, and if we could have lunch together.

"I'd love that," I said. I told him I was excited to meet him. He said he was excited as well.

The next day, Wednesday, we met up at a train depot. He was adorable — he brought me stickers from his cousin's t-shirt company.

We sat down to lunch, and conversation flowed easily. Although we had never met before, it was easy to talk to him. He was a great listener, and such a gentleman. He shared that he was into fitness, and eating healthy in moderation. He really enjoyed his cheat days. He lived an hour or so outside of New York City, and had driven to meet me that day.

I had a buzz from my margarita with an extra shot of tequila. He was so excited about his cheat meal, and had also had a margarita.

After he paid for lunch, we hopped on the subway to get to the Met. On the train we stood very close to one another, facing each other. My pulse began to quicken. I wasn't sure if he was going to kiss me. I wasn't sure if we were even on a date. Or if he was romantically interested in me. I certainly hoped he was, because my GOD, he was hot. Half Dominican and half Haitian, 6'3, with lots of muscles. Like a big teddy bear.

We got off the subway and headed to the Met. We chatted as we walked through the museum. I told him about my favorite game — the Pose Like a Statue game: you find a statue in a weird pose, and then you take a picture next to the statue making the same shape. He was down to play. I found one that was clearly some sort of goddess, and decided to take that pose. One arm over my head, the other across my waist, knee dipped in and hip tilted to one side, I smiled innocently at Michael, and he snapped a photo. (That photo, by the way, became one of my online dating profile pictures. It's one of my best flirtatious photos.)

Michael, on the other hand, chose a statue of a ballerina, with her leg kicked out at a 90 degree angle from her body. I snapped a photo, stifling a laugh. He was trying his hardest to keep his leg up, but he was struggling.

We continued through the Met, and we decided we needed a little break. He bought me a cup of coffee, and we decided to head to Central Park to walk around, and do some yoga.

On Instagram, Michael had been working on his handstand, but without much guidance. I had a few pointers I wanted to give him to make his handstand stronger. We headed to Central Park and walked around. We found a grassy spot spotted with trees, and Michael climbed a tree to do an inversion. He handed me his iPad to take video of him lifting himself into a handstand in the tree. He tried about three times before he got it. I recorded all three tries.

Then he took video of both of us doing headstands. He promised he'd send me the video as soon as he got home. I looked at the time and told him I needed to get up to Harlem to meet my friend. He asked if I wanted a ride.

I wasn't sure I wanted to be in the car with a stranger, but he seemed nice. I told him ok. We took the subway back to his car, and took off towards Harlem. As we drove, I thought of how I was going to end our time together — with a kiss? Would I ever see him again? I mentioned that two days from then I was going to do a food tour in Greenwich Village.

"Oh, really? I may be able to join you! Send me the link and I'll see if I can get a ticket."

I was ecstatic. I would get to see him again! How fun!

As we approached my destination I told him I'd send him the link. He said ok, and slowed down to let me out. Unfortunately, it was on the side of a very busy road, so there wasn't really the opportunity to kiss him.

I slammed the door shut, and he sped off, heading towards home, and I met my friend in Harlem for drinks.

The next day Michael texted me. **Hey, I can't buy my ticket. Would you mind getting it for me and I'll pay you back?**

Damn. My untrusting ass figured that if I bought the ticket for him, I needed to be prepared to eat that money. I had no idea of knowing if he would actually show up, or if he was actually going to pay me back. I decided to take the risk.

**Sure.** I replied. I bought the ticket right then, and sent him the info of where and when to meet.

On Friday, Lauren and I hopped on the subway to meet our food tour guide in Greenwich Village. On our way there I received a text from Michael.

I checked my phone, expecting bad news. I figured he was going to cancel, or let me know that his car broke down somewhere, or that he wasn't going to meet up with me after all. Wow, am I a Debbie Downer or what?

**Hey! I just got here and checked in with the guide. Where are you?**

I smiled, and breathed a sigh of relief. He wasn't going to flake after all!

**We'll be there in five!** I texted back.

Lauren and I finally exited the subway, and made our way to the meeting point. About a half block from our meeting place, I spotted Michael among the crowd of people, just as he spotted Lauren and me walking up. His face broke into a grin, and he waved excitedly. I saw him reach into his pocket just as we walked up. He pulled out the money that he owed me for the ticket, and handed it over to me.

"Thanks so much for getting the ticket for me," he said. "I'm so excited for this food tour!" He threw his arms around me and squeezed me tight.

"No problem!" I squeaked. Although I knew it had been a problem. I had been so frightened that I was not going to see him again, and that I wasn't going to get my money back. With his arms around me, all of my insecurities melted away.

We started the food tour. Michael was the hit of the group. He cracked jokes and was genuinely excited with each tasting. When the tour guide announced to the group that there were seconds available for anyone who wanted them, Michael leaped at the opportunity to get another slice of pizza or bite of a bagel. He always checked that no one else wanted any first, and then dove right in, taking as big a bite as his mouth would allow. I adored every quirky move. What a gentleman, and a big kid at heart.

When the food tour ended, Michael decided to stick with Lauren and me. We checked out a wine bar down the street, and MrKnight and his boyfriend joined us (they were in town to see Neil Patrick Harris on Broadway. Yup, that happened).

The afternoon devolved into a pub crawl.

And I was okay with that. As long as Michael stayed with us.

We first went to a bar that was a couple hundred years old. Big kid Michael thought it was super fascinating, and proceeded to take about a thousand photos of the place with his iPad. After finishing a beer (on top of the wine I'd already consumed), my head started to swim with fantastic ideas of falling in love with Michael and moving to New York to be with him.

The five of us left the old bar and traveled to a dive bar, complete with pool tables and "cash only" signs. Lauren and I sat at a table while MrKnight, Boyfriend, and Michael all stood at the bar chit-chatting. I admired the way Michael got along easily with my gay friends (something that is definitely on my list of must-haves in a partner). MrKnight and Michael started a game of pool, and I made my way to the back of the bar to use the restroom.

As I exited the bathroom, I was immediately met by Lauren and Boyfriend. They surrounded me, and frantically told me of their plan to get me alone with Michael.

"He clearly likes you!"

"You've got to get alone with him so you guys can make out!"

They had clearly decided on this while I was in the bathroom. Boyfriend and MrKnight had to leave to go to another Broadway play, and Lauren was going to say she needed to meet up with another girlfriend.

Great, totally foolproof.

I still wasn't even sure he wanted to kiss me. I told them as much.

"You're being ridiculous. He TOOOOOOOOOOOOOOTALLY wants to make out with you!" Boyfriend exclaimed. I felt like I was in high school, having a conversation in the bathroom, plotting how I was going to get some guy to make out with me.

How did I get here? This felt completely absurd, and yet so fun at the same time. Glad to know that the thrill of the chase never gets old.

We ended up at our third and final bar. This one was more of a restaurant, and we all crammed into a booth. Michael sat next to me, and I tensed up. I could feel the heat of his body radiating against mine. My pulse quickened. I kept staring at his mouth every time he spoke. I really wanted to kiss him. My mind moved to dirty thoughts.

Each of us ordered another drink, and some food. Conversation flowed easily. We each chipped in for the tab, and MrKnight and Boyfriend said they had to go.

Lauren chimed in that she had to take off too.

Oh Jesus. This was not smooth at all, guys. It's completely obvious that you're trying to get him alone with me. Abort mission! But it was too late. Everyone was already on their way out. And before I knew it, we were alone.

Alone. Just Michael and me. Heads full of drink. What to do? We're standing in the middle of the sidewalk, in daylight, in New York City. Not exactly romantic make-out scenery.

"Hey, we're right down the street from the 9-11 memorial," he points out. "Want to take a look?"

This moment just keeps getting more and more romantic.

"Sure," I say, unable to figure out a better plan. "Just..." I hesitate. I know these kinds of memorials make me cry. And I am not very good at being vulnerable. It's really tough to let other people see my waterworks, including my closest friends. Not sure I can handle having an almost-stranger watch my emotional reaction to such an event. "...Just be aware that I am probably going to cry," I finally blurt out. It was difficult for me to even state that I might cry.

"It's ok to cry." He responds.

Jesus. What an adorable man. I start planning our wedding in my head.

We head into the memorial. The gravity of the space is palpable. I can feel a lump forming in the back of my throat as I think of all the lives lost.

Michael leans over to whisper to me. "It's probably not acceptable to do a handstand here, is it? I bet I could get some cool photos with my iPad"

"No!" I whisper back a little too harshly. His childlike nature is going to get him in trouble one of these days.

We stand in front of the fountain, in silence, among the other observers there to pay their respects. I am overcome with a wave of emotion, and I start to cry. Tears stream down my cheek. Michael glances over at me. All of a sudden, I feel his arm around me.

And I feel safe. Comfortable. I know he is not judging me, but he is there to support me. He doesn't want me to feel alone in this moment. And I don't. Being vulnerable with someone allows me to feel a deep connection to that person. In this moment, I feel extremely close to Michael.

I finally get myself together, and we leave the memorial. We pass the time walking along the streets of New York, chatting and laughing. I finally get up the courage to put my arm through his. We stop at a bodega so he can get a bottle of water. I wait outside. When he comes back out, he walks right up to me, and grabs me by the waist.

And kisses me.

I am taken by surprise at the suddenness of his movement. It takes me a moment before I can absorb the feelings — his soft lips on mine, his hand on the small of my back. I inhale his manly scent. His tongue is slightly cold from the water he just tasted before kissing me.

He pulls away after a few seconds.

"I have been waiting for you to do that all afternoon!" I tell him. He chuckles. "What took you so long?"

"I don't know," he responds sheepishly. "Well, it's not like we had a ton of time alone together all day."

"True," I respond. My heart is pounding. I feel tingly. I want to keep making out with him...and other stuff. Why are we so far from a bed?!

We stand there with his arms wrapped around me for another minute before he says the dreaded words.

"I have to go." No. NO! Just when we're getting started! "I promised my cousin I'd help him out with something tonight." He looked regretful, like he didn't want to leave. "We should catch a cab back to my car."

Car, eh? I started daydreaming about our hot make-out session in his car before he would take off. Things could get very interesting....

We catch a cab, and we make out the entire way back to his car. Things were so heated that we didn't even notice when the cab stopped to let us out. We finally stopped and both stumble out of the cab.

The cab drives off, and I am still picturing this amazing make-out session in Michael's car.

Insert mood-killer: "My iPad!" Michael cries out. "My iPad is in the back of the cab!" As we stare ahead into traffic, all we can see is a sea full of cabs. There is no way to figure out which cab was ours. Apparently we were making out so hard he forgot that he even owned an iPad.

His iPad is gone.

So are my chances of a make-out session. He's now fixated on getting his iPad back.

We spend the next 20 minutes on the internet — trying to figure out which cab company it was (a yellow one?), how to report a missing item (a $50 fee), and what he was going to do (apparently, nothing. We had to come to terms with the fact that it was gone forever).

He seemed most upset about losing all of our memories from today.

Finally, I walk him back to his car before I get on the subway to go back to Lauren. At this point in the game, more kissing is out of the question. He is clearly upset and does not have his head in the sexy-time game.

He gives me a hug goodbye. I tell him I had a fantastic day today, in spite of him losing his iPad. He sighs, and says he's trying to forget about losing it. He subscribes to the belief that everything happens for a reason. There must be a higher purpose to why his iPad is gone. Someone must need it more than him.

Even when he's down, he finds a way to be positive. This guy is amazing.

I tell him to text me when he gets home. He promises that he will. I walk towards the subway as he gets into his car.

And I never saw him again.

We exchange a few texts and still follow each other on Instagram. He has a girlfriend now, and I am happy for him. I can see that he's made progress on his handstand, and he's definitely working towards other inversions as well. I know that things would never work out between the two of us, but I am thankful for the time that we spent together. It reassures me that there are good men out there, ones that can allow me to be vulnerable and accept me as who I am. I love the experiences that we shared together, and this is one of my most vivid memories of my trip to New York. I wouldn't trade it for the world.

# 63
# New Orleans

Picture it: New Orleans, October. I'm left to my own devices during the early evening. (My friends, Kate and Tom, who live there are working and aren't off until later on.)

So, what else would I do to keep myself busy on a beautiful evening in the Big Easy? Have a few drinks in the French Quarter, and then swipe left and right, of course. Ah, the joys of Tinder.

I match with a cute Latino dude named Martin, and we start to chat. Gotta love the French Quarter: he's only a few blocks away from the bar where my friend Tom is working as a bartender.

Martin shares that he, too, is a teacher. He's in New Orleans for a history teacher conference (man, how do I get that gig!? My last conference was in Sacramento). Turns out he, too, is from Los Angeles, and we live about 10 miles apart.

A date in another state, and the guy only lives a few miles from me back home!? If this works out, it would be kind of nice.

But then again, the reason I date in another state (man, I got sick rhymes!) is because I am open to the idea of living somewhere else. (That, and it's fun to have a hook-up in another city. I guess if the guy is from LA, he doesn't do me much good in that department.)

I ask Martin to meet me at Tom's bar. I've already had a few cocktails, so I've got some liquid courage. And if things go south, Tom can just kick this guy out of the bar.

I am sitting at the bar, glued to my phone, when suddenly I get a message. It's Martin.

**I'm behind you.**

I turn around, and he's standing against the wall. Why the fuck didn't he just sit at the bar next to me, if he already knew it was me? I walk over to "pick him up" from where he's standing. He sits at the bar, and we begin to chat.

"Is this your first time in New Orleans?" I ask him, out of curiosity. He says it is.

"Mine too," I reply. I see Tom give Martin the once over as Tom approaches where we're sitting.

"Can I get you a drink, man?" Tom asks, trying to be casual. I can see under his cool exterior that he's giving Martin the side-eye. I love when my friends are protective of me.

"I'll take a diet coke." I turn to study him.

"You're not having a cocktail?" Maybe he's already been drinking, and that's why he doesn't want a drink. Maybe he's trying to be good, since he's here for a work conference.

"No. I don't drink."

Oh.

Is this date over yet?

No? Fine. I'll play nice. But I don't have to like it. I believe in the saying "never trust a man who doesn't drink." I can already tell this isn't going to work out. But, at least there will be someone to chat with until Kate gets off work and we can hit the town.

We begin the usual chit-chat: where in LA we grew up, our favorite sports teams, where we went to college. After I mention that I went to UCLA and have a Bachelors in Mathematics, he suddenly decided he wanted to play a game.

"Oh, you like math? You must love puzzles."

I stare at him. "Not really." Sure, sometimes I love puzzles. But not when I'm on a date. Not when I'm at a bar. Not when I'm on vacation. C'mon bro. Read your audience. He flags Tom down and asks for a napkin and a pen. Tom hands over the items, and looks at me sympathetically. I tilt my head a little bit and widen my eyes just enough so Tom knows I'm not having a good time, but this date doesn't need to end immediately. Tom gives a slight nod, and I know he's keeping an eye on us.

Martin draws a bunch of lines on the napkin in an order so that it he creates an equation out of match sticks. It reads 3+3=6.

"Okay, you can only move one match stick to make another true equation." He looks at me with a big grin on his face.

"Oh, yeah, I've seen this one." I tell him. "Move the vertical line from the plus sign to the front of the three. Then the equation will read 9-3=6. Then it's true."

"Ooh, look at you!" he exclaims. I'm not sure if he's being sarcastic, or he is truly impressed with me. Either way, I can't say that I care. I'm trying my hardest not to roll my eyes. "How about this one?"

He draws another puzzle on the reverse side of the napkin.

"Do you know this one? Do you know the answer?" He pushes the napkin toward me.

"No." I barely look at the diagram. I'm not interested in solving puzzles on a date. Or in playing his stupid game. I shove the napkin back toward him.

"WHAT!? You don't?! C'mon, it's easy." He scoots the napkin back over to my side of the bar. "You've got to know how to do it. It's a piece of cake."

That's when it dawns on me. He's trying to prove he's smarter than me. He needs to put me in my place. He's not testing my mathematical prowess, he just wants to make sure he's got something to hold over my head. How insecure.

I'm not playing along. I don't need anyone to make me feel stupid. On purpose. What kind of a date is that?!

I thrust the napkin back towards him. "I'm not interested in doing any more puzzles, thanks!" I grumble at him. He picks up from my tone of voice that I mean business.

"Okay, okay. Wow, what a spoiled sport!"

"No, that's just not what I feel like doing right now. I'm on vacation."

He backs off. He sits quietly. A moment later he chirps, "I should go! I have an early day tomorrow, and it's getting kind of late."

"Yeah, you should."

"Have a good night, and enjoy the rest of New Orleans."

"Same to you." I smile politely, but I clearly don't mean it.

He walks out of the bar. I continue to sip my drink. Tom saunters over.

"That was quick!" he points out. He looks down at the napkin in front of the now-empty barstool. "What was he doing with the napkin?"

"Puzzles!"

His mouth drops open. "You're kidding me."

"No! And he essentially said I was stupid for not automatically knowing one of the answers!"

"What a douche. Well, good riddance. At least you have a good story."

And I never heard from Martin again.

# 64
# Rome

In 2012 I went on a yoga retreat to Monteriggioni, Italy led by Jennifer Pastiloff. (By the way if you haven't taken a Jennifer Pastiloff yoga retreat, do yourself a favor and go. Even if you're not into yoga. Life. Changing.) I couldn't find anyone to go with me, so I traveled to Italy by myself, went to the yoga retreat, made friends, and ended up hanging out with some of them on the rest of my trip to Florence and Rome.

One such friend I met, Danielle, and I ended up overlapping part of our time together in Rome. She had convinced me to extend my trip by a day so that we could fly out together — she, back to the US, and myself to Munich so I could hang with my friend Natalie, who I used to work with at my first job. Since I had already given up my Airbnb, Danielle agreed to let me stay with her at her Airbnb so we could ride to the airport together. She was staying in a one-bedroom apartment near the Vatican.

After I dropped my stuff off at her place we grabbed dinner together at an amazing restaurant.

Over prosecco and pasta on our last night in Italy, I put it out into the Universe: I had made out with a man in every city I had been to thus far on this trip. I would make out with some guy within an hour! Danielle laughed at my declaration and said she loved my enthusiasm. We finished dinner and decided on one more drink (famous last words) in the square.

We ordered a glass of wine, and by this point we are both a little tipsy. We continue our conversation about dating, about life, about success, about who knows what the fuck else, when I see them out of the corner of my eye. Two men. Definitely Italian. One was 6 feet tall, very muscular, with olive-colored skin. The other was slightly shorter, with a more stocky build. He was wearing a hat, and had a thin mustache.

The taller of the two was definitely making eyes at our table. His target had been acquired. I locked eyes with him as he walked by, and just as they walked past our table, they began conversing. I thought maybe the opportunity had been missed. I wondered if they were going to come back. My heart quickened. I love the chase.

"Did you see them?" I asked Danielle. "They were so hot."

Danielle nodded, looking past me. "They're turning around." Before I could comment back to Danielle, they were already at our table.

"*Ciao, bellas*" the shorter one said, his mouth thick with his Italian accent. He introduced himself as Danny, and his taller friend as Giovanni. According to Danny, Giovanni didn't speak much English. Danielle used what little Italian she knew to communicate with Giovanni. Apparently they were hitting it off. Danny and I sat, talking, while Danielle and her man looked longingly into each other's eyes.

Danny was an engineer, and had worked in Iowa for a little while for John Deere. I knew he was just playing wingman for Giovanni, who was doing extremely well with Danielle. Danny made small talk just to keep me entertained, but I wasn't sure he actually liked me. After Danielle and I finished our glasses of wine, Danielle said we should go back to her place. Danny had parked his car not far from the plaza, so the four of us walked back to Danny's car. I sat in the front seat while the lovebirds sat in the back. Danielle tried to direct Danny where to go, but she kept being interrupted by Giovanni's kisses. If we didn't get them back to Danielle's place soon I was pretty sure they would start having sex in the backseat.

Danny drove us through Piazza San Pietro — the plaza in front of the Vatican, and made a left under one of the archways. I was so shocked he had driven on the cobblestones where hours earlier we had stood in line to get inside to see the Sistine Chapel. The whole area had been blocked off with cones and long panels meant for crowds, but in the evenings it was fine to drive over the cobblestone plaza!

Finally we arrived at Danielle's place. We left Danielle and Giovanni to go about their business, and I promised Danielle I would be back in a few hours. I had my cell phone and could reach her if needed.

Then, I got in the car with Danny. Alone.

We sat in the car outside of Danielle's apartment, parked under a street light. Suddenly Danny leaned over and kissed me. His lips were warm and soft, his hands lightly lingering over my face and back of my neck. My head was spinning, still slightly drunk from the wine but also drunk off the masculine scent of this handsome and brilliant Italian man. He pulled away just as suddenly as he had come towards me, breathing heavily.

"Too much light," he grumbled, squinting as the streetlight shone directly on his face. "I know place." He started the car, and we took off.

Alright, not one of my brighter or finer moments. Yes, we all do stupid things. It happens. Going off with a stranger in his car in a strange country sometimes makes me wonder how I'm still alive. But, I'd like to think I have pretty good radar when it comes to people. And Danny seemed to be a good person, so I trusted him. Besides, his friend was still with Danielle in the room, and I doubted he would abandon his friend.

We drove for just a few minutes and pulled into a giant empty parking lot. He pulled into a space, but his car seemed so tiny in the massive spots.

"Why are these spaces so big?" I asked him.

"Bus," he responded. "Tourists for Vatican."

Oh. We were in the Vatican Tour Bus parking lot.

I am going straight to hell. Do not pass go, do not collect $200.

We fooled around some more in the Vatican tour bus parking lot. I wouldn't have sex with him because he didn't have a condom, but we both got ours in the end. There was even an "Oh God" in there somewhere.

Yup, definitely going to hell.

When we were finished, Danny asked me if I liked coffee. I said I did. He started the car, and drove me outside of the walls of the city of Rome. He stopped at a gas station, apparently open 24 hours. Inside was the cutest coffee shop that I have ever seen. It was well past 3 am, and there were a half dozen people inside.

Let me tell you, there is something amazing about Italian gas stations — they have great espresso bars in them! You can get great coffee and a glass of prosecco — and thong underwear from a vending machine.

Danny held my hand as we walked up to the counter, and ordered us each a cappuccino. It was the best damn cappuccino I've ever had. We stood there drinking our coffee, and suddenly exhaustion hit me. I had been up since before 8 am that morning. It was well past 4 am. After we finished our coffee, Danny drove me back into the city, and parked in front of Danielle's place. We took the elevator and knocked on the door. Apparently the coast was clear, because Danielle opened the door right away. Giovanni was just putting on his shirt, and ready to go. Danielle and I said our goodbyes, and Danny and Giovanni left.

"Oh my God. You are a witch!" Danielle said accusatorially. "You totally called that. It was like an hour after you made that statement that we met those guys!"

"I told you. I just had to will it into existence!" I exclaimed. I told her I wanted to hear all about her night. She cursed, said she had been so good for 8 weeks, but the last night of her trip was when she slept with someone. She showed me the giant hickey on her neck.

"It's a good thing I'm going to this wedding in Oregon before I head back to see my man," she yawned, "we are only going to get three hours of sleep before we have to get up and catch our flights. We went to sleep, woke up extremely exhausted, mildly hung over, and ready for our next adventures.

I still talk to Danny every once in a while over skype. We emailed a few times, and he was working on getting a job out here in the US. I haven't heard from him recently, but I would like to thank him for being such a gentleman, and a good wingman. We'll always have the Vatican Tour Bus parking lot.

# 65
# Munich

From Italy, I stayed with my friend Natalie who lived in Germany. She agreed to let me crash with her for a few days, and would show me around Munich.

We had a great time — Natalie took me to Neuschwanstein Castle, and I met a few of her friends. I told her I really want to see Hofbräuhaus, and she argued that the only way to attend a bier garten was to wear a dirndl, a traditional Bavarian outfit.

So we went dirndl shopping. After trying on what felt like a hundred dirndls, I finally found one that I loved — a black dress with small white polka dots and bright green trim. The whole thing was topped with a green apron.

We (myself, Natalie, her friend Liz, and Liz's friend Helen) put on our respective dirndls and headed out to Hofbräuhaus. We were a hit! People actually lined up to take pictures with us, thinking that we were Bavarian. I enjoyed two steins of beer, and when we shut the place down, we headed to an Irish pub down the street.

As we sat down, I took note of a gorgeous black man watching "football" on TV. I whispered to Liz while making bedroom eyes his direction, "Did I mention I love chocolate?" In my drunken haze, I couldn't stop staring at him. I was hoping to make eye contact with him, but he seemed so intent on watching the game. After becoming frustrated and deciding that I'd never get his attention, I walked to the bar to order a drink. While at the bar, a German man decided to ask me my name, and I told him "Desirée," which he then butchered into Desire, and made some stupid joke about being filled with desire. I rolled my eyes, and went back to the table. As I got close I realized Liz was talking to my man! In my head, I began to curse her and plot her demise, when all of a sudden she said to my man, "Have you met Desirée?"

I immediately backtracked every evil thought I had about her, and gave her a grateful look. As I started to chat with my delicious chocolate hunk, I realized his accent was *not* German, and his English was almost perfect.

He grew up in France and England, and obtained a Masters in Mechanical Engineering from the Netherlands. Fucking gorgeous. His name was Tanyi (Tawn-yee), and I wanted to marry him right then. He was working in Germany for an aerospace company that modified the process of making helicopter parts to be environmentally sustainable. Could he get any more perfect for me?

Seriously. I think he hit every box on my checklist. Smart, hot, interested in math, black, environmentally conscious, and speaks French. If I had to list my ideal man, he was it. And he was completely enthralled with me. Win-win!

In my drunkenness, I accused him of not being interested in me. I confessed to him that I couldn't stop staring at him when he was hanging out with his friends.

"I noticed," he whispered in my ear in his beautiful French accent. "I couldn't concentrate on the game because I knew you were looking at me. You are fucking gorgeous and I was having trouble not staring back." At this point in the conversation, we decide to go outside so he can smoke a cigarette.

Ew. One of my pet peeves, but I guess I could live with making out with an ashtray for the rest of my life if this ashtray is hot and brilliant.

As we stand outside, he asks me how long I'm in town for. I tell him tomorrow is my last full day, and I leave the day after. He is angry with himself for not meeting me earlier. At some point in the conversation, he says he would love to take me out tomorrow night, if I don't have any plans.

I ask Natalie if that's alright with her, and she says sure — she could use some alone time anyways. I tell Tanyi that Natalie and I are going to Salzburg, Austria on the train tomorrow to go to the Sound of Music Tour, and I'll email him on the train ride home. He tells me he loves the idea.

And then he kisses me. The most amazing, most passionate kiss I think I've probably experienced. I know I want to marry this man.

Natalie drags me away from Tanyi kicking and screaming, with the promise that I'll get to see him the next evening.

Natalie and I enjoy the train ride to Salzburg, and the Sound of Music Tour. Of course, in the back of my mind, all I can think about is my date with Tanyi, and what to wear. I'm almost out of clothes, considering it's the last night I'll be in Europe after my three week vacation.

On the ride home, I email Tanyi to tell him I'm on my way, and he emails me back immediately. We negotiate plans — he'll pick me up from Natalie's apartment at 10 pm.

Natalie tells me it's fine with her if I bring Tanyi back to the apartment. I hadn't even thought that far ahead, and told her that wasn't necessary, but thank you anyways.

Tanyi calls me to let me know he's outside. I walk out of Natalie's building, and I find him looking as gorgeous as ever, and very European — leaning against the side of the building in tight black jeans, a patterned t-shirt and a black leather jacket, smoking a cigarette. He greets me with a kiss on each cheek.

We walk down the streets of Munich, and he takes me to a little cafe where he orders beer, and I order wine. We talk about American culture: TV shows, music, and movies. As the alcohol flows, so does the conversation, and I am absolutely thrilled to be on a date with such a brilliant and attractive man.

After we finish at the bar we attempt to enter some dance club that has a ridiculously long line. Instead, we head for the only open bar down the street, since it's now extremely late. I've lost all track of time. Tanyi heads to the toilet the minute we enter the bar, and I order a wine. As I look around, I realize we're at a gay bar.

I tell Tanyi, and he doesn't seem to care.

He's perfect. He's not one of those men who's completely put off by the thought of gay men (because I've come across those, and it bothers me, since one of my favorite people in the whole world is my gay friend MrKnight).

After we finish our drinks, and they proceed to close the bar, Tanyi tells me that he doesn't want the night to end. I tell him I don't either — why doesn't he come back to the apartment?

I make a mental note to thank Natalie in the morning for her earlier blessings.

As we get to the apartment we chat a while longer and eventually we start making out.

Of course, the making out doesn't stop, and only escalates. Into the best. Sex. Ever.

Passionate, giving, strong, and a marathon man. We went a few rounds that night, and took intermittent naps. After only having slept for probably a total of two hours all night, I told him he should probably leave, since the sun was rising and Natalie would be getting up soon. He told me that he didn't want to leave, he didn't want this night to end, he didn't want to say goodbye.

It takes him twenty minutes to leave, since neither of us wants him to go. We promise to email, Skype, and WhatsApp to text as soon as I get home. He texts me the minute he gets home to tell me what a fantastic time he's had, and how he misses me already. We spend the day emailing back and forth, until I get on my plane to head back to the states. We talk about him coming to the US, visiting California in November, during Thanksgiving. I promise him a fantastic time, and talk about all the amazing things to see in California.

We use WhatsApp to message each other at least once a day. We Skyped a few times a week for months. At some point, he tells me he doesn't want me to date anyone else. I agree. He makes a good point — if we're dating other people, then why bother doing this? I agree, and change my Facebook status to "it's complicated." Because it is: he lives in another country!

As the days go on, we continue to Skype. I show him my school. He shows me his room at his mom's house in Paris. We discuss our future together, having children, him moving to California. I Skype with him on Halloween and show him my costume.

One day, in early November, I message him to say hello, and never get a response. Weird, I think to myself. I know he's visiting his family in Paris. I wait. And wait.

And wait.

I get a little crazy. I text him a few times. I email him to ask him if it's over, and if it is, will he please let me know?

I never hear anything. I am heartbroken. I truly thought I was going to marry this man. I change my Facebook status back to single. Again.

Now that I've had some time to think back to the amazing time I had with this man, I am actually not sad about this experience, but hopeful. Hopeful because it helps me realize that somewhere out there is a man that will have all of the things that I am looking for. Hopeful because there is a wide world out there, and Los Angeles is not the only place that I can find love. Love can appear in any city, as long as I keep my heart open. And somewhere out there is a man who can make me feel beautiful, smart, and sexy, and that I can have an instant connection with. I'm writing this as a reminder to myself that I need not settle on anything less than amazing.

# 66
# San Francisco

About six months after Danielle and I had our stint in Rome, I visited her in San Francisco. My favorite football team (UCLA Bruins!) was playing at Stanford, and I wanted to watch the game. We decided to make a weekend of it, reminiscing about Italy, catching up about life, and generally gossiping about the people on the retreat.

The day of the game, Danielle and I bought some Cokes and mixed them with some vodka before we got on the train at 10 am. As we sat on the train drinking our spiked diet cokes we swiped on my Tinder account. I forgot about it as we got off the train and headed to a college friend's tailgate in the parking lot.

I felt pretty good by the time we met up with my grad school friend, who I hadn't seen in ten years. We reminisced and drank in the parking lot before the game started.

As seems to be the norm when Danielle and I get together, we were approached by two men, and we all chatted in the parking lot before the game began. The four of us talked all through the first quarter of the game before heading in to our seats. The two gentlemen decided to stay with us through the game.

By the time Danielle and I got to the game we were in a good place. I definitely had a buzz going. UCLA lost big time, so we ditched the game and headed to a bar in Palo Alto.

At the sports bar, we chatted and continued to drink. Danielle seemed drunker than me, so by the time we hopped back on the train she passed out and I was left to find our way back to Danielle's stop. On the 45-minute ride home, I chatted with some of the guys I had matched with on Tinder.

I wasn't ready to be done for the evening — it was only 9pm — and Danielle seemed down for the count, so I tried to find a date. I had been drinking most of the day, though, so I was mildly intoxicated (to say the least) while choosing a date on Tinder.

One of the men I matched with was a tall, lanky Indian man who worked in the tech industry. After chatting for a few minutes I asked him to meet at a wine bar around the corner from Danielle's place.

I put Danielle to bed and walked to the wine bar. I arrived first, sat down and ordered a drink. When he arrived, he was just as tall as he looked in his photos. As we began to chat I knew, even in my drunken state that something was off about this guy.

He began to tell me that he was divorced. He said that his family frowned upon his divorce. He seemed obsessed with the idea — it had been over two years but it was clear he hadn't processed it yet. I tried to find common ground by asking him about his life here in San Francisco, his interests.

After I finally got his mind off of his divorce, we chatted about our favorite places in San Francisco. The date was friendly, but nothing romantic. There was nothing in our interactions that was particularly flirty or sex-driven. Suddenly, out of nowhere, he leans over and asks, "Can I kiss you?"

I pull back, staring at him quizzically. "No!" I respond. In the middle of the bar? In the middle of the date? After you've been weird and awkward? Not a chance in hell, buddy. Clearly you don't know how to read signals very well. Big ole red light and WRONG WAY DO NOT ENTER all over my face.

He seems unphased, and continued with the conversation as if nothing has happened. I am ready to leave. I finish my wine, and I tell him I am going to go back to check on my friend. He insists on walking me home. I try to tell him in the nicest way possible that no, he doesn't need to do that, but he is insistent.

He pays the tab, and we head outside. He asks again if he can kiss me. I tell him no.

As we walk along, he tries to put him arm around me. I shrug it off, telling him no again.

I am starting to feel extremely uncomfortable. I don't trust him to walk me to my building. In my drunken state I try to formulate a plan of how I am going to get rid of this guy. I'm wondering if he finds me to be the weakest gazelle in the pack, if he's got a plan of attack. Fortunately it's early enough in the evening that there are still people on the street as we walk along for the seven minute walk to her apartment.

About a block from Danielle's place I tell him this is far enough, that my place is down the street.

"Are you sure you don't want me to walk you further? I can walk you to your front door."

"No, it's fine," I grumble. This dude does not know how to read tone of voice or body language at all. Who doesn't read major cues?

More importantly: what man doesn't take no for an answer?

Weirdly enough, I never felt scared. Just uncomfortable. I felt sorry for him, mostly.

"Can I kiss you?" he inquires one more time.

"No!" I cry out. "Thank you for the drinks, nice meeting you."

This guy just does not get it! I turn to walk away. He insists once more, "Are you sure you don't want me to walk you home?"

"NO!" I practically scream this time. I walk away, never looking back. I am done with this guy and his persistence. Some men just can't take a hint.

# 67

# Boston

Matching with men on Tinder is one of my favorite out-of-town past times. One year for Spring Break I stayed with a friend in Boston for a week, and Tindered my face off. I managed to match and set up dates with two guys. (See the next story for the other date.)

Boston's minimal profile (hello, it's Tinder) stated that he was a feminist, and had attended some prestigious University. He was also into the environment. After a few messages, he seemed adorable enough, and we set up a date to meet at a brewery along the waterfront later that evening. I arrived early, and ordered myself a flight of beer.

By the time Boston arrived about 30 minutes later (traffic, or work or some other obligation that kept me waiting — don't worry, I entertained myself!) I was halfway through my flight of beer. When I hugged him, I realized how absolutely thin he was. He was slightly taller than me, but I likely outweighed him by at least 50 pounds. (I wasn't necessarily feeling insecure about my weight, but the idea of outweighing my date doesn't sit well with me.) He was 5'8, thin build, with dark hair, dark eyes, and a beard. He wore jeans and a plaid button down over a white t-shirt. He seemed nervous, or at least slightly awkward. As he ordered his own flight of beer, he seemed to loosen up just a bit.

We chatted for hours. It was one of the best dates I had been on in a long time: good conversation, respectful, good listener. He paid for our beers once we decided we needed to grab some food before everything closed. We walked, arm in arm, through the cold to some restaurant about a half-mile away. He ordered a beer, and I switched to wine. Drunk with wine, and loving the evening, I opened up to him. I let myself be vulnerable with him. We talked about the environment, my past, his future, and everything in between. I felt safe with him. Comfortable. Damn travel dates. I felt like I could see myself with him, a future with him.

Dammit. This was just supposed to be fun!

After he paid for dinner (he paid!) he offered to drive me back to where I was staying.

"Are you sure?" I asked.

"Of course," he replied. "It's not a problem."

Cool.

I gave him the address of where I was located, and as he entered it into his GPS, he told me what a nice time he had tonight. I told him I felt very much the same way. As we neared the building where I was staying, I asked him if he wanted to park and come up. He said he did.

As we entered the house, the girl I was staying with wasn't home. We decided to utilize her room to...uh....entertain ourselves for a while. We started making out, and one thing leads to another, and suddenly I'm not wearing any clothes.

How did that happen?!

Suddenly, there's a knock on the door.

My friend is home.

Uh oh.

I unlock the door, peek my head out, and tell her to hang on. I give her my most innocent smile. She pouts at me, and cocks her head to the side, as if to say, "Are you fucking serious right now?"

I tell Boston that he has to go. He nods, understandingly. I feel bad. For denying him, and for locking my friend out of her room.

Mostly, I feel bad for not getting off. It's been so long.

I walk Boston to the door, and ask him to text me when he gets home. He kisses me and tells me that he will, then walks out the door.

I apologize to my friend, and she accepts my apology. She understands that it's been such a long time since I've gotten laid.

He ends up texting me the next day to let me know that he had a good time. I write back and say that I did, too.

I go back to LA, and we end up texting periodically about one thing or another. In the summer, my job ends up sending me to Boston for a week for a conference. I text him to let him know that I will be in his area, and that I would love to see him.

He says sure, but doesn't say anything after that.

I text him again as I get closer to arriving. I have other people to see in Boston, so my schedule is filling up quickly. It takes him a day to respond, but he says that he's got Thursday night open. I tell him that's perfect.

On Thursday during my time in his city, Boston texts me to say that he won't be able to make it unless he can stay the night with me — his commute is too far.

Unfortunately, I'm staying at an Airbnb which specifically requests no guests.

I tell him he won't be able to stay.

He tells me he's sorry, but he won't be able to make it to see me.

I'm devastated.

The story I make up in my head is that all he wants to do is get in my pants. Our time together didn't matter, he was faking interest so he can sleep with me.

There's another part of me that understands that he might not be able to commute so far in one evening, and he can't make it to see me, even though he really wants to.

Ah, yes. There's that constant battle. It's the "I'm amazing, I'm good enough!" teetering on the edge of "I am not worthy of dating, I'm only good enough for a hook-up." It's a struggle to stay constantly single, go on a string of bad dates, find a good one, and then have him decide not to see you again when he has the opportunity. I brush it off, and try to pretend it's okay, but sometimes it hurts. But I have to keep going.

And I never heard from him again.

# 68
# Cambridge

Have you ever taken someone's virginity?

Me neither.

(Yes, this story is going to be disappointing. Aren't they all?)

At least, I haven't physically taken someone's virginity. I did take their dating virginity. Let me explain...

The night after my amazing date with Boston I matched on Tinder with a guy who lived in Cambridge. And people from the area will tell you: Cambridge is not Boston — don't confuse the two.

What I knew about this guy before we met was that he was 26, worked for his family's business, and was born and raised in Cambridge. We met at a nice bar in Cambridge, not far from Harvard Square. I arrived before he did. He showed up and introduced himself. We hugged. He was adorable — tall, dark hair, and a full beard.

I could instantly tell he was nervous.

He struggled to formulate sentences. When he finally managed to string a sentence together he stammered his way through it. His forehead shone with perspiration. He avoided eye contact with me. I asked him a variety of questions, and he did his best to answer. Between his response and my next question was complete silence. He struggled to come up with any questions on his own.

I felt bad for him. Jesus, I'm an easy first date, too. I make conversation easy. At some point in my dating career I read something that said you should pretend it's your job to make the other person feel at ease. So far, it's worked on all of my dates — they usually ask me out on a second date at that point in time. I do my best to ask questions, be relaxed, and make the other person feel comfortable. My techniques did not appear to be working on this guy.

"Is this your first Tinder date?" I inquired.

He nodded. I knew it!

"It's my first date ever," he continued.

"*Ever*!?" I asked incredulously.

"Ever," he replied sheepishly.

"How is that possible? You're 26, right?"

"Yes, but I was very overweight until recently. I didn't have the self-confidence to go on a date."

I wasn't sure he had the confidence to be on a date *now*. He was really struggling with eye contact; I could see the sweat glistening on his forehead.

How do I tell him how lucky he is to be on a first date with me without sounding like a cocky asshole? Did he realize he could have ended up with some bitch that would walk out on him in the first ten seconds of the date? I'm kind and compassionate.

I continued to ask him questions about himself — what were his hobbies? Where did he grow up? Did he have siblings? Did he collect things? Where was his favorite place to travel to?

He tried to answer to the best of his ability — I listened patiently while he stuttered his way through the answers. He collected classic firearms from wartime eras — which sounded real fucking creepy coming from this guy. Like, if he attempted to use it as a line on a girl at a bar it would sound a little too *Silence of the Lambs* for anyone's comfort. He was extremely active in his Greek Orthodox church, and he proceeded to tell me all about the religious ceremonies he had participated in. He showed me pictures of firearms, religious precessions, and the house he was building with the family business.

This dude was going to make some woman very happy someday, if he could just get over his initial anxiety. He was well intentioned, and was clearly not looking for a hook-up. I told him he needed to get off Tinder.

"Why?"

"Look, Tinder is not for guys like you. The women you'll meet on Tinder are not kind. You're too nice for someone to treat you like garbage on this app. You need to be on something like OkCupid or PoF. Ladies will treat you a little more nicely there. They probably have similar intentions to what you're looking for anyways."

He didn't respond. Again, I wanted to tell him how lucky he was that I was his first date. I wanted to shelter him from the rest of the dating world — I felt responsible for his confidence and well-being. It's a fucking cruel world out there in the online dating arena. People act like assholes for no good reason.

I knew we wouldn't stay in touch after this but I could only hope he would heed my warning. Since I'm pretty independent, I said that I would walk myself to the T station. He insisted on paying for my drinks, and walking me the entire way to the station while holding his umbrella over my head. His old-fashioned chivalry was impressive.

When we arrived at the T, I reminded him again of my advice: get off Tinder. He said he would consider it. I thanked him for the drinks, told him it was nice to meet him, and that I hoped he would find what he was looking for. He said thank you, and waited for me to enter the station.

I walked into the station, and never looked back. I never heard from him again.

# 69

# **Madrid**

I found a cool feature on OkCupid where you can set your location to be anywhere in the world. When I was planning a trip to Europe, I would set my destination to somewhere I was planning to visit, and I would end up with messages from men who lived in the area.

One night, I set my location to Madrid. Armando messaged me.

He was adorable, and his English was excellent. He was a sports journalist in Madrid, and had lived in Madrid his entire life. He was about 6'1, with dark hair and dark eyes. He was gorgeous. We exchanged information and began to chat about two months before my trip on WhatsApp. We chatted on a regular basis, just sort of checking in on how our days were going.

A few days before the trip, I told him, "I'm excited to meet you!"

"That's nice," he said. I was hoping it was a translation error, and that he was actually excited to see me too.

Finally, I arrived in Madrid. I told him I wanted to meet up. I had been dying to try out Mercado de San Miguel since I had passed by the local stalls that afternoon on a tour. The food and wine from each vendor looked amazing. I figured it would be a fun date idea (strike 1: why am I coming up with a date idea halfway around the world?).

He goes in for the European kiss on both cheeks when he meets me. As an American, I'm not used to it, and I came off a bit flustered.

Then he went in for the kiss. Not a European kiss, but an actual, full-on, with-tongue kiss in the first thirty seconds of knowing me.

I push him away, and give him a look, trying to play coy but I'm a bit weirded out. Okay, I'm going to give him the benefit of the doubt that I don't quite get Spanish culture, so maybe they're a bit more forward here? I'm not amused, though.

We head inside the market, and he stops at one stall so that we can have a drink. He orders us a red wine. I do have to say, it's nice having someone who speaks the language around. We stand against the counter, drinking our wine.

He puts his arm around me.

And kisses me. With tongue. Okay, now it's been five minutes since we've met in real life.

I politely push him off of me. "You come on strong, huh? I've only just met you," I tell him.

"We've been talking for a long time," he responds, and puts his arm around my waist. I'm not exactly sure how I feel about all of this, but I decide to stick it out. I was smart when I made this date, because I've got limited time to spend with him before my Flamenco show three hours from now.

"I know a rooftop bar not far from here where we can see a view of the entire city," he tells me. I look at him. Clearly he doesn't want to stay here. He's already told me before over text that he thinks this place is too touristy. I'm sad I won't sample all the amazing foods, but I figure I can come back the next day on my own. I agree to go with him. It's still light out, I've got my GPS on my phone in case anything happens, and I vaguely know where we are. I'm on my guard, just to be cautious. Better safe than sorry.

He takes me to Circulo de Bellas Artes, to the rooftop bar there. The view is amazing. He kisses me again, and I tell him I am not a big fan of PDA. He says he understands, and backs off a bit.

I tell him we should take a picture together. I am thinking he'll put his face next to mine so we can get a selfie — no, he stands behind me, arms around me, face against mine like we are a couple. I internally roll my eyes and snap the photo.

After we finish our drink, we ride the elevator back downstairs, he kisses me again. I'm just not that into it. The conversation is pretty good. He knows a lot about LA, and has a strong desire to visit the States, so I tell him all about my travels. We walk to the gay neighborhood in Madrid, the epicenter of World Pride 2017. He wants to hold my hand, to kiss me. He takes me to another Mercado, another rooftop bar. The view is not as nice, but it's fun to people-watch in the gay district during Pride.

I tell him I'm writing this book, and he asks for a dating story. I tell him about *Shouting Match*, and he is shocked. He tells me a hook-up story about him and a girl he met in a club, who he ended up going home with. He asked me if I had any hook-up stories. I told him I did, and he wanted to hear them.

I tell him a story about the time in Vegas that I ended up in the shower with this guy, and my bra and underwear got wet, and my hair and makeup were a mess...

He interrupts me, puts his arms around me and purrs deeply into my ear, "So he enters you..."

I pull away, "Uh, I'm not talking about that." Clearly this guy wants a sex story. It's weird that he wants to hear about me, someone he clearly wants to sleep with, having sex with some other guy. No thanks.

Our time together is almost up. He pays the tab, and insists on walking me to my destination, which is a good twenty minute walk from where we are. I tell him I can do it, but he insists. I figure he knows the city better than me, so it'll be easier if he navigates. I'll be ten minutes early to the flamenco show. He takes me down some major shopping avenues. After what feels like a very long time, I check my map.

He's been taking me the wrong way.

Now, instead of being early, I'll arrive late. I'm frustrated and upset. He apologizes, and we rush to get to the show. Now, instead of enjoying the scenery I have to practically run, breathless, to the entrance.

He apologizes a few times, but I am so concentrated on walking quickly that I don't really say anything.

"Calm down," he tells me.

"Please don't tell me to calm down," I tell him. It's one of my least favorite things in the whole world, and always has the exact opposite affect. Besides, I am calm. I'm just rushing, and I'm annoyed.

We finally arrive at the entrance, and I am out of breath. We are standing in front of the doorman, and Armando plants a giant kiss on me — tongue and all — before dropping me off at the show.

"Maybe we can meet up for a drink after the show," he says to me.

"Maybe. I've been pretty tired since I'm trying to get used to the time zone," I tell him, before rushing inside.

"Text me!" he calls as I run in.

He texts me about an hour later, during the show, then again an hour after to see if I wanted a drink. I told him I was going to bed. He texted me twice the next day to see if I wanted to get together.

I told him my plan was to head back to the Mercado de San Miguel (someone didn't take the hint that I wanted to see it the first time) and to check out the Prado. He didn't seem interested in doing touristy things. I never heard from him again.

# 70

# Bordeaux

"Hi, I'm Ted," he looked at me across the van seats as he introduced himself. No one else was doing introductions; then again everyone else who was sharing a row already knew each other. We were the only strangers, ready to embark on a wine tasting adventure in Bordeaux, France for six hours, so I suppose introductions might be necessary.

He was about 5'8, with salt and pepper hair, a muscular build. His voice was rough, like he smoked cigarettes in his twenties. He was in his forties, and his olive skin suited his green eyes perfectly.

I introduced myself, but I wasn't on the trip to make friends. I was there to enjoy and learn about the wines of the Bordeaux region in France.

Our guide, Franck, started to talk about French wine as we settled in to our 45 minute ride from Bordeaux to the Medoc region. It turns out that the two girls in the front and the couple in the back had never been wine tasting before and didn't know much about wine in general.

I'm not a sommelier or anything, but I know a bit about wine. Ted piped up that he was "in the industry." When I inquired what that meant, he said he had a sommelier certification and had previously worked for some wineries. He was originally from Washington, D.C. and was in France checking out wine for work.

Okay, so he knows a bit more than me about wine? Now I know who I'm spending the day with — we can chat about wine. I love talking about the complexities of a wine: the body, structure, aroma, acidity, and taste of a wine.

We go to the first chateau and tour the grounds. Afterwards, we end up inside and we taste the wine. I lean over to Ted and ask what he thinks. He spouts off a bunch of words about the wine that I can follow, but my palate isn't quite as sophisticated as his. I nod, and he continues to tell me about the wine.

At this point, I'm thinking it would be fun just to have someone in Bordeaux to hang out with, have a glass of wine, and chat. I don't want to drink alone, and it would be nice to have someone around who knows wine. As we continue the tour, I casually mention this in the van. He says he doesn't have any plans, and pulls out a big tourist map of all the wine bars in our area. We pick one, and decide to check it out after the tour.

After six hours of riding together through the countryside and chatting about wine we are fast friends. We head to a wine bar in town and get some food and a glass of wine. He tells me all about his travels in the South American wilderness. He brags about hitchhiking from a French beach. He mentions a Costa Rican girlfriend. I am surprised that he's traveling alone for eight weeks without his girlfriend, but I don't say anything about it.

We leave the wine bar and take the tram to another wine bar. Here, he orders us a bottle of wine. We share and my head feels swimmy. We've been drinking all day, but in such small spurts it's finally caught up to me.

At some point, he mentions Tinder. "I thought you had a girlfriend?" I inquire.

"No, that was a while ago. I've been using Tinder while I'm here in Europe. It's been a lot of fun." We talk for a while about online dating, and what it's like. Then the conversation turns to sex.

"Yeah, I like it when my women are dominant. Like, I bet you like to be on top."

"Actually, I don't. I spend all day being in charge, I don't really want to do it when I come home." Of course, at this point, I think we're talking hypothetically. It's a casual sex chat that I've had with a ton of different guy friends. Then he drops the bomb.

"I would love to bend you over, take you from behind, and choke you. Just a little bit. Maybe pull your hair?" I stare at him. I couldn't tell whether the warmth in my face was from the alcohol, from embarrassment, or from the idea he had put into my head. I had no clue he was even remotely interested in me.

"You're exactly my type: blond hair, blue eyes, very pretty, and intelligent," he said. "By the end of the night, I'm going to have you." His confidence was a bit of a turn-on. He ordered us another bottle of wine. I wasn't sure how much of it I could actually drink. I also wasn't sure if I was going to sleep with him or not. We finished the bottle of wine after some more conversation — some about sex, some about work, some about travel, and we grabbed an Uber back to my place.

Of course I slept with him. Adventures in travel include lovers in other countries. We had sex twice, and at the end I kicked him out at 4 am so that I could sleep. I had to catch a flight that day to Lyon.

He has kept in touch with me since. He wants to visit the wine region near where I live in California since he hasn't been there yet, and he's asked me to come and stay with him when he gets there. I told him I would consider it.

# 71
# Dublin

"I'm glad I met you. I hope the story isn't shit," he wrote in my travel journal.

I met Davin in Dublin — we had been chatting for quite some time before we actually met, since I had set my OkCupid account around the globe before I ever actually made it to the cities on my trip.

I knew that the date was going to devolve into sex from the minute our conversation began online, but I can't say I was upset about it.

He walked up to the bar where I was sitting and opened with, "What's the story?" with his fantastic Irish accent. He was about 6 feet tall, with brown hair and a beard. He seemed quiet, reserved, and very serious.

We chatted over a pint while I used all of my brain power to listen to and understand him. His quiet tone and accent made him difficult to understand in the loud bar setting.

He took me to a locals bar on the north side of the river, where there was a loud rock band playing. This time, he had to speak directly into my ear for me to hear him. Our conversation had been rather innocent, discussing my trip, his work, our online dating experiences. I shared with him that I keep a travel journal of everything I experience when I travel — where I go, what I do, who I meet.

"So what will you write about tonight?"

"That I met a handsome Irishman," He leaned over and kissed me. A slow, tender kiss that left me wanting more.

"And what will you write about the rest of this evening?" he asked me to predict.

"I don't know. We'll just have to see what happens," I said coyly.

Suddenly, he leaned in, brushed his face against the side of mine and said, "I want to taste you. Is that bad?" A warmth gathered at the base of my legs. I pulled back, looked him right in the eyes and shook my head sweetly.

Jesus, when were we gonna get out of here already?!? I patiently waited through one more beer. In that time, he asked me what color underwear I was wearing, then asked me to go in the bathroom to take them off. I declined. "It's actually hotter that you turned me down. Classy move," he responded.

He led me out the bar, down the street back towards the place I was staying. When we got inside, he became an entirely different person. He was domineering and in charge. And I liked it. Although, he did have some strange requests while we were together.

For one, he asked me to sing him a song. While he was going down on me. Do you know how difficult that is? The concentration required is extremely high, and my voice got all breathy and skipped a few notes.

He also wanted me to tell him a story while we were fucking. Again, strange request. But it was kind of fun, not going to lie.

Eventually I got to the point in the evening where I was exhausted and just wanted to sleep. He stopped, and disappeared into the living room. He was putting on his clothes to leave.

"You know, I didn't cum because condoms are shyte," he tried to explain to me.

"I've heard this story before," I told him.

"It's not a story," he argues, "it's the truth." I tell him he doesn't get to fuck me without a condom, sorry.

He finishes getting dressed, writes something in my travel journal, kisses me goodbye and walks out the door.

I look at my journal. At the top of the page, he's scribbled, "I'm glad I met you. I hope the story isn't shit."

And I never heard from him again.

# 72

# Belfast

*Dear Man in Belfast:*
*Thanks for the constant texts over the last few months. They were nice.*

I think my favorites were the ones on WhatsApp where we joked about you moving to LA and becoming my househusband. I really loved your personality — you were funny, kind and smart.

*I also appreciated the recommendations you sent me when I was in Dublin earlier in the week.*

You told me to check out Gravity Bar (even though it was already on my list), and you checked on me every day to see if it was raining. When I texted you a picture of myself in a poncho, you texted me back a picture of yourself in your raincoat. I found you adorable. You recommended that I should buy an umbrella for Belfast — it came in handy during my days in Dublin just before I would come to your city.

*And I'm sorry you were feeling sick yesterday, so I'm glad you said you were feeling better today.*

It was my first day in Belfast, and I wasn't really eager to meet up either, so it was good that you were sick. But since I only had a few days in Belfast, I really wanted to meet you. I'm glad

I sent you a text the next day asking if you were feeling better. I said I would be back from my tour around 6:30 pm, and asked you what time you were thinking of meeting up.

*The time range of 7:30 to 8 sounded fine.*

That's fine. It gives me time to grab dinner after my tour. I didn't hear from you after you sent that, so while I ate dinner (alone), I decided to send you a text since we hadn't really solidified a time or a place yet.

*But I didn't really appreciate it when I sent you a text at 7:30 and noted that I had been blocked.*

I didn't get the usual two checkmarks on my WhatsApp message to signify that you had received the message. Instead, I got one gray checkmark, the one that shows I've been blocked. I waited thirty minutes, checked again, and noted that I still had one gray check mark. I sent you the only thing I could think to write.

*Wow, not cool. Dick.*

After that, I went to a bar to grab a drink. I thought I was doing fine. I convinced myself that maybe you had a girlfriend and you were fine just chatting but it was another thing if we were actually going to meet up. The three men at the bar asked me if I was okay — and I burst into tears. I told them I was okay, but I'm not sure they believed me with tears in my eyes. After another beer, I felt fine and had forgotten about you. However, I had to send you one last text.

*Thanks for nothing, asshole.*

I walked home and opened my OkCupid. I won't give up.

# 73

# "Bald Guys Are Good
# at Going Down"

You know what school districts shouldn't do? Send 23-year-old teachers to conferences in Las Vegas to learn about Professional Learning Communities. It's really just an invitation for trouble.

My school paid for me to stay at Caesar's Palace. I was a good girl and attended all of the sessions I was supposed to. I also enjoyed a little bit of the Vegas nightlife as well...by getting wasted and walking the strip by myself. Because when you're 23, you can bounce back quite easily from a couple of shots and hardly any sleep.

The last night I was there, I went out alone and walked the strip. Somewhere inside Mandalay Bay, I met two guys, one named Steve. He wasn't the most attractive man, but he was sweet. He was originally from Orange County, had moved to Vegas for college and stayed out here. He worked for the Aladdin hotel (when it was still the Aladdin; now it's Planet Hollywood). After we'd had a few drinks, I told him I needed to go home, because I had to be at a conference at 8 am (it was 5 in the morning). He asked me if I wanted to take a cab; I told him I'd walk. He proceeded to walk me from Mandalay Bay back to Caesar's Palace (which, if you know the strip, is no small feat)! When we'd gotten to the lobby, he kissed me. It wasn't terrible. He had my number, and said that he'd call me.

I made it to the conference the next morning!

About six months later, I returned to Vegas with some friends for a weekend of debauchery. I texted Steve that I was going to be there. He wanted to meet up with me — he set up a date for 5 pm at Mandalay Bay. I met with him and he was sweet: he told me the reason he set up our date at 5 pm at Mandalay Bay is because we met there at 5 am. How romantic! We chatted for a while, and then I told him I had to get back to my friends.

At 23, I was too young to realize what a great guy he was, and I was hung up on the fact that he was balding. I never called him again.

My best gay friend MrKnight told me I missed out. "Don't you know," he preached to me, "bald guys are good at going down on girls." Is this common fact? I missed out.

# 74
# Postage Stamp

Remember Foursquare? It was the precursor to "checking in" on Facebook — the whole app was dedicated to "checking in" somewhere, and if you checked in there more often than anyone else, you would become the mayor of that place. Then anyone who checked in there could see that you were the mayor. You could also be friends with people, and see where they had checked into at any given time. My Foursquare was linked to my Facebook account as well.

During my Foursquare heyday, I was the mayor of a few places — my gym, the school where I worked, a local coffee shop, and a restaurant down the street from my place.

One day a friend request showed up in my Foursquare feed. Instead of clicking on "view profile" my fat fingers slipped onto "accept request" instead.

Okay, well, I guess we'll make the best of this. I checked his profile: his check-ins seemed to be mostly places in Las Vegas. I wonder how he found me. Since there was a messaging feature, I sent him a message to find out how he discovered me.

Turns out he had attended the school I was teaching at (he was in his mid-thirties, and I was in my mid-twenties, so there was no way that he was a student while I was teaching there.) and saw I was the mayor of the school on Foursquare. He decided to friend request me.

He was Mexican, bilingual, and divorced. He had a ten-year-old son, and had moved to Vegas to share custody of his son with his son's mother. He worked in a school district training teachers on how to work with students with autism. I could tell he had a big heart, and a kind soul. He had kind eyes, and by stalking his Facebook a little bit I could tell he was a nerd — he was interested in comics and collected action figures.

We spent hours chatting on Facebook Messenger. He would write me beautiful poems in Spanish, talk about wanting to meet me one day. I fell madly in love with the idea of him, the idea of a man writing me poetry, declaring his infatuation with my beauty using a tangle of words.

We commented on each other's Facebook posts, and it felt as though we had known each other forever. We exchanged numbers, and texted each other daily for months. We shared secrets through texts, had intimate conversations, discussed our passions, likes, dislikes and desires. I discovered that he was extremely shy, introverted, and didn't believe he was attractive. I knew otherwise: he was a handsome man with a beautiful heart.

During our time chatting, I went to Mexico on vacation with a girlfriend. She and I decided to get our hair braided in cornrows so we wouldn't have to deal with it while we were there. It seemed like a good idea at the time. When I finally unbraided it, my hair looked like a bad 80's crimp-job. It was giant. I felt like a lion.

I posted a photo of my ridiculous hair on Facebook. My new Facebook friend commented that he was going to take that photo and make it into photo postage stamps to send letters to all of his friends with. I told him it sounded like a fantastic idea. From that moment on, he was known as Postage Stamp.

At some point, Kendra and I went to Vegas. I told Postage Stamp that Kendra and I were going, and that I would love to meet up with him. He agreed. After almost a year of talking, we were finally going to meet in person.

Kendra and I partied in Vegas, including drinks and clubbing. Postage Stamp and I agreed to meet on my last morning there.

He was waiting for me when I arrived at the cafe. He was dressed in a button down shirt and slacks. I was impressed with the outfit he has chosen for 9 am on a Sunday morning.

We sat down to eat, and I will admit it, I was nervous. At this point in the dating game, I didn't get nervous often, but I knew that I liked him, and it was a big deal to finally meet someone after talking for almost an entire year. He also appeared to be nervous, in the way that I could tell he actually cared whether I liked him or not. It was refreshing to be on a real date with a real man, as opposed to what felt like the emotionally stunted men of the Internet I had been dating through all of the apps.

We chatted through breakfast, laughing along the way, cracking jokes and flirting pretty hard-core. He paid for breakfast, and I thanked him. We walked out of the cafe, back onto the casino floor, and I told him I had a fantastic time.

"Me too," he said. We stood close to each other, face to face. I touched his arm, wondering if maybe he would kiss me. He leaned in and hugged me. I felt his warmth, his energy radiating from his body. I leaned into the hug, hoping it would turn into something more. After a few longing moments he pulled away.

"It was really, *really* nice finally meeting you," he looked deep into my eyes as he said it. I could feel the sexual tension between us.

"Same here. I'd really like to do this again." He agrees, and tells me to drive home safely. He backs up slightly, and the tension is broken. We say our final goodbyes, and I pick up Kendra so we can start our drive. The whole way home I have mention-itis — Postage Stamp this and Postage Stamp that. He texts me when I get home to tell me how gorgeous I looked, how much fun he had. I mention that I have the opportunity to come back in three weeks if he wants to get together again. He says he does, so I tag along on a trip with another girlfriend.

I fly into Vegas on a Friday night to meet up with another girlfriend who is already there. Postage Stamp has already said that he is excited to see me. We have plans to see each other on Saturday. I text him when I arrive to let him know I've made it.

He doesn't message me back.

Okay, I try not to panic. It's fine, right? ...Right?

He doesn't text me back the rest of the day. I try to distract myself with a variety of Vegas-style activities: drinks, dancing, gambling, shopping. I wonder if there is something wrong with his phone. There must be, right?

I'm trying not to be that girl that blows up his phone, but my GOD, we made plans, I'm out here to see you, and you won't text me back?

Then I see that he has checked into somewhere on Facebook. Oh, his phone is working, alright. It's now Sunday. I text him one more time.

He says he's out shopping with his sisters. I ask him about our plans, about what happened, but he just kind of shrugs me off. I tell him fine, that we're done here, and I delete him from Facebook. I also block him on my phone. I go back to my Vegas trip and try to enjoy myself. I am overcome with sadness and loss of someone who I thought was a friend, but is apparently another flaky person. I begin to wonder if maybe he's married, or has a girlfriend or something going on that he is not telling me about. I had already stalked a bunch of his Facebook pictures — there are a bunch with himself and his son, but none of any woman at all. Apparently he's just a disappointment. A flake. Another one. My heart aches, but I have to go on. I move on, continue to date, and try to forget about him.

Two years or so later, enough time for the pain to dissipate, and for my selective memory to only recall the amazing poetry he had written me, he sends me a Facebook friend request. I grudgingly accept.

Turns out he's moving back to the area and wants to see me. This time his messages are not sweet poetry, but raunchy and dirty. He wants to fuck me. To feel my mouth on his cock. And I play along. Because there's a certain sense of power I feel when I own my sexuality. We go back and forth for a few months this time, continuing with dirty texts. He only lives three miles from me. In all the time that he's here, he never bothers to try to see me. He uses his son as an excuse for why he can't get away, but I know damn well his parents live close enough to watch his son so he could get away for an hour if he wanted. We continue the cat and mouse game, the sexual innuendos.

He moved back to Vegas after seven months of living near me. We continue our game, and I'm sure he's feeling safe now since there's no way we could actually run into each other somewhere in the neighborhood.

I tell him that I'll be back in Vegas for a wedding. He finally says he wants to see me, wants to make plans. We decide on a night to get together. Somewhere in his plans, he starts in with the sexual texts.

I bring him back down to earth for a second, killing the mood with talk of condoms.

"I haven't been with anyone for years. I don't have any diseases, and I don't want to be with someone who thinks that they need to wear a condom."

What.

What the fuck is that supposed to mean? Does he think I'm some whore, who just sleeps around with everyone she meets? It's called being safe, jackass, but if you don't believe in condoms, then we don't need to sleep together.

He stops all communication with me.

I'm not even certain he was actually going to meet up with me in the first place. I honestly believe that was his way of backing out before it was too late. Apparently he was all talk, no action. He can't handle a woman who knows her sexuality. I am a strong woman, and won't let anyone make me feel otherwise.

I never heard from him again.

# 75
## JC

I went to Vegas a few years ago for a bachelorette party. I'm known in Vegas for getting into a little bit of trouble. I mean... it's Vegas, right?

We went to Revolution Lounge inside the Mirage. The night is slightly hazy — I got involved with this super hot guy with snakebite piercings. We danced and I tried to take things to the next level (yup, I'm that girl), but told him I couldn't invite him back to my room. He said he had a car, but I told him I wouldn't go anywhere with him.

So we had sex in his car. In the parking garage of the Mirage hotel. And it was *good*.

Well, cross "Sex in a Car" off my bucket list! (I know, I know, what did I *do* when I was a teenager? The answer, my friends, is *nothing*. I was a nerd who studied all the damn time.) And for the record: apparently the way to do it is with the girl in the passenger's seat, lay all the way back, and the dude with his feet on the passenger's side floor. In case you were wondering.

He was really sweet afterwards — he walked me down to the taxi line, and gave me his number so that I could text him to tell him I got back to the room okay. He texted me the next day to meet up and have lunch, but I had bachelorette plans. And the worst hangover in the world.

We ditched both of our sets of friends that evening and had sex in the car *again*. Same dude, same car, two nights in a row in Vegas. Who does that?!

We stayed in touch after I returned to regular life. We Skyped a few times, talked on the phone, and I planned to come visit and stay with him. A few days before I was supposed to go, he called and made up some excuse about his friend being in jail, how he was the liaison for the family, and he was going to have to cancel. I said I was going to fly in anyways, and stay with some friends in their hotel, and I'd love for him to take a few minutes out of the weekend to hang out with me (it's not like they have visiting hours all the time, right?) I flew into Vegas, called to tell him I was there, and he didn't pick up the phone. Nor did he proceed to answer the other two texts I sent him that weekend. I got the hint. I deleted him from Facebook and vowed that would be the last time I flew into Vegas to see some guy!

## THERE WAS CRYING INVOLVED

*These are painful to write about, painful to think about, and were painful to live through. They're also the dates that made me reflect on who I am and what I want from my relationships.*

## 76

# Frozen Lemonade

One fall Monday evening at a game night with the girls a few towns over from mine, I remarked to the homeowner that the hotel bar next door to her house looked amazing.

"I know! I've been meaning to check it out for a while!" she exclaimed.

"Well, how about we check it out next Friday?" I suggested, hoping she and a few of the other girls would say yes. I had big plans that Saturday to go to a UCLA football game, so I knew I needed to stay in that Friday night. But I knew I was free the following Friday.

The girls agreed, and twelve days later we found ourselves at the bar, seemingly alone for happy hour. We chit-chatted for a while, and suddenly, in walked a group — there seemed to be a man dressed in a collar (oh my god, is that a priest!?), a woman, and two other gentleman. Each appeared to be in their mid-to-late forties. They all took a seat at the bar. We ignored them as we continued to sip our cocktails and catch up about the events of that week.

Suddenly, a cackle burst from the woman at the bar. The priest had clearly said something hilarious that everyone seemed to be laughing at. One of the gentlemen, a tall, handsome Black man with dreadlocks down to his shoulders, had a deep, booming laugh that resonated throughout the bar. As he laughed, I couldn't stop staring at him. I felt like maybe I had seen him before. Or maybe I just had a magnetic attraction to him. Either way, it was really distracting.

I tried to forget about him while I continued conversation with the girls, but I kept staring at him out of the corner of my eye. He clearly had a big personality: he laughed loudly and was constantly smiling. At one point he got up and walked by our table on his way to the bathroom. His eye caught mine, and he made a flirty comment about the group of girls at the table. His baritone voice carried throughout the table, and he never skipped a step as he kept eye contact with me until he disappeared around the corner.

I blushed. My heart beat faster. There is something about this man that is definitely magnetic.

"His voice sounds so familiar," I told the girls, trying to remember where I'd heard it before. "Is he famous? How do I know him?"

"I haven't heard his voice before. But it's really sexy," one of the girls exclaimed.

Okay, not famous. I must know him. I must have met him before.

But where? I was never going to be able to concentrate on what the girls were talking about. Suddenly, the girls became background noise while I concentrated on listening to this guy speak. I was determined to figure out how I knew him.

Suddenly, it came to me.

"Frozen Lemonade!" I scream-whispered to the girls in the group. "I met him at the UCLA game last weekend!"

"Stop." My friend blew me off. "We were drunk at that game. I'm sure you're mistaken. They probably look similar."

"No." I replied adamantly. "It's him. I know it's him." I recalled the Frozen Lemonade story to the rest of the girls in the group:

After game night with the girls that Monday, we had a UCLA football game that Saturday. I met up with my group of friends for six hours (yes, six) of tailgating before the game started. It was the first home game of the season, and I brought my brother with me for a little sibling drinking time.

We met for tailgating at 8 am and started drinking while we were making breakfast at our tailgate tent. My brother remarked that he hadn't eaten anything yet, as he grabbed his beer and shot of whiskey.

Uh oh, this isn't going to end well.

We proceeded to laugh and drink while we waited for kickoff. Eventually, we cleaned up the tailgate, and pounded a beer on the way to the gate. Since the stadium doesn't serve booze, you gotta get drunk before the game. My brother pounded his last beer, and we headed into the stadium.

As we headed up the stairs to our seats, I saw my brother sway and practically topple over into the guy on the aisle. He is clearly drunk. It's the beginning of the second quarter. I look over, and he has his head in his hands. I lean over and ask if he's okay.

"I'm kinda dizzy. I feel like I might throw up."

I escort him down the stairs to the bathrooms near our entrance gate. My head was still kind of fuzzy, but I was clear-headed enough to know that my brother's needs come first.

I sat on the planter while he headed to the bathroom to throw up. I couldn't help but worry — what was I going to do if he passed out in the bathroom? As I stared in the direction of the bathroom, I noticed I was seated next to a frozen lemonade stand.

The line was sort of long — it was a hot day — filled with parents and their kids.

Except for one set of customers. Two grown men. No kids to be found near them. I was intrigued.

Once the men got their frozen lemonade, I watched one of them open a water bottle and dump half of the water bottle into the lemonade.

Being drunk, my filter was off, and I yelled to them. They were only standing a few feet away.

"Something tells me that's not water!" I flirted to the guy holding the water bottle over the frozen lemonade.

"No," he replied in a smooth baritone voice. He shook the dreads from his face. "It's vodka. Want some?"

I politely declined, and told him I was waiting for my brother. We flirted until my brother reappeared from the bathroom, and plopped down next to me on the bench.

Frozen Lemonade remarked that that must be my brother, it was nice chatting with me, and that he was going to head back to the game.

I wanted to give him my number. But I just didn't know how to go about telling him. I let him walk away, with so much regret in my heart of not giving him my number. I knew my brother was my first priority — he wanted to sleep it off in the car for the rest of the game, so I gave him the keys to the car and told him to sleep in the backseat while I finished watching the game. He didn't want to ruin my good time.

I walked back to my seat, disappointed that I didn't have the courage to give Frozen Lemonade my number.

"Wow," one of the girls at happy hour responded, "and that was in Pasadena. And he's here in San Pedro!? What are the odds?"

I felt like the Universe was giving me a second chance to give this guy my number. Now all I had to do was get up the courage to say hi to him.

"I'm going to say something to him the next time he walks by," I promised out loud, more for myself than for the girls.

Sure enough, not ten minutes later he got up to go to the bathroom again. On his way back, I finally got the nerve:

"Hey! Were you at the UCLA game last weekend?"

He stopped dead in his tracks, and looked at me inquisitively. "Yeah..." he started slowly.

"And did you buy some frozen lemonade?"

"You're the girl with the brother!" he exclaimed excitedly. He recognized me! Oh, this was so happening.

We ended up talking about how we each ended up here, at this bar. It turns out he lived just down the street from where I worked, and just happened to check out this bar with his friends today. He was a filmmaker and coached soccer at a local private high school down the street. He was also a UCLA alum — with a major in business.

"Are you going to the UCLA game next Saturday?" he asked me. I nodded. "Well, come find me. I'll be at the lemonade stand at halftime."

"How about if we exchange numbers?" I held my breath while I waited for his response.

"Sure!" He whipped out his phone and I casually gave him my number. Inside, I was bursting with joy. This guy seemed great!

We exchanged a few texts throughout the week, but ended up missing each other at the UCLA game.

The following week, I invited him out for wine tasting with Kendra and me. We wine tasted together for a while, then Kendra made some excuse to leave. It was just he and I. Suddenly, I was feeling nervous. Was he going to kiss me? I certainly hoped so. He had made me laugh all night. He was funny, witty, and made me feel safe. In the most gentlemanly way possible, he walked me to my car. I told him I had a good time, and he said he did too.

And then he leaned in and kissed me.

In that moment, I was the happiest woman in the world.

When he finally pulled away, he asked if I wanted to hang out this weekend.

Sure, I told him. I was free Sunday, after I get done doing some work.

"Great, text me when you're done and we'll get together!" Normally I hated spontaneous, but this seemed to be a good plan.

After I finished my work on Sunday, I texted Frozen Lemonade. He asked me to meet him at a restaurant at our local mall for a drink. I parked in the structure, and on the way out I noticed a giant tent in the parking lot nearby. I wondered what it was, but didn't think much of it.

I met up with Frozen Lemonade, and was greeted with a warm smile and a giant hug. We grabbed a drink, and he convinced me that we should go bowling at the bowling alley upstairs.

I'm not a bowler. But I agreed.

He decided we should bet on each frame — whoever lost the frame had to give a kiss to the other person.

I'm so in. There are no losers here. And how cute is that?!

Of course I lost. But I had so much fun doing it. As we chatted with the cocktail waitress, we discovered the tent outside was a circus. And the next show started in 20 minutes.

"C'mon! We gotta catch the show! Who doesn't love the circus?" He grabbed my hand and dragged me to the circus. On the way there, I was freezing, and he took off his jacket and placed it over my shoulders.

I. Can't. Even. How adorable is this man?

I cuddled up next to him while we watched the circus. He placed his arm around me, and I snuggled closer. I felt safe.

When intermission came, he escorted me to the bathroom, and waited for me — like a true gentleman.

Still waiting for the downside. He seems perfect.

After we finished at the circus, he walked me to my car and kissed me goodnight.

I thought that was the most amazing date I had ever been on. So fun, and so spontaneous!

We agreed to get together again that week.

We watched a movie together at my place. He showed up in sweat pants and brought over his favorite movie, *The Guy's and Girl's Guide to Getting Down*. If you haven't seen it, it's a party movie about early twenty-somethings trying to do drugs and get laid. I thought it was weird that a forty-something would love a movie like that, but I tried to brush it off. I told him I wanted to get frozen yogurt, and he agreed to go — as long as I could pay. He had forgotten his wallet. I told him that was fine. (Although, really, second date and you can't even pay for ice cream? C'mon.)

The following weekend, I asked him to escort me to my friend Lila's birthday party downtown. We decided to take the metro. He met me at my place, and when he hugged me, I noticed he smelled like weed. Not like he had smoked, but like fresh plant. At this point, weed was still illegal in California.

"Why do you smell like weed?" I inquired.

"Oh, I brought a joint in my pocket. I also have a flask of tequila!"

Interesting. I'm a bit too straight laced for that. I was worried that he would get caught with it, and I'd be guilty by association. I'm a big rule-follower, so I'm not down with all of that.

We hopped on the metro (yes, in LA some people actually take it), and they were doing construction on the blue line, so we had to hop on a bus to get to our actual stop. When we finally got off and joined Lila, the party was in full swing.

Lila was charmed by this man, as was I. She whispered in my ear that he was cute, and I smiled back as if to say, "I know!" She took a bunch of photos of us together. I felt happy.

At some point during the party, he decided to take Lila into the stairwell and get stoned with her. Buttoned-up me wouldn't join; instead, I just sat there super worried until they came back, stoned and a little bit drunk.

Eventually, Frozen Lemonade and I decided to walk back to the bus to get back to the metro station. Unfortunately, we couldn't find the bus stop. Frozen Lemonade decided to ask the cops around the corner where we could pick up the bus — I annoyingly nagged that he shouldn't get too close, since he still smelled like weed. He just looked at me like I was being overprotective and paranoid. He escaped without incident, and we made our way to the bus stop.

By the time we got back towards my area we decided to go to one of my favorite bars. We grabbed a drink and sat at a table near the door. He went out for a smoke, and was there for quite some time before he came back in. When he approached me, he leaned over and said, "I did something bad."

I looked at him, concerned. "What is it?" My heart dropped. What the hell could he have possibly done in the ten minutes he was outside?

"You'll see when we get back to the car."

What the hell. Did he scratch up his car? He didn't even go anywhere. A thousand scenarios crossed my mind. My heart started to race.

Eventually, when we left and walked to the car, I noticed a huge bouquet of flowers sitting in the passenger's seat of his car.

"Oh my god!" I shrieked with joy and surprise, "Where did you get these?"

"There was a woman who walked by with a bunch of flowers. She asked me if I wanted to buy some. I figured you would like them."

What a sweetheart! I couldn't stop grinning as he drove us back to my place. I suggested that he should stay the night — although, I warned him, I wasn't ready to sleep with him yet. He said that was fine.

When he left in the morning, I was floating on air.

We texted throughout the week, and that weekend he went out to a bar with some of his friends. He asked me to join him at the bar. I thought I was going there to pick him up, since it sounded like he had had too much to drink.

Instead, he wanted to drive himself back to my place once I got there. We argued in the parking lot that I didn't think it was safe for him to drive himself to my place. He said he was a grown man and knew when he was too drunk to drive. Ugh. I followed him back to my place, carefully watching his every move to make sure he didn't do anything dangerous.

When we got back to my place, he flopped himself down on my bed and passed out. I took his shoes off, got ready for bed, and hopped into bed myself. I got up and went to yoga in the morning, leaving him to sleep it off in my bed.

After yoga, I returned back to my place. He was just starting to wake up. He wanted to fool around. I still wasn't ready to have sex with him — mostly because I had seen the size of his dick. There was NO way that thing was going to fit inside of me. When I had tried to give him head that morning, I had to use my mouth and two hands to try to even run the length of his shaft. I wasn't ready to even communicate with him that that was part of the problem.

One of my (many) issues I have struggled with is communication and my ability to be honest with people when prompted. I used to be embarrassed and unwilling to share my thoughts, because I had previously been shot down whenever I shared my opinion. I've been berated, belittled, and made fun of for sharing my point of view. It's taken me a really long time to feel like I can have an opinion, I can share it with the world, and as long as my view doesn't encroach on anyone else's rights,

I am valid for speaking my mind. It's something I continue to work on.

He, however, was clearly upset that we weren't going to have sex. He wanted to know when. I shared that I just wasn't ready yet, and to give me time. I hadn't even known him a month, and we hadn't had a discussion of where we were in terms of our relationship. I wasn't sure if we were friends with benefits, if he was interested in courting me, dating me casually, or being in a relationship with me. I also didn't feel comfortable sharing this part with him yet — it meant I had to be vulnerable and put myself out there, and I wasn't ready to do that yet.

He left, and we seemed to be on good terms. We agreed to meet up at the UCLA game that weekend.

Somehow, through miscommunication, we missed each other at the game. I was frustrated, and we texted a few times after that, but nothing else happened.

I was upset, but I think I was more regretful that I hadn't been able to communicate my thoughts with him. I didn't think in the long run it was going to work out, though, because he seemed to be a bit too much of a party-guy for my taste. I felt like he never actually worked! Any time I messaged him, he was always willing to get together spontaneously. That can be fun sometimes but it's not something that my obsessive-planner self can handle. We never texted again, but we remained Facebook friends until I had to delete him. Although I knew it wouldn't work out in the long run I still cared about him.

Two years later I was running errands on a Saturday and I was kind of a mess — my hair wasn't done and I was PMS-ing. I was bloated, no make-up, and had a giant zit on my chin. I had looked down at my feet and noticed that that morning I had thrown on two different color flip-flips. What a disaster.

As I walked through the mall, looking at my phone, I felt someone watching me. I looked up, and there was Frozen

Lemonade, walking out of a baby store, arm-in-arm with some woman.

And she was pregnant.

We had pleasantries, and he introduced me to the woman.

I immediately regretted every decision I had made that morning. Why was I wearing that outfit? Why didn't I do my hair? I should have at least done my make-up. These flip-flops are ridiculous. I hope he doesn't look at my feet. Jesus Christ, is there any way I can disappear into a puddle on the floor? I struggled to find words to say to him. My face was probably the deepest shade of red possible.

Finally, we said our goodbyes, and I walked off as quickly as possible.

And immediately burst into tears.

I wasn't exactly sure what made the tears start — if it was a longing to be with someone who would care about me the way he would, if I missed him, or if I wanted to be in that woman's shoes.

All I knew was that I fully enjoyed the experiences I shared with Frozen Lemonade, and he helped me to recognize the way I wanted to feel with my future partner.

# 77

# Dave

I was in love with Dave from the first minute I laid eyes on him.

I also knew he was going to be bad news. One look into his beautiful deep-set hazel eyes, with his pouty lips hidden underneath a well-kept beard was enough to inspire mystery. Who was this gorgeous man? I re-read the message he had sent me: **You are absolutely beautiful, and I would love to get to know you.** He was interested in me? He was incredibly hot —

most often wearing a hat in all his photos, and his profile stated he was 6'3. I noted from his pictures he had quite a few tattoos — including one on his neck. Stereo-typing him as a bad boy, I was surprised when his profile stated that he had a Masters degree from a local University. His profile also stated that he was divorced, but had no children. He also had an Annual Pass to Disneyland and was looking for someone to go with him.

I messaged him back almost immediately. I was truly excited about this one. The first guy in a long time I was actually thrilled about. After a few messages back and forth, we exchanged numbers.

He texted to see when I would be free to talk. On the phone. Like a gentleman. He called me while I was at an outlet shopping mall by myself, and we talked for 45 minutes while I sat outside a Kate Spade store and watched people walk by. I couldn't stop smiling to myself. Our conversation seemed to be so natural, so easy. He was thrilled I had so many diverse interests and would fit into his various friend groups. He liked that I was smart. I liked that he was knowledgeable about a lot of things, and that he kept complimenting me.

Rather abruptly in the conversation, he stated that he had to go, and that we would talk soon. Shortly after, the line was dead.

I sat on the bench, wondering what I had said wrong. Why did he hang up so suddenly? I started to panic. I began to obsessively replay the conversation in my head. I couldn't think of any red-flag things that I had said. I tried to let it go, and consider that I just might never hear from him again.

But I did, the following afternoon. He asked me out for coffee, and wanted to meet immediately after I was out of work. He would just be getting off of work, too, and wanted to see me before traffic got too bad, since his drive home in traffic could take up to two hours. I agreed, and told him I would see him the following day.

I arrived at Starbucks before him, and my heart fluttered when I saw him in person. He seemed so confident when he walked in, and gave me an amazing hug. He smelled good — not just his cologne, but his musk. (I have a big thing about scent — someone has to smell right to me in order for me to be with them.) I felt like I fit into his arms.

As we sat and drank our coffee, the chemistry between us was notable. I wanted to sleep with him so badly (this doesn't often happen to me on an online date. I get this feeling more often when I meet someone in person). He made me laugh multiple times — even more of a turn on. At one point he noted that I made him nervous. I was taken aback at his statement. He seemed so confident! I can't believe *I* made *him* nervous!

After an hour, he reluctantly noted that he needed to get on the road. I agreed, and was sad to see him go so soon. We decided we would definitely go out again. He walked me to my car, we hugged again, and he drove off. I got in my car for the five minute drive home. As I pulled into the driveway, my phone rang.

It was Dave.

"I really didn't want to leave, but I have to get on the road before traffic starts. I thought maybe we could chat while I drive home?" I smiled at this adorable gesture. Clearly it was going well.

Turns out he owned a trucking company that was doing some work near LAX, but he was living in Pasadena. I lived close to LAX, so it was nice that at least I was close to where he worked. I thought of the possibilities of him staying the night before heading into work.

We worked out the details for our next date — he would pick me up after he got off work later in the evening, and we would do happy hour and dinner. He stated that he didn't really drink but he'd be glad to take me out for a drink.

As we sat at the bar, enjoying our wine, he told me about how he had taken a wine class in college. He had enjoyed the elements of the class, but he really didn't drink too often, he told me. We had dinner, and eventually the waiter came by to inquire about dessert. I didn't want anything, but Dave insisted on the chocolate cake.

And then he fed it to me.

Holy hell. It was the sexiest thing.

Being an overweight woman in LA, I often feel like I have to watch what I eat when I'm on a date — like the man will suddenly be absolutely disgusted with who I am. Like he'll suddenly discover that, *my god*, this woman actually eats food. Yup, it's fucked up. It's also LA.

Dave feeding me chocolate cake affirmed that not only did he find me attractive, but that I could be free to be myself around him. I really felt that he accepted me for who I was, and that he liked it. He made me feel sexy.

I knew at that moment that I loved him.

As we finished the cake, we talked more about his job. I confessed that I had never been in a big rig truck before.

"Let's change that." We hopped in his car, and he drove me to his work site. He pulled his tiny Honda up next to a giant truck. He opened the passenger's side door of the truck and helped me into the cab. He ran around to the driver's side, found his way into the cab, and started the engine. The noise was almost deafening.

Dave drove us on a quick drive around the perimeter of the job site, then on a quick drive around the block. After about 5 minutes, we headed back. I smiled the entire way. I was definitely interested in this guy. What an experience!

He helped me down out of the cab, back into his car. We both didn't want the night to end, so he suggested a drive down to the beach.

I knew where this was going. This guy was going to try to kiss me. And I couldn't wait.

Dave parked his car in the parking lot near the sand. We sat in silence, listening to the radio. My whole body was tingling with electricity, waiting for him to kiss me.

He opened his mouth to speak, and then stopped. I looked over at him, encouraging him to speak.

"You know when you're super nervous, and you are worried you're gonna screw something up, so you just don't do anything?" he blurted out.

"Are you talking about kissing me?" Sometimes I'm kind of blunt.

"Yes." In the pale of the streetlight I could see him blush.

"Just do it."

And just like that, he leaned over and kissed me. It was magic. The touch of his lips to mine. The feel of his beard on my chin. The softness of his tongue darting in and out, finding mine. It was a soft and sweet kiss but full of desire at the same time. Finally he pulled away.

"Wow."

"Wow indeed." I definitely did not want to stop. I knew, however, that if I didn't stop, I'd eventually get to what I have affectionately coined "the point of no return" where I know I'm going to sleep with him. And I wasn't emotionally ready to open up to him that way. I wanted him to get to know my mind before he got to know my body. My soul is much more difficult to get into than my pants.

He kissed me again, this time much more gingerly. I could feel him holding back. I wanted to give him all of myself in this kiss, but knew that neither of us were ready for it. Eventually he stopped, and with a breathless whisper he sadly stated he should take me home. On the drive home, we held hands in the car. After we arrived, he walked me to my door and softly kissed me goodnight. He promised to text me tomorrow. I told him I was looking forward to it.

We texted the next day, and he was at the Renaissance Faire. I didn't really feel like that was his scene from how he had described his friends. I asked him to send me a picture, and he sent me a selfie with some of the guys who worked at the RenFaire. Weird that he wouldn't get someone else to take the photo, but maybe he didn't want to let his friends know who he was texting.

After a few days of texting he let me know that he was going to start working nights. He wanted to come over and hang out with me before he went to work a few times. We spent multiple nights over the next few weeks watching TV on the couch, sharing about ourselves. I felt comfortable in his arms. I could see a future with him: he was motivated, and stated that he had recently lost 30 pounds. He wanted to start running with me. We were beginning to get into a routine. I still had my PoF profile up, and through my stalking I noticed that he did too. I was nearing the point where I wanted to have a conversation with him about being exclusive.

One evening in particular we had talked about going out to dinner together on Wednesday of the following week. I was excited about the prospect of spending some quality time out with him. We still hadn't slept together, but I thought maybe Wednesday would be the night.

I awoke on Wednesday morning, excited to spend time with Dave that evening. He usually texted me mid-morning, so I patiently awaited his text.

It never came.

I tried to justify it, saying he was probably busy with work. I decided to make the first move, and text him. I waited — no response.

I began to worry. Thoughts of him preoccupied my brain throughout the work day. He never texted me back. I texted again, asking if he was okay. Again, no response. My brain spiraled into panic mode. Was he dead?

I logged into PoF to check his profile.

He had blocked me.

I felt all of the blood rush from my face. Why? Why had he blocked me? I couldn't send him a message. Was he seeing someone else? I can't believe he didn't have the nerve to even tell me he wasn't interested in me — even through text.

I began to wonder what I had done wrong. Over the next day and a half, I played our last conversation over and over in my mind. Nothing stood out to me as being weird. I didn't say anything red-flag-ish. I was mad, sad, hurt, and disappointed all at the same time.

After three excruciatingly long days, I composed a text message. In the nicest way possible, I told him it was really disappointing that he didn't have the nerve to break up with me over text message. I stated that I wasn't sure what I had done, but I wish he had said something to me instead of the radio silence.

I didn't even know if he had actually received the message. Since he had blocked my PoF profile, I assumed he had also blocked my phone number as well.

I was angry and sad for quite a long time. It was the not-knowing. The disappearing. The wondering. I hated it. I need to know. I have a desire for answers, so it was killing me.

I had forgotten about him, dated around a bit, and lo and behold, two years later — TWO YEARS — I received a message in my inbox.

It was Dave.

I couldn't believe I would hear from him after all this time.

The message was extremely long. Somewhere in there, he apologized: he was making amends for disappearing. He didn't expect me to understand, but he wanted me to know he recognized the wrong he had done. I recognized the language he was using.

"Are you in a 12-step program?"

He said he was. He actually disappeared because he went to rehab the day we were supposed to date. He had been abusing pills and wanted to stop. Dave stated that he didn't actually expect me to respond to him. He hemmed and hawed, and finally got around to asking me if I would give him another chance. He asked for my number.

I was in shock. I truly thought I would never hear from him again. Now, he reappeared two years later, and wanted to get together after stating that he was an addict.

And, in my fucked up mind, I truly considered going back to him. I thought maybe I could deal with it. I loved the way he made me feel. I loved our conversations. But I know addicts — both my parents are alcoholics. I don't trust them. I can't. They have lied to me multiple times. I hesitated.

Eventually, I gave him my number. I still wasn't sure I could handle it. All I could remember in that moment was the time we had spent together on that first date, the one where I felt so sexy and amazing in his eyes.

We texted a few times, but then I decided I couldn't go through with it. I needed to keep my guard up. I ended up texting him to tell him that I couldn't see him. He said he understood.

A few weeks later he messaged me to tell me he was moving to my neighborhood. He said I was the only person in the neighborhood he knew so he wanted to be friends and hang out. I figured it was a game he was playing to try to get me back, but I let it happen. I invited him to a friend's birthday party, figuring he could at least keep me company. I wasn't 100% sure that I could trust him, but I decided to try. I told him there would be drinking involved, and I asked him if it was okay, since he was in a 12-step program. His answer? "Oh, my program is just for pills. I don't have a problem with booze." Famous last words.

He showed up to my apartment. He looked fucking hot, as usual. I felt on edge — that electricity was back. It was hard to be in the same room with him. I didn't trust him, but I was still extremely interested in sleeping with him. Damn his pheromones.

I brought wine to share with the table at the restaurant. Dave insisted on going to the bar to buy his own drink. He purchased an entire bottle of wine. I thought he was going to share it with the table, but no. He drank the whole thing, by himself. The. Whole. Bottle.

In the time that I had had two glasses, he drank an entire bottle. What happened to the guy who claimed he "didn't really drink"? Not shockingly, he was schwasted. I tried to blame it on being nervous because he was around a bunch of people he didn't know. He slurred his words, embarrassing himself in front of a room of people who were still fairly sober. While I was in the middle of a conversation with a girlfriend, he leaned over and slurred quite loudly in my ear, "These people are boring. Let's get out of here!" I shot him a death stare and snapped that he could go if he wanted, but I was still talking to my friends. With a forlorn look he plopped down on a chair and waited for me to finish. I ignored him for an hour, hoping he would sober up. Eventually, I decided to go. We walked to another bar to share a drink.

As we sat at the bar, just the two of us, he opened up his Instagram to show me a photo.

After scrolling through a few pictures, he showed me, "And look at my kids. Aren't they adorable?"

Wait.

Wait.

What?

I swear, on my life, on my mother's life, he told me he didn't have kids. He said he divorced and there were no kids involved. Suddenly he has two kids? Has he been lying to me? He's been lying to me! I confronted him about it. He says he for sure told me he had kids. I argued that he didn't. How can I trust this guy? He then tried to confess how much he cared about me, and how he could see a future with me. So much for being friends. I told him I couldn't handle something like that with him. Eventually

I got tired, and we headed back to my apartment since that's where his car was parked.

He slurred to me that he couldn't drive. I let him sleep on the couch, and made him promise he wouldn't come into my room and try anything. He didn't, and in the morning he left. I figured since I'd turned him down I wouldn't hear from him again. I knew I couldn't be with him. He had lied about having kids — what else had he lied about? When I looked at his PoF profile, suddenly his schooling said he had only graduated from high school — what happened to this "Masters degree" he had? Was anything he had told me true? Was he actually divorced? I tried let the whole thing go, but I was hurt. I felt like I didn't know the man I had spent so much time with in the past. Is this why he was so abrupt in our first phone call? Did he need to leave from our first date to get home to his kids? Had he really gone to rehab? I tried to forget about him.

However, a few weeks later, in a giant moment of weakness and vulnerability, I texted Dave. I wanted to have someone make me feel sexy, so I made plans to go see him. Hello, dick!

I parked down the street from his apartment complex, and texted him that I was there. He greeted me at the front door with a giant hug. He reeked of booze and was visibly drunk. I saw him stumble as he pulled away.

I didn't care — I was only there for one thing. As long as he could perform, that was what mattered to me.

We went inside, and I headed to the bathroom. In the bathroom trash, I noted there were four empty wine bottles. That seems like a weird place to throw away a wine bottle, but I tried to ignore it. When I went back to the living room, he was drinking wine. From the bottle. At 8 pm on a Monday.

I glanced in the kitchen trash. It was filled with empty wine bottles. This guy definitely has a problem with alcohol.

Yes, I realize I'm judging. But at this point, he's showing me who he really is, and this time, I'm choosing to believe him.

As he chugged wine from the bottle, I walked over to him with the intent to seduce him. He looked at me with glassy eyes, swayed slightly, and kissed me.

It still felt nice. Even after all of his stupidity and mistrust. Damn my fucked up brain. We made our way over to the couch, where he took off my top and my bra. His hands were warm as they felt their way down my body to lift my skirt. His breath became ragged as he discovered I wasn't wearing any underwear. I spread my legs to let his fingers find their way.

Eventually he scooted himself down so his face was buried between my legs. His tongue felt soft and warm against my clit. I could feel the tension building until I released and my body shook as I rode the wave of my orgasm to completion.

"Wow." I said as he made his way back up to snuggle against me. I tried to catch my breath and he pulled me close to him.

"I want to date you." He suddenly replied.

"Oh." I froze, completely taken aback. I thought it was common knowledge that we were just hooking up. And who says that when they're drunk, with the taste of pussy still on their lips? Jesus.

I laid there in silence, in the dark, unsure of what to say next. Eventually, he got up to go to the bathroom. After he didn't come back for a while, I went out to the living room. He was there, drinking wine from a different bottle. He had finished the other one, and had opened a new bottle.

"Let's dance," he slurred, and put on some music. I held his hand, and put my head against his chest as we danced in the dark. I couldn't help but think how this moment could have been perfect, was exactly how I wanted to feel with someone, except that he was the wrong someone for me. I wanted to feel adored, to feel beautiful, to feel secure in his arms. I felt all of that *in that moment*, but knew this was fleeting. This was one moment in time, and this moment didn't outweigh all of the bullshit that had I had already experienced with Dave.

After a few minutes we collapsed together on the sofa. Dave had grown more drunk, and could no longer speak completely coherent sentences. His phone rang, and he answered it. Apparently it was one of his kids, calling to say good night to him.

Dave responded with, "Not tonight, buddy. Daddy's got a tummy ache," and hung up. My heart broke for that kid. I felt pity for Dave. A man who was too drunk to answer his son's phone call. I knew then that this would be the last time that I would see him. The phone rang again. Dave asked me to answer it.

"No."

"C'mon. It's gonna be my ex-wife. Answer it."

"I'm not answering the phone for you." There is no way in hell I'm having a conversation with his ex.

"Answer it, Asshole."

I stared at him, trying to control my rage. No one fucking calls me a name. Treat me with some dignity and respect. I got up from the couch.

"Where are you going?" he inquired, watching me put on my shoes.

"I'm leaving. You don't get to call me a name."

"I was just joking. I'm kidding. Come sit back down." He grabbed for my hand.

"Don't fucking touch me. I don't care if it was a joke, it's not funny to me." I snapped at him. I grabbed my sandals, and searched for my keys and purse. "I'm leaving. Do me a favor and lose my number."

"Please don't leave." He whimpered quietly. If I wasn't more filled with rage at this moment, I would have felt sorry for him. He looked pathetic. I stormed out the door, and slammed it on my way out. I stomped my way to my car, filled with anger and fury.

When I finally got behind the wheel I collapsed into heaving sobs. Fuck you, Dave, for making me feel like this. I felt small, invisible. I decided at that moment that I was better than this, and that I wouldn't put myself into these situations again. When someone shows you who they are, believe them.

I never heard from Dave again.

# 78
# Stood Up

Not too long after I started writing this book, my younger brother got engaged.

Now, my brother and I are alike in a lot of ways, but we are polar opposites in the dating world.

My brother has been in relationships with exactly three women in his entire life. I think those are the only women that he has actually dated as well. He and his now-wife dated for ten years before they got married. They have witnessed my dating horrors. Neither of them understands why I can't find someone decent to date.

Look, when you've been in a relationship for a long time, you forget what it's like to be in the game. It's fucking terrible out there. It really is like trying to find a needle in a haystack. And when you find one that might even resemble a needle, you tend to cling pretty tightly...even if it turns out to not be a needle.

So, Brother gets engaged. And, don't get me wrong, I'm ecstatic for the two of them. They absolutely deserve all of the happiness in the world. It's perfectly clear that they're made for each other, and that they love each other. And I know that they'll continue to do so until death do them part.

All of that aside...fuck them. Fuck them for finding each other, for having such a perfect relationship, for being together for so long. For my brother to have someone so amazing to be his best friend and partner, and for my now sister-in-law to get to experience such an amazing love from a really great guy.

When my brother told me they were engaged, I screamed and shouted congratulations.

And then promptly burst into sobbing, hysterical tears.

Having been on a hundred first dates, I have to wonder, when's it my turn?! Most of the time I am perfectly alright being alone, enduring these bonkers dates. But every once in a while it hits me, and I am not the happy-go-lucky woman that I appear to be. Sometimes I let down the wall, and am vulnerable. Sometimes I am not a robot, and feel emotions. And goddamn if they aren't the most raw, real emotions there are. Thank God for my therapist, because she has put up with my crazy for the past ten years and knows how to let me just cry it all out, without any judgment.

But I digress.

So, my brother tells me he's engaged on a Saturday.

I have a date scheduled with some guy from Tinder on Sunday. Oh joy. Yup, another Tinder date. Still haven't learned my lesson. Let's say his name was Charlie.

Charlie and I had been messaging back and forth for a few days. He seemed nice enough, and wanted to meet for coffee. We exchanged numbers, and scheduled to go on a date on Sunday, and on Saturday he texted me to confirm.

Always a good sign. I approve of the confirmation text. I let him know that yes, indeed, I will meet him at the coffee place tomorrow at 7 pm.

The day of the date, I put on my best coffee-shop-date outfit (jeans, heels, a cute shirt that shows off a little cleavage — not enough to look desperate, but just enough to keep him interested), and arrived at the coffee shop 15 minutes early to get some reading done.

I texted him:

**Hey! Just got here. I know I'm early, but I'm sitting near the door getting some reading done. See you soon!**

No response. Okay, well, I guess that's not that weird. He's probably driving, and it's safe not to text and drive. I think nothing of it.

Seven o'clock rolls around, and still no word. I check my phone. No response. I go back to reading.

At seven-ten, I text him again:

**Hey! Are you coming?**

I start to get a little panicky. It's weird that he hasn't texted anything. He texted to confirm our date yesterday. I also feel anger starting to build. This guy is wasting my time, and hasn't messaged me at all. I go back to reading, jerking my head towards the door each time that someone walks in. Every time it's not Charlie, I get more pissed.

At seven-twenty, I've had it. I send him a final text.

**Wow, really you're going to stand me up? FUCK YOU!**

I put my book back in my bag, and head to my car. I'm fuming mad. I get in the car, and slam the door shut.

I burst into tears.

How dare he? How dare this man waste my time? What gives him the right to disrespect me?! He just confirmed our date yesterday! And, on top of that, I am still dealing with this bullshit after years of watching my brother be in a functional and loving relationship! I'm tired! I'm tired of doing the "getting to know you" questions, the fake smile, the pretending to be interested while you tell me some shit I don't want to hear, and answering questions that no one in their right mind should ask a total stranger. I can't stand it anymore!

I sit in my car, heaving sobs, for ten minutes. When I finally get myself together and check the mirror, I wipe the mascara from under my eyes, and sigh deeply.

I can't quit. That will never get me to my end result.

I want a partner. Someone I can love, who loves me. A best friend, a travel companion, a lover. And the reason I am on this journey is because the Universe hasn't shown me who he is yet.

And, I think it goes without saying...I never heard from him again.

## MAYBE HE'S THE ONE?

*I have a tendency to head into a date thinking that the guy is "The One." I try to picture a future with them, and see if I can imagine the two of use living a long, happy life together.*

*Nope.*

# 79
# King Bill

The story of King Bill can only be told if I share the amazing story of how I met the Canadian Boy Band. Canadian Boy Band (CBB) is not a date, but it is an amazing encounter.

I worked with Dan at my first teaching job. Dan is a character and has a strong Serbian background. His parents are from Serbia, and are friends with many other Serbians within the US and Canada. Dan approached my group at lunch one Monday, and asked us if we would go see his friends perform on Friday. I told him I couldn't because I was going to Oktoberfest that weekend.

After lunch, I was teaching an Algebra 1 class with 36 rowdy fifteen-year-olds. It was difficult to get them to focus in general, when all of a sudden there was a knock at my door. I opened the door, and standing there is a gorgeous light skinned Black man. He had large curls piled on top of his head, and beautiful green eyes. He looked like he could have been a model.

"Are you Ms. Kent?" he inquired.

I paused. He wasn't a student here, but he looked like he could have been the older brother of a student. He definitely wasn't the dad. But why would they send a student's brother down to pick him up? Or to talk to me about grades? That's not usually how we do things here.

"Yes," I replied slowly.

"Hi, I'm Dan's friend, CBB. I just wanted to invite you to come to the show this weekend!" He smiled a thousand watt smile, and my heart melted. This guy was adorable. I flirtily asked where he was going to be performing, forgetting that my entire class was watching my every move. We chatted for another few seconds, and somehow his charm convinced me to possibly go see the show. I closed the door, grinning from ear to ear.

And turned around to a classroom full of "ooooooh!"

Shit.

I had so little control over them already, never mind trying to control them now that they had just seen me flirt with a hot man. I blushed, and then tried to maintain decorum. I struggled to get through the rest of the lesson.

That Friday during the same class period, there was another knock at my door. It was CBB and his friends. Turns out they wanted to attempt to sell tickets to my class.

Everyone refused to buy until they performed.

So that's the day a Canadian Boy band danced in the middle of my classroom. And I don't know much about Canada, but it appeared as though they're about ten years behind the US — because these guys were trying to be N'Sync. They sang and danced the exact same way. When they finished, my class applauded. The Canadians tried to convince all of us to go. I told them I'd think about it.

In my mind, I already knew I was going. I cancelled Oktoberfest plans and hitched a ride with Dan to the performance.

When I get there, CBB is wearing all black, with a red and black leather jacket, and sunglasses. He looks a bit like a bad Michael Jackson impersonator. Another of the members is wearing one glove, and a big white blazer like he belongs on Miami Vice.

We watch the other acts while we're waiting for the boys to perform. I realize this is a talent showcase: some agents are sitting in front of the acts looking for new talent to represent. And most of the acts are teens.

Eventually the guys perform, and it's every bit as amazingly cheesy as I hope it is. They dance and sing their way through the pop song, with each Canadian taking his own solo. Each guy does some version of the move — you know the one, the power stance, legs spread wide, and raises his arm, hand spread, to the ceiling as he belts out a note. When they finish, more acts perform, and we wait for the manager to announce the winner. It was a set of young teens. The Canadians are thoroughly disappointed. I've had two glasses of wine so I don't much care about their loss — I just can't wait for this venue to turn into a club so I can dance.

Dan and I dance while the Canadians are interviewed on some red carpet in the lobby. We stick around a bit longer before we head back to Dan's house (which, coincidentally, is down the street from my house). As we leave, the boys run into the promoter of the event, and we chat for a minute. He's also from Canada, and introduces himself as King Bill.

He slips me his card, and tells me to find him on Facebook. As we get to the car, one of the guys in the band tells me that King Bill asked about me. I was flattered, but didn't want to hear it at the time. I had my heart set on my Michael Jackson impersonator from 1996.

When we get back to Dan's house, I turn off any semblance of decorum and throw myself hardcore at CBB. Eventually, when everyone else is too drunk or passed out, I convince CBB to walk back to my house with me.

Score.

We have a cocktail when we arrive at my house. He tells me he can stay, but he needs to be back early in the morning for church.

Even better.

We lay on my bed and talk for what feels like forever. He tells me about himself — his family, where he's from. I learn he's half Black, and half White. This explains his caramel skin and light eyes. I wait for him to make the first move. It takes a while, but he finally does. We have sex, and it's just not as impressive as I would have hoped. More jack-hammer, less pleasure.

Damn.

In the morning, I drive him back to the house. He can sneak in and pretend he was there the whole time so he can go to church.

I don't see him again, but I do keep in contact with him on Facebook. Fine by me. He's still pretty to look at.

A week later, I get a Facebook message from King Bill. He asks for my number. I give it to him, not thinking about the sticky situation that this could provide, since he knows CBB.

Turns out King Bill lives in the Valley. I agree for our date to meet him at Macaroni Grill in the Valley at 9 pm on a Wednesday night. I drive all the way to his neighborhood.

He's 45 minutes late.

The conversation between us is amazing. He's smart, funny, sweet, and has just a little bit of "fuck you" to him that I like. He tells me he didn't finish high school, and is divorced with two kids in Canada. I can, of course, look past all of his faults to recognize him as attractive, and sweet to me. (Never mind the gigantic red flags of being ridiculously late, not finishing school, and having two kids. That should have been a lot for me to take in at 24. Along with the fact that he's a promoter/party guy at the age of 35. Yup.)

Partway through the date he talks about the boy band. He mentions CBB. I attempt not to blush.

At the end of the date, he walks me to my car, and we make out under the lights of the mall parking lot in front of Macaroni Grill. Amazing kisser. I'm beginning to think we're going to get married soon.

For our second date, I pick a location halfway between us. We agree on a date and time, and I drive myself home, floating on cloud nine.

We chat throughout the week on Facebook and text. He tells me about how he's "working" promoting an event at the Playboy Mansion. Tough Life. I tell him about how a student broke down and cried because his father went back to jail, and I attempted to console him. We're both doing God's work, right?

When date night finally comes (which, by the way, is another weeknight. Since he's a promoter, he works every weekend night and sleeps during the day on the weekend to recover), I arrive at the bar on time, 9 pm, just like we agreed. I order a glass of wine while I'm waiting for King Bill to show up. I take my time and sip on the delicious cabernet. Then I order a second glass.

Again, he's 45 minutes late.

Not okay. Not on a weeknight, when I have to be up super early to teach. I finish my glass of wine while we chat, but I'm just not that into it. Time for me is a *huge* factor. I couldn't place it then, but it's not just about time, but about respect. You respect me by respecting my time.

I can excuse being late once. I understand things happen that are outside of your control that may make you late. It's happened to everyone — crazy day at the office, forgot you have a stack of papers you have to grade before you can go out, accident on the freeway prevents you from being where you need to be. But twice. No. It's clearly a habit.

The first date charm had worn off. I began to realize that I wasn't thrilled about the idea of dating someone who never had a Friday or Saturday off and was a glorified frat boy. Who never finished high school. And who had two kids. Habitually late. This isn't who I want to spend my time with. Or waiting on. The date ended amicably, and we remained Facebook friends. He's apparently still promoting.

# 80
## Aaron

I had a crush on Aaron since the day I met him. A friend of MrKnight's, at the tender age of twenty I thought it was just *so cool* that he was in a band. Although MrKnight and I were in college, Aaron was in the Navy. Before he deployed, a few of us had a get-together where Aaron and I ended up getting drunk and making out in the bathroom of my college apartment. At that point, I thought it was the best day of my college life. He was so cute.

Fast forward ten years, and I hang out with MrKnight, Aaron and some other friends at the Redondo Beach Pier. Aaron and I haven't seen each other since that night, but he would message me on Facebook every once in a while with some crazy song lyric. I was pretty certain he liked me, and I knew that I liked him. That night at the pier confirmed my feelings for him. We ended up singing Oasis's "Wonderwall" together for an entire bar (it wasn't karaoke, but the guy playing guitar at the bar didn't know it?!)

Aaron came back to my place, and we made out and snuggled for most of the night. We chatted about life, and he finally admitted feelings for me. He said he wanted to go out on a date. I couldn't have been more excited. As I lay in his arm looking up in his eyes, oxytocin flowing through my bloodstream, I said yes! We agreed on a date the following weekend. He left after the sun rose, and I got some much needed sleep.

The following week, he showed up at my door to pick me up for our date. I was thrilled to finally have the opportunity to date a man I'd been thinking about for ten years. We chatted about our lives — I had been teaching math for seven years and was thrilled to be helping my students get into four-year universities. He was at a community college as an astrophysics major. He was taking advanced mathematics classes, which I found to be super hot. He was living at home while going to school, and enjoying his regular online gaming Tuesday night with his friends.

I was so blinded by my feelings for him that the fact that he still had a lot of growing up to do didn't bother me. I was a grown woman, working full time and in charge of an entire program at my school. He was living the college life I had lived ten years earlier. I didn't care.

We chatted through dinner, then went back to my place to watch a movie. During the movie I leaned over to kiss him, and he backed away.

"We need to talk."

Uh oh. That's never a good sign.

He then went on to tell me that I was a grown, independent woman, and he felt like a boy who had a lot of growing up to do before he could be on my level. I told him that I didn't care (again, blinded by my feelings), and that it would be fine with me if we were to date.

"But, see, I know one of these days you're going to want me to do something on a Tuesday night, and I just can't let down the guys that I game with. I take my gaming very seriously. I can't cancel on them, and you're just going to end up being mad at me, and I'll feel bad. I don't want that to happen."

What? What is with the made-up scenarios in your head? And if the game is that serious to you, fine. But I think it's all an excuse you want to use to not date me. Fucking wishy-washy bullshit.

"Maybe we can try again when I've graduated."

Oh, you just want me to wait around for you for four more years? Think again, homie.

He leaves after that. I cry. I'm heartbroken.

We don't talk again for over a year.

Suddenly, early one morning he sends me a Facebook message.

"I wish we could date! But I'm Mormon and can't date anyone who isn't Mormon!" he exclaims in his message.

Is this guy just trying to rub it in? Is he a little psychotic? What's with the stringing me along? I can't stand it. One minute he wants to date me, the next minute he doesn't, and in the next breath he *can't*?

Whatever, Aaron. I stop responding.

He finally leaves me alone. He's dating some other girl now. I hope they're happy.

# 81
# Lyft

I hopped in the Lyft car, complete with my insulated bag of wine and a blanket for sitting on.

"Hey Desirée!" The driver greeted me cheerfully. I replied with a smile. His eyes looked kind and jolly in the rear view mirror as I situated myself in the back seat.

"Just so you know, you are using Lyft Line, so we'll be picking up another rider!" He explained as we took off. Clearly he was new to Lyft. I had picked the Line option when I had opened the app.

I thanked him for letting me know. He asked where I was off to, and I told him I was on my way to a movie in the park in Culver City.

"Wow, what a cool idea! And food trucks? Really?!" He asked incredulously. He seemed so easy to impress.

As we came to a stop, I noticed we had pulled up in front of a building I had lived in ten years ago. Waiting outside was a girl of about 22, who was dressed in fitted jeans, a strapless top, and high heels.

Her hair, unfortunately, was a wreck.

The driver greeted her as she hopped in. I commented that I used to live in the building, and then asked where she was off to.

"Santa Monica to meet a girlfriend. We're getting our hair done and then going out for drinks. I'm newly single so she wanted to take me out." Oh good. I'm glad to hear that hairstyle was not the final product.

"Oh! I love Santa Monica! Where are you guys going?" I asked. I always have recommendations at the ready for anyone who needs them.

"We aren't sure yet — got any recommendations?"

She said the magic words!

"Well, you could try the Viceroy. Or the Bungalow. Or there's..." I spouted off about four more places before I felt satisfied with the recommendations I'd given her.

"Wow, you know a lot of places!" The driver piped up from the front seat.

"Well, I like to stay active, so I go out a lot. I'm not really one for sitting in my apartment doing nothing," I remarked.

"That's so cool!" he replied. "I never really go out. We just hang out in my friend's garage and watch football most of the time. What kind of places do you know about around this area?" he inquired. We were cruising down the freeway, but still in the neighborhood I'd lived in for years.

I spouted off about ten different bars to check out, some amazing restaurants, and my favorite old-timey theatre near the airport.

"Silent movies with an organ?! That sounds really neat."

"Yeah, it's pretty cool," I was thrilled someone appreciated my recommendations. The girl in the back seat with me was too busy texting to even pay attention to what we were talking about.

As we neared my destination the driver commented that he would love to have my information, you know, for recommendation purposes. Because, like, I just know so many cool places.

Famous last words.

I hadn't seen his face the entire time we were in the car, but he had kind eyes. And his photo on the Lyft app wasn't bad looking. At this point in my life, who am I to say no when an interesting opportunity presents itself?

I gave him my card, and told him to feel free to reach out. I thanked him for the ride, exited the car, and went about my evening. I forgot all about him as I sat on the blanket watching *Office Space* in the park.

A few days later, he texted me. I had forgotten I'd even given him my number.

Him: **Hey Desirée, it's Bill, your Lyft driver from the other night!**

Me: **Hey Bill!**

Him: **Hey, I wanted to see if maybe you wanted to have drinks somewhere soon. You seem like a really cool person!**

Me: **Sure! I'd love to!**

Him: **Any recommendations where?**

I suggested a spot a few miles from me, close to the beach. He knew exactly where it was — in fact, he says he used to go there about 13 years ago.

Him: **All those places you know, and you end up picking a place I used to hang out? Interesting.**

Look, if this is something where I'm just getting to know you, I'm not going to spend a bunch of money to Lyft it somewhere out of the norm. Let's just meet up at one of our local spots to see if this is going anywhere. I don't have time or money for bullshit.

We met at a great spot that overlooks the ocean on a Sunday afternoon. As I walked up, I noted that he was just as attractive as his picture. He was, however, slightly older than I originally thought. He also had a bit more of a beer belly than I would have liked. But, I guess that's what happens when it's only a tiny picture of someone's face on an app, and eyes in a rear view mirror.

We chatted over drinks and got to know each other better. After going on so many online dates, it was different to meet someone in real life — I knew virtually nothing about him. I wasn't able to click on his profile and just get random tidbits of information about who he was — I had to ask for myself.

I soon learned he had three kids, with the youngest being 15. He worked in a welfare office. He had been single for a few years, but didn't get out much — he mostly kept to himself. He had never done online dating before. And he was 48.

That motherfucker did not look 48. I'd say 40, maybe. I was 30 at the time. It didn't matter much to me, but I could tell we were in different places in our lives. I didn't necessarily want a family, but I wanted to travel the world. I wasn't ready to hang out in some guy's garage and watch football all day.

He was nice, though. I tried to play out the scenarios in my head, to see if I could picture a future together. Oh Magic 8-ball, will I marry this sheltered Lyft driver? My sources say no.

After we finished a drink at the first place, we moseyed down to have a drink at another bar that overlooked the ocean. Then he wanted food. By that time, I was bored of the conversation — he kept talking, and I was uninterested in what he had to say. It was so mundane.

At the end of the date, I told him I was going to grab a Lyft home.

"You got a Lyft here?" he seemed surprised.

"Well, yeah...any time I drink I use Lyft."

"You should have asked me! I would have given you a ride!"

"But would you have charged me for it?" I joked.

"No!" he seemed hurt. "Of course not!"

I told him I was only joking. That seemed to calm his nerves.

"Do you want a ride home?" I thought about making a joke about turning on his app to give me a ride home, but thought better of it.

He drove me back to my apartment. I thanked him for the drinks. I got out of the car.

He texted me once after that, but I was out of town. He never bothered to text me again.

# 82

# 20 minute date

I should have known we weren't a match right away.

Mr. Smiles messaged me on OkCupid about how beautiful I was. He wasn't someone I would normally be attracted to — he seemed to be blue collar, and shorter than someone I would typically date. He did have an attractive smile though.

A friend at the time was on this push for me to date outside my "comfort zone." She claimed that her sister went on a date with someone she wouldn't normally have said yes to, and that's the man she ended up marrying.

So, against my better judgment, I engaged in a conversation with Mr. Smiles. I tried to keep an open mind. Maybe he would be the one I would marry? After just a couple of messages, he jumped to wanting to exchange numbers and meet. Figuring it's better to know sooner rather than later if we had chemistry, I agreed. I gave him my number. He texted me immediately.

**Hey, it's Mr. Smiles. Want to meet now?**

Eager much? I got shit to do, that's not happening.

**Sorry,** I messaged him. **How about on Saturday afternoon — I'm free then. I can meet you for coffee?**

**Ok. Let's meet on Saturday at 3 pm at the Starbucks on Hawthorne and El Segundo Blvd.**

**Do you mean the one in the Albertson's Plaza?** I clarified.

**Yes.** He messaged back.

**It's a date!** I texted back. I tried to psych myself up for the date, but I had some mild reservations.

Saturday rolled around, and I had a full day planned: favorite cycling class with my favorite instructor and crew of friends, a catch-up lunch date with a girlfriend, a date with Mr. Smiles, and then dinner with some girlfriends.

As I rolled out of bed to grab my morning coffee at 8 am, I noticed I already had a text from Mr. Smiles.

**Hello — can we meet this morning instead?**

**No, I'm not available until 2 pm.** I texted back.

**Ok, how about 1 pm?**

What part of "I'm not free until 2 pm" is hard to understand?

His difficulty in understanding my schedule really makes me question this date choice. Now, not only do I have reservations, I'm resentful towards this man.

And yes, I realize I'm being petty. But I will say — my schedule is not very flexible. I'm extremely busy, and I pack my day pretty tight. If I carve out time for you, it's because I want to spend time with you. If you can't respect the plans we've made, then this isn't going to work. I find it to be disrespectful to not honor plans that have been made (I understand things come up. I'm very forgiving in that arena, but trying to adjust day of just usually isn't flexible on my schedule. At least give me a reason. C'mon.)

**I can't meet until 3 pm, unfortunately.**

**Ok, see you at 3.** He replies.

I arrived at Starbucks a few minutes before 3 pm. I grabbed a table, and pulled out a book I brought along to read while I waited. Just after 3, Mr. Smiles texted me.

**I'm outside.**

I peered out the window. I didn't see him. I decided to head outside to locate him. I peered around the building. No sign of him anywhere.

**I don't see you — where are you?**

**Standing outside Albertson's.**

What the fuck? Didn't you ask me to meet you at Starbucks? Why the fuck are you standing outside Albertson's, across the parking lot, thinking that's where we're supposed to meet? I'm not fucking meeting you at a grocery store. Get real! I was instantly angry that he couldn't follow his own directions. I text him that I'm at Starbucks...like he asked.

I watch him saunter across the parking lot to meet me at Starbucks. He gives me a hug, and we sit at a table.

He doesn't offer to buy me coffee.

In fact, we sit at the table without purchasing anything.

He tells me about his time in the military. He traveled to one city internationally.

"Oh, so you like to travel?" I asked him. That could be a commonality between us. I kept looking for a bright spot in this bullshit.

"Uh, no, I don't really like to travel." I stared at him incredulously.

Strike One. Yes, I realize by now it should be more than that, but I am forgiving.

"So, you are a teacher. Tell me about your school."

I begin to describe my school to him. He looks at me, clearly impressed with what my school has to offer, and my position at the school.

"Wow, so you know a lot of math?" He asks me. I get this question all the time.

"Yeah, my degree is in math."

"Do you have any other schools in your organization?"

Seems like a weird question to ask...unless he had kids. His profile said he didn't. That is definitely something I check for. I want to be a priority in someone's life, and I know I can't be if he has kids. I told him that we had two middle schools.

"That sounds like somewhere my daughters might like."

He said daughters! With an s! Plural!?

"Oh, you have kids? You didn't mention that in your profile."

Another strike. At this point, I knew it wasn't going to work out, but I thought I would wait it out just to be polite.

He asked me what Europe was like (if you want to know so bad, why don't you travel there?), and somehow we got on the topic of drinking.

"Oh, I don't drink," he announced.

Strike 3. He's out. Clock's ticking. How do I get out of this?

He continued, "So you drink?" I noted that I do. "Why does anyone drink? Like what does it do? How do you feel? I've never done it."

Jesus, this man is sheltered. I tried to explain, but by then I was so over this date that I'm sure it came off as bitchy.

He nodded slowly, as if trying to understand. It was clear he didn't get the appeal.

"Well, I have to go back to work," he announced suddenly. "I have to get back to my security job. It was nice meeting you."

He got up and left abruptly.

I never heard from him again.

# 83
# Engagement Ring

He messaged me on OkCupid. I wasn't super attracted to him physically, but his profile made it seem like we had some things in common: a love of wine tasting, being physically active, and a desire to find the right person to be with. I figured at that point it was worth a shot. Maybe I should date someone based on similarities instead of physical attraction.

After a few messages on OkCupid, we were getting along so we exchanged numbers and agreed on a dinner date.

I know, against my better judgment. From our messages he seemed really sweet, so I thought it might be alright to sit through dinner with him. Try something new, ya know?

He wanted to meet at a spot in Culver City — it wasn't too fancy. In fact, we ordered at a window and they gave us a number and brought us our food. I tried not to be too judgy about it. It was, after all, our first meeting. That awkward moment where you're unsure if you are even going to be able to stomach dinner with this person, or if you're just going to walk out because they're racist.

Fortunately, he was not racist.

He was from Kentucky, and had only lived in this neighborhood for the past 6 months. Before that he lived in Hollywood. He was in "the Industry" as they call it. I usually try to steer clear of guys in the Entertainment Industry — it's just not a scene I dig. My work (and therefore my values) lies in the realm of compassion, reflection, listening, and caring. I don't find that Hollywood often embodies those values. Not saying that men in LA can't find that, but I feel many of the men I've come across in the Industry don't value the same things that I do.

As we bantered back and forth through dinner, I tried to get a feel for whether or not I could see myself spending more time with this man. I tried to picture waking up next to him on a Saturday morning, or divulging to him my deepest secrets from my childhood. I couldn't get a read on whether I was a yes or a no yet. I was already thinking that I'd have to give it at least one more date.

But, of course, a maybe is already a no. Right? I should have known better.

After dinner we decided to walk to a coffee shop across the street. I sat with my tea, and he with his coffee. The shop was quiet, with folks mostly typing away on their computers.

He began to ask me questions, rather loudly. I tried to answer him in hushed tones, hoping he would take the hint, but he didn't.

"SO HOW LONG HAVE YOU BEEN SINGLE?" He asked in a tone that reminded me of Will Ferrell in *Anchorman*.

"Oh, a while now. You know how online dating goes sometimes," I responded in a half whisper. "Hey, did you want to sit outside?"

"NO, I'M FINE IN HERE. SO WHEN WAS YOUR LAST RELATIONSHIP?"

Oh Jesus Christ. Great. I glanced around apologetically at all the faces staring back at me.

Alright, this wasn't my favorite thing in the world, but I'm not exactly known for being quiet myself most of the time, so I can forgive this. The world would just have to deal with a loud couple if it came down to it.

Finally, it was getting late as it was a school night. I told him as much.

"You don't get the week off for Thanksgiving?" he inquired. I told him I didn't. "Well, I'm headed home to Kentucky for Thanksgiving, but I'd like to see you when I get back."

I agreed, he walked me to my car (as any Southern gentleman should) and gave me a hug, stating that he'd be in touch.

Like a perfect gentleman, he called me on Thanksgiving to say Happy Thanksgiving.

Like a bitch, I didn't pick up. I should have known then I wasn't that into him.

I texted him and said I was with family, and couldn't talk (which was, in fact, sorta true.)

He texted me on Black Friday to ask me if I was shopping.

I told him I wasn't.

He said he was out at the mall with his grandma.

Then he said he picked up a gift for me.

I was taken aback. Was he serious? He couldn't be serious... could he? We just met.

Then the picture came through.

Shockingly, not a dick pic.

I almost wish it were a dick pic. At least that is something I can reason away.

No, it was a photo of an engagement ring.

An.

Engagement.

Ring.

The band was beautiful, silver with a giant princess cut stone in the middle. Surrounding the gem were a bunch of smaller diamonds that flowed down to the band. The price was originally in the $7,000 range, marked down with a Black Friday special to $3,700.

My heart was pounding, my palms sweating. I was a mixed bag of emotions. Was he serious or was he joking? It's not really a funny joke to pull on a woman you are potentially going to date. But then again, it shows he's alright with commitment. Was this a story I was going to tell our grandkids? And he definitely had good taste in rings. But was I insulted that he decided on one that was on sale, or impressed that he was sale-savvy?

I texted back **That's a beautiful ring, but maybe you should wait until after our next date to show me an engagement ring**. That seemed less accusatory than the **Are you fucking crazy!?** text I was going to send him.

I decided I was done with him. I didn't find humor in joking around about such a big commitment. Or maybe that was the excuse I was telling myself, when in reality it was just the little thing I needed to confirm my suspicion all along — that I just wasn't into him.

He messaged me again the next day, and I told him that I just didn't think it was going to work out. Weirdly, he texted me back with options of either deleting my number, or keeping it in his phone as friends. Although kind of him to offer the option, I already have my life full of friends that I don't see often enough as it is. I chose the former.

And I never heard from him again.

# 84
# How I Dodged a Crazy Bullet

My latest dating (mis)adventure is brought to us by OkCupid. Since I've started writing this book it's been challenging not to approach every date as a potential story. I've also been attempting to open myself up to men I wouldn't normally be attracted to, since whoever I've dated up to this point hasn't worked out for me so far.

Simon messaged me with a super thoughtful message. It stood out from the typical **hey** that dominates my inbox. He wasn't someone I'd traditionally be interested in, but I could tell from his message, combined with his profile, that he might be a genuine person.

I decided to message back, and we traded messages until he asked for my number. Soon into texting he asked if we could chat on the phone.

Ugh. I am not in the mood. It takes a lot of energy to chat with someone on the phone that I don't know, and don't know much about. I reply that this time isn't good. Plus, it's fucking Monday. Don't make me date on a Monday.

He texts me the next day to find out when we can grab coffee. I tell him that Sunday would work. We set up a time for a phone date that evening so we can make sure we have chemistry before committing to coffee.

His phone voice is timid. He speaks slowly. I am already unsure this is going to work, because I have a big personality and speak quickly. I try to withhold judgment though, because clearly whatever I've been doing hasn't been working. He drops the bombshell that his current job is driving for Uber. Put another check in the "no thanks" box. But, I'm still going to keep an open mind until I actually meet him. He's a writer. I try to envision us writing together in the future, spending Saturdays at a coffee shop, our laptops screen to screen, face to face, creating beautiful poetry together.

Then he tells me he doesn't have social media, and doesn't really text that often.

Ugh. I understand many conversations when dating need to take place on the phone, not over text (this is how many miscommunications start, and I get that), but sometimes I don't have a bunch of time to dedicate to talking to someone on the phone. He says he understands, and isn't opposed to texting altogether. We make a plan to go to coffee that Sunday. At the very worst, if the date sucks, at least I'll get a cup of coffee from my favorite coffee place.

I chug through the week, almost forgetting about the date. On Saturday night at 8 pm, I receive a text:

**Hey. I won't be able to meet tomorrow. Since we spoke on the phone I actually had a date that went really well and**

**so I'm no longer single. I wish you all the best. It was great talking with you.**

Can we just analyze this for a second? First, I find it super polite that he let me know ahead of time that he couldn't meet. I'm happy for him that he met someone. But after one date, can you honestly say you're not single? Are you expecting this girl to think she's not single? Or that you're not single? That choice of words is strange — I'd honestly prefer that you just said you were planning to pursue something with this other person. But to say after one date that you're not single? I definitely think this guy did me a favor. I dodged a crazy bullet with that one.

# 85
# Damien

My first eHarmony date was with a man who reminded me a bit too much of an ex. I'm sure that's why I agreed to go out with him.

He sent me an online eHarmony message, and we went back and forth for a few days through eHarmony. If you're not familiar with how eHarmony works, there are stages of communication in order to get to "open communication" where you can actually email.

Damien was 38, 5'8, and worked in television for the Nielsen rating system. He was extremely athletic and had photos of himself doing triathlons. He seemed cute, and I was really into the fact that he was active.

When we finally got to the open communication stage, I was disappointed by his first email to me:

**Desirée -**

**Let's exchange phone numbers so we can go out.**

Dude, we've already been through this whole section of getting-to-know you, but I'd like your first email to me to have a bit more personality than that. I send him my number, and he texts me. **It's Damien. Would you like to go out this Friday?**

I tell him that will work, and he sends me a time and address in downtown LA. We're going for drinks. I try to appreciate that his texts are short and to-the-point. He seems no-nonsense, which I can appreciate when it comes to making plans. I'm a little leery, though, that he's done nothing to try to engage with me in any other capacity. I guess I should respect that online dating means dating multiple people, so he could be creating plans with many women in the meantime.

With the date five days away, I assume I'll hear from him at some point during the week just to check in and see how my week is going. I don't. Thursday night I get a single text. **Still on for Friday?**

Alright, at least I get the reminder text so I know he's not going to flake. I text him back that we are. I begin to wonder if this is going to work out. One of my "must-haves" is a guy that texts me. I try not to be too closed-minded as I go into this, but I'm already struggling with his style. I start to think about the long journey downtown since I'll be taking the metro. If the date doesn't work out, I'll be spending more time on the metro than I will on the actual date. I asked my friend Patrick to meet me downtown about an hour and a half after I'm supposed to meet my date — that way, Patrick and I could enjoy our Friday night, and I could get a ride home instead of taking the metro.

I meet Damien at the bar after I've already purchased my first drink. He has also taken the metro to get there (point for Damien:

I like a guy who can take public transportation!) as he lives in Chinatown. He apparently also takes public transit to work. (I begin to wonder: does he have a car? In LA, it's a big deal to NOT have a car. A car is necessary for getting around, otherwise it's REALLY inconvenient. Although, mostly, in my case, I need the guy to have a car just because it shows he earns enough money to afford one. I've dated a few guys in my day who don't have enough money to have their own car.) He's quiet, kind of shy. He was also actually 5'6, slightly shorter than I expected (I'm 5'5). Not only that, but he runs Ultra Marathons.

If you know nothing about Ultra Marathons, I suggest you get out there and read Dean Karnazes's book *Ultra Marathon Man* — he talks about running fifty to one hundred miles at a time. FIFTY MILES?!?! Are you kidding me?! I won't even *drive* fifty miles in a day! I ran a half marathon once and was super excited that it was over, and vowed never to do it again. And that's only a quarter of the distance! It's an inspiring book that makes you want to go out and run, but more like to improve your 5k time. Dean Karnazes just seems a little off. I think you have to be to *want* to run that far in one sitting.

Damien seemed a little off himself.

Not in any way that seemed like he was a serial killer. And not in the engineer awkward kind of way either. Just in the way that he wants to run 100 miles without stopping, and wants to train for it six months out of the year. I was so fascinated with his story that I asked him a thousand questions, but not because I wanted to see him again. He was boring, although he had an interesting story. He kept telling me how beautiful I was. Eventually, I saw that Patrick had texted me. I tell Damien that I have to go, because I'm meeting friends (I half lied, because I think it would look shady to leave a date to go hang out with another guy — even if that other guy is just a friend), and he insists on walking me to the bar where I'm supposed to meet Patrick.

The bar is *seven blocks* away.

That is a really long walk in awkward silence.

I'm assuming at this point that he is picking up on the fact that I don't want to go out with him again. About a half-block from the bar, I insist that I can walk the rest of the way by myself. I can't let him see that I'm meeting another guy, even if he is just a friend. He gives me a hug (thank GOD he didn't try to kiss me!) and he leaves after I vehemently tell him that I can make it to the bar, which is just at the end of the block.

I head inside the bar to tell my friend about my night, and he can't help but laugh. We enjoy the rest of our night together.

The next day, Damien texts me.

**Would you like to go out again on Friday night?**

Dude. First of all, what's up with Friday night only? Second, NO! I send him my typical response text:

**Thank you, but I don't think things are going to work out. It was a pleasure meeting you, and good luck in your search.**

He sends back a response text:

**Ok.**

A man of few words, indeed. This was not a good introduction to eHarmony.

# I NEED A BREAK!

*After returning from Europe and my crazy travel adventures, I was not in the mood to write anymore. I'm not in the mood to date. I don't want to talk about dating, and I feel like it's the only thing my friends ever ask me about. I'm done. I'm tired of thinking about it, expending energy on some bullshit that just seems to be the same waste of time, every time.*

*That's the definition of insanity, isn't it? Doing the same thing over and over, but expecting different results?*

*Jesus, I might be insane. It really might be true.*

*I'm tired of being fucking optimistic about dating. I'm tired of hearing "good things come to those who wait!" or "he'll show up when the Universe is ready to present him to you!" or "he'll show up when you least expect it."*

*Well, guess what. I don't fucking expect it. I'm miserable. I'm so over writing about these dates. I'm bitter and angry and wallowing in this self-pity that is being single. Over the weekend, two of my friends got married, and three others announced that they were pregnant.*

*And a friend put it in perspective, that I got the opportunity to spend 6 weeks in Europe because I was single without a bunch of responsibilities (such as kids) holding me down.*

*That doesn't make my trip any less lonely.*

*And all of the dates I have to write about after this point suck. Not in a funny or fun way. They're just experiences that I've had, and giant wastes of time. And I'm trying my best to report reality, and not that Instagram or Facebook appearance of reality. Not the shiny shit, but the real-life "this fucking sucks" shit.*

*So here it goes.*

# I QUIT DATING

*The following stories are just ridiculous. They're the ones that when the date was over, I couldn't help but say "I quit!" and run away from dating with my tail tucked between my legs. Although — I was down, but not out. I'm a glutton for punishment, and so somehow I always came back for more.*

# 86
# The Engineer

The Engineer responded to my Craigslist post during my first year of teaching. He was an engineering student at UCLA at the age of 25, and lived close to the campus with two roommates.

The first time we went out for sushi to a little place in West LA. We ate sushi, almost in silence. He struggled to communicate: he was socially awkward and unaware of anyone else's feelings.

Back then, I thought this was all okay. I thought he was the only option, the only one who was going to care about me, so I had to latch myself onto this opportunity while I could.

We got together a few times after that — once, I brought him to a student's birthday party. We stayed just long enough to make an appearance, then went back to my place to fool around.

The biggest thing I remember about him is his scent. Not in a good way, though. He had this musk that was like he hadn't showered, except he had. It was B.O. buried underneath cologne and deodorant. The worst was giving him head: stuck down there, with a mouthful of that smell was terrible. Once I gave him a hand job, and no matter how many times I washed my hand I could still smell his musk on me for two days straight.

We would see each other every once in a while, but never for any regular intervals. He would just show up when he wanted, and I would allow it, even though it didn't make me happy. At this point in dating, I didn't know how to express my feelings, how to open up to someone, how to be vulnerable. I was too emotionally scarred from my childhood to actually express what I needed.

He would text me sporadically to get together, but our relationship was never going to go anywhere. I was always waiting around for his messages, but never thought we were going to be together.

I just kind of gave up on him. I didn't think I was going to hear from him again, and then of course, out of the blue, he would call me. Then I would go six months without hearing from him, and he would try to contact me again. The third time he did it, I told him not to contact me anymore, that it wasn't going to work out between us.

Again, six months later, he texted me to say hello. I ignored his messages. I had moved on, was trying to date someone else.

Then he texted me again. And again.

He continued to text me for two years after I had told him I didn't want him to contact me anymore. I never felt in danger, never even questioned that it was strange or stalker-ish until a girlfriend pointed it out to me. He even found me on Ok Cupid and sent me a message.

I really think it was obsessive behavior because of his awkwardness, but not because he was actually obsessed with me. Or maybe I'm just fooling myself.

I've blocked him on all forms of social media and dating sites. Hopefully he's found someone and he's happy. To this date, I haven't heard from him again. And I will never forget that smell.

# 87
# Motorcycle

There was something about his profile photos that struck me. In one photo, he was on a motorcycle. In another, he was propped against a boat, wearing a snorkeling mask and white tank top, a stark contrast against his chocolate skin. His body wasn't that of Adonis, but he was definitely in good shape. The way the tank-top hugged his body made me imagine there was a six-pack underneath. I hadn't dated a guy with a motorcycle before, and I was excited at the prospect of possibly riding one in the future.

We chatted on the phone a few times, and somehow he suggested a 9 pm date at a Starbucks near me. I show up, and notice that the Starbucks has just closed. He showed up on his motorcycle a few minutes later, wearing his helmet and motorcycle jacket. He takes off his helmet, and I explain to him that the Starbucks is closed. We decide to sit in my car and chat.

He takes off his jacket, and I can't help but notice. He's got quite the beer belly. He's let himself go. The pictures are obviously not current on his profile. He's not working out or something. There are extreme differences between the photo and real life. This is not attractive.

Okay, I get it. I'm not the skinniest girl in the world. But I never misrepresent myself. I show current pictures. I show pictures of my whole body, so when a guy messages me he knows what he's getting. No one can ever say that my profile pictures didn't accurately portray what I look like in real life.

But this guy...this guy is at least 30, if not 40, pounds heavier than his profile picture. And slightly balder. I'm trying not to hold this against him, but partnered with the lack of planning — considering we're sitting in my car in front of a closed Starbucks, along with having to meet so late at night, it just annoyed me. Okay, it obviously doesn't take much. But that also tells me I'm just not that into him.

The conversation was okay. I don't remember much of it. He texted me a lot after that just to tell me what he was up to. Never to ask me what I was doing, or to ask me out again. After a while, it just gets old. I get it — you're just not that into me. And that's fine. But don't waste my time.

Eventually, the texts stopped.

# 88

# Bar Date

I emailed a guy online a few times and he asked me out to a bar. He mentioned that he enjoyed the Wednesday karaoke that this place had to offer. He told me he would be there at 9 pm.

I texted him to tell him I'm leaving my place, and he tells me to wait: he and his friends are running late.

Friends?! Who said anything about friends? I thought this was a date. At the time, I don't have the nerve to ask him about it, so I wait a bit longer before I leave.

By the time I get there, he's there with five other friends. There's are two couples, some girl that works at his bank job, and himself.

How am I on a "date" and yet I feel like the 7th wheel? He spends most of his time talking to bank girl, and doesn't chat much with me. I talk with his other friends, who seem to be understanding and sympathetic to my situation. They were great listeners.

Eventually, after entirely too long of being ignored, I tell him I'm leaving. He seems disappointed, like it's so soon and he hasn't gotten a chance to talk with me. How could he, when he's spent all his time talking with this girl from the bank?

I leave, wondering to myself if this guy tried to have a date with two different women that evening. I cringe when I think how long I sat there being ignored by him. I will never again waste my time on a man who doesn't give me the attention I know I deserve.

# 89

# James

I met James on OK Cupid. We actually went out a few times. He was somewhat awkward, and I wondered if he was on the autism spectrum. He struggled to show emotion sometimes, and often would get hung up about certain things.

For one of our dates, we went to a concert in the park. I shared that usually when I went with friends I would bring some cheese and crackers, and a bottle of wine. He said he would handle it — he planned to pack a picnic for us. I was thrilled he would put together such an awesome trip for us. When he arrived at my house, however, it was clear that he had just gone to Trader Joe's about 10 minutes before arriving at my house — one can of green tea, one can of iced coffee, and a sushi sampler pack tray. But where is my wine!? The concert ended up being really good, even though I was sober the entire time. That was our second date, and when he walked me to the door, he hugged me goodbye. We still hadn't kissed, even after our second date.

My request for our third date was to go to a museum exhibit on Houdini that I wanted to see. I knew that the third date would be the deciding date. If the first date isn't a total disaster, I try to give myself three opportunities to decide if he's someone I want to see on a regular basis (many of the men in this book didn't even make the three date opportunity).

So, he picks me up and we head to the museum. We check out the exhibit, but he spends most of the time ahead of me in each room. It was a very rare point where we were together. I hoped to start a conversation about some points of the exhibit, but he was off in his own little world. I tried to shrug it off, not think too much of it. When we got to the end of the exhibit, I suggested that we get something to eat. He heard what I said, but I feel like he wasn't listening to me. He ignored my suggestion and we headed back towards my house. At this point, I figured the date was pretty much over. He was giving off the vibe that he wasn't interested in hanging out with me much longer — he didn't hang out with me in the museum, and he didn't want to grab a meal with me. I could tell this was going to be the end of our time together — as I had weighed my options about seeing him for a 4th time, it didn't make me sad to give up seeing him, and that's how I knew I wasn't actually that interested in him.

When we arrived back at my place, he walked me to the door. Of course, this date is when he decided to go in for the kiss. He smashes his lips on mine, puts one hand around the back of my head and one around my waist. He thrusts his tongue in and out of my mouth, jabbing my tongue in the process. He takes his hand from around my waist, slides it down my back and grabs my ass. A nice, firm pinch. He repeats this move three times. Three. What kind of a move is that? That's the first kiss that you have with someone you are dating? That's one of those moves that makes me feel like I'm in a bar at 1:45 am, it's last call, the lights just came on and we're going to hop in a cab together to see where the night goes. That does not feel like the respect and admiration that I would want from a man I was dating. It reaffirmed the idea that I didn't want to continue to see him.

A few days later he texted me to see if I wanted to go out again. I sighed. I knew I had to compose a careful message to end it between us. I decided to use the "I just don't feel the chemistry between us" line. It usually works pretty well, and isn't something that the guy can argue against — I know what I'm feeling, and you can't deny that I'm feeling the way I feel.

I took a deep breath, and sent the text. My phone buzzed with his response.

**Why? What did I do wrong?**

**Nothing**, I replied. **I just don't see things working out between the two of us.** This was weird. Usually a guy just says okay when I tell him it's not going to work out.

**But what specifically? I am just going to quit dating. I can't find anyone. What's wrong with me?**

I scoffed. He must be joking. He'd told me previously that he had been online dating for a month. At that point I'd been at it for three years. Jesus Christ, you can't assume you'll find your soul mate in a month, buddy. And don't you dare bitch to me about how long it's taking you to find your mate. C'mon.

I tried to tell him we just had different interests. He was clearly getting angry in his texts. He finally texted me **Enjoy the highlight reel.**

Hmmm that's weird. I don't understand what that means. Maybe he is saying I should enjoy the moments we had together? That's kind of a weird way to put —

My phone buzzes again. Another text.

**Hi James, sorry, I just don't think we're a match. Good luck in your search!**

And again

**I think we'd just be better off as friends.**

And again.

**We're just not compatible. Thanks for the coffee.**

It took me a second to realize what he was sending me. Oh my god. He's sending me his breakup texts. My phone continues to buzz. I can't believe he's got these saved somewhere. He was sending the messages so quickly he must have them saved in a file somewhere.

I can't believe he's sending them to me. That's really weird and awkward.

After the twelfth message, my phone stopped. I ignored every single one. I had nothing to say to console him — it's not my job. He needs to face the idea that sometimes it just doesn't work out — whether it's the twelfth or hundredth time.

I never heard from him again.

# 90

## Lou

Tinder is not a place to meet someone to date. It's taken me a while to realize that.

I know, I know, sometimes I'm a slow learner. Or just really hopeful.

All the crazies come out on Tinder. Every. Single. One. Because there are no consequences. They can open with anything they want, because they don't have to look me in the eye and watch me cringe. Or experience me throwing a drink in their face.

I once had a dude ask me *as his opening line* if I would peg him. Another asked me if I wanted to fuck. Well, about fifty have opened with that. Jesus, put in just a little bit of effort to get me to sleep with you, will ya?

Here's the deal: they can get turned down 99 times, but if that one hundredth girl says yes, guys think it works. So they'll keep using it. And if I am one of the 99 that say no, they'll just move on and ask someone else on the list.

Although, I suppose, the Internet has created a world where people can be more open about their fetishes, which might make it easier for you to find someone who not only tolerates your fetish but enjoys it just as much as you do.

Okay, back to Lou. We match on Tinder. We begin a conversation. He seems perfectly normal — lives in Santa Monica, in construction, has friends and hobbies.

I know, I'm setting my standards high here.

Then somewhere in the middle of one of our conversations, he lets me know that he has a foot fetish.

That I can deal with. I like to keep my feet pedicured. I am pretty clean in general. And who doesn't love a good foot massage from a man every once in a while? Hell, if you want to stick my big toe in your mouth because it gets you off, then fine. I can handle that — it's one of the less creepy fetishes.

He asks to meet, and I tell him about this great coffee place I know near me. We meet, and he's cute. Like, so cute. And kind of adorable. We each order coffee, and he pays (score!), and I choose a table outside. It's a four-top, and he chooses the seat next to me instead of across from me.

Ok, that's cute. Makes me feel like he's going to pay attention to what I say. He seems interested. This is a good sign. My heart pounds, and I can feel the blood rushing through my ears. I blush a little. I wasn't nervous before, but now I am. It seems to be going well.

At some point, there is a lull in the conversation. Lou looks down at my feet. I am wearing flip-flops, and a pair of capri pants. My legs are crossed towards him — you know, in that body language way that says, "I want you."

I watch him look at my feet. He compliments my feet, and says he's happy I wore flip-flops. He then grabs my foot, and puts it in his lap. Without asking.

I jokingly make a comment about what he's just done, and I take my foot out of his lap. I'm sort of weirded out. He grins, and takes my foot in his hand again. This time he starts to caress it, and massage my leg.

Look, I am all for a nice foot massage. I can get behind expressing yourself, and speaking your mind. It's fine with me if you want to experience your fetish. But you need to *ask permission*. You need to make sure it's ok with the person you're with. Because it's weird when an almost-stranger invades my personal space. I was creeped out. It was just too much too soon.

I finally put my foot down (pun intended) and told him it was not okay for him to massage my feet. Or touch me in such an intimate way, in fact. He backed off, but it was clear that I had bruised his ego. I thanked him for the coffee, and we went our separate ways.

And I never heard from him again.

# 91
# The Stutterer

The Stutterer, the first guy I met on eHarmony, seemed great on paper. He had gone to a good school, and we liked some of the same things. However, he was geographically undesirable — he lived 30 miles away in Pasadena. In LA terms he may as well have lived in another country. Pasadena to South Bay can take up to two hours in traffic on any given night of the week. Strike one.

We met for drinks on a sunny summer afternoon. I picked my favorite Mediterranean restaurant on the Hermosa Beach Pier for some sunshine and people watching. He was totally adorable.

He had quite a stutter when he spoke, however. I can sometimes be a patient person, so I figured I could stand that.

I did have some trouble with his spitting food while he was speaking though.

There were two things about him I couldn't take: 1. His constant trying too hard to impress me: he mentioned his family had a mountain-home in Montana, a house in Santa Barbara, and a boat in the Marina. Clearly, his family was rich. (And I say his family, because it was clear none of these possessions belonged to him.)

2. Every story that he told was about his parents. His parents were his best friends (or maybe his only friends?) and he lived with them. He was taking over the family business and was spending much of his time with his family. He told a story about how he had brought home some pot brownies and his parents ended up accidentally eating some, and were both high. Then at the end of his story he laughed for like a minute straight. Apparently I had to be there.

At some point during the date, the property-dropping got so bad that I had to stop him to tell him I wasn't actually impressed with what properties his family owned, so he didn't need to keep telling me about it. That seemed to take the wind out of his sails quite a bit. I think we both knew from that point on that this wasn't really going to work. We clearly had different values.

We finished our drinks, walked on the pier for a bit, and we decided to part ways. He walked me to my car, we said our goodbyes and left.

And I never heard from him again.

# 92
# **Wallet**

His profile seemed promising. He was working on his psychology clinical hours before becoming a full time school psychologist. He was living in Orange County.

And, according to him, we had spoken before.

He remembered who I was — he gave some clues about what was happening in my life at the time, which led me to believe we had spoken about two years prior. I found it endearing that in the sea of Internet dating he remembered who I was. I found a blur in the back of my mind that maybe we actually had spoken before — I remembered he had a daughter that lived in the area.

We exchanged numbers, and talked on the phone for 45 minutes before he asked me out. I was feeling really positive that he might be someone I could date for a while. We agreed to meet on Sunday evening at a coffee shop in Culver City.

I've been on a date to this coffee shop before: it's kind of quiet, but the coffee and teas are pretty tasty. I arrived before he did. When he walked up, I was impressed with his dress: jeans, button down shirt and blazer.

"Sorry I'm late, I just came from studying at Starbucks in the Valley."

I told him thank you, but it was no big deal that he was five minutes late. LA traffic is a beast, so you just never know how long it's going to take to get somewhere. A five-minute delay is no reason to get upset.

"Are you hungry?" he asked me. "I'm hungry."

"Not really." Since we had plans just for coffee, I had already eaten before I came.

"Let's go eat. Where do they have good food?"

I was already annoyed. I don't like to be stuck for a meet-and-greet. I also don't like the change in plans. I picked out this coffee place with intention. Already he is disrespecting my ideas and going against the plan. (Yes, I realize I'm blowing this way out of proportion. Deal with it.)

I mention there's a Cuban spot across the way. We begin to walk across the street, when he feels in his back pocket.

"My wallet is missing." He insists we go back across the street to look for it.

He spends the next twenty minutes looking for his wallet: he checks the coffee shop where we met, the area around the crosswalk, the trunk of his car, his laptop bag, the backseat of his car, and the driver's side. He calls the Starbucks to see if they've seen his wallet. No dice.

He eventually gives up, and still insists on going to eat. He has twenty dollars in his pocket.

"I hope you don't mind paying for yourself." Wow, what a gentleman. Not only do you not have money for a date, you still want to eat, and now you want me to pay for myself? Why aren't we doing coffee again? It's cheaper on both of us...

Fine.

We sit down to eat, and the server brings us bread. We each take a slice, and he opens up the foil on a pat of butter.

He rudely snaps his fingers to summons the server. "Do you have honey?"

The server looks at him like she doesn't understand. English may not be her first language, but she is confused because this is clearly not the kind of bread you eat with honey.

"HON-NEY. DO YOU HAVE IT?" He demands rudely.

She looks at him, then looks at me, disappears, then reappears with the honey. I'm already turned off: why can't you treat another human being with some respect?

He squirts the honey on the bread, takes a bite of the bread, and then eats the butter straight from the foil.

I'm sorry, did you get that? HE ATE BUTTER FROM THE PACKAGE.

Ew. And this is why I don't like a meal to go with my meet-and-greet. Now I'm stuck with this fool. Also, I feel bad for the server and the bullshit she has to put up with.

He continues with "conversation" — and by that, I mean he tells me all of his opinions and asks nothing about myself. I eat my side order of plantains while he chows on his chicken, beans and rice.

At one point in the conversation, he proceeds to tell me about his time as a school psychology intern at an inner city school.

"Man, let me tell you about those inner city schools. They're nuts."

Oh, you're going to proceed to tell me about education in an inner city school? I worked in one for seven years, and you interned for three months. But please, tell me more. Tell me what I don't already know. He knows I'm a teacher, and doesn't even think to ask me about the environment of the school I work. But please, tell me more about the education system, Oh Wise One.

I've completely checked out at this point. I am so turned off by this guy, but I stick around for entertainment purposes.

The waitress returns to ask how everything is.

"I didn't like the chicken. It was too dry," he complained to the waitress. I look down at his plate. He's been chowing down on that thing the whole time he's been talking (yes, with his mouth full). Almost ¾ of it is gone. How can he say he doesn't like it?

He repeats to the waitress that he doesn't like it. She takes the plate away. He gets up, and follows her.

It takes me a second before I recognize what he's doing.

He's trying to get the meal removed from the bill.

I was appalled. I can't believe his nerve. Is he broke? Because if so, we didn't need to go for dinner. Is he testing me? I mean, I could see if he's testing to see if I'm the kind of woman who is just trying to get a free meal — but I didn't even request to eat — I just wanted coffee!

I'm not sure what kind of game he's playing, but I'm not interested.

I figured he would pay for my $3.50 in plantains, since he got 50% off of his meal. He didn't. And he left less than a 10% tip. I chipped in a few extra dollars to pay the woman for being so polite to such a rude man.

When we left the restaurant, his car was out front, so he said his goodbyes, and left me to walk to my car alone.

Wow. No manners at all. I sulked my way to my car. What a waste of my time.

And I never heard from him again.

# 93
# **Corey**

As of the writing of this book, this is the most recent date that I have been on. I still have a lot of anger tied to this date, so I'll try to refrain from cursing too much.

Fuck that. No I won't.

I went to Vegas during Christmas Vacation. While I was there, I decided to Tinder a bit, as I'm prone to do while I'm traveling.

I happened to match with a 26-year-old cutie named Corey. We chatted back and forth a few times, and when my friend ditched me at the bar at 10 pm to go to bed, I texted Corey.

Turns out Corey wasn't far from where I was having a drink. He came to join me, and we chatted.

He was Southern gentleman sweet. He was from Florida, in Vegas for business. He worked for a company that made him travel a lot. He even mentioned that some of his clients were in Southern California, so it was possible he would be in my state sometime in the near future.

He also mentioned he had no social media, as per company policy, but he decided to download Tinder while he was in Vegas to meet people. I was the first date he'd met.

How quaint.

Conversation with him seemed easy. He was extremely laid-back and non-judgmental. He was polite, and paid for the beer that I drank before he got there. He offered to walk me back to the hotel I was staying in when the bar we were in closed.

"Just so you know, you're not going home with me," I warned him. "My friend is asleep in our room."

"I know. I wasn't expecting to." He responded. Wow. A true gentleman. Even in Vegas!

We walked arm in arm along Las Vegas Boulevard back to my hotel. When we arrived, we both decided we didn't want the night to end. I offered up the hotel bar. We each got a drink, and sat on a love seat together, legs touching. I could feel the electricity flowing between us.

Yup, attraction.

We continued to chat, he touched my leg, I touched his arm.

Ah, the mating dance.

Eventually I said I was getting tired.

He said he would walk me to my door. I said okay. I mean, I've already warned him that he is not coming in. I don't even believe he's going to try. He's genuinely nice. We walk, arm in arm again. When we arrive at my door, he kisses me. A soft, gentle kiss. Loving, not hungry like some guys who just want to hook up. He caresses my face as he kisses me. It feels nice.

I finally end the kiss (we both know it's not going any further!) and we plan to get together the next night. He then leaves.

We text back and forth the next day, but our timing is off. We don't meet up, and eventually I end up going back to LA. He continues to text me over the next few weeks on a fairly consistent basis. We have casual conversation and he maintains that sweet Southern charm.

Eventually, Corey texted me to say that he was staying in Anaheim, at one of my favorite hotels. I texted back that he must be telling me because he wants to see me. He confirmed that this was true. I knew exactly where this was going. On Wednesday, I gave him the days that upcoming weekend that would work for me, and he texted back that Friday would be the best day for him. Cool.

I then texted him that I don't drink and drive, so if we were going to go out for drinks that I would need to spend the night. I figure this way, I'm setting up our evening so that he already knows that after he gets laid, I'm staying over. He's staying at a beautiful, expensive hotel, so I'm not going to let that go to waste if I have the opportunity to stay there. I let him know that I will be coming straight from work, and will be there about 5:30pm. He says he gets off at 5pm, so he'll be ready by the time I arrive.

On Thursday, I texted him that I hope he likes to snuggle, because I'm definitely in the mood to snuggle. Come on, that's a clear sign that you're going to get laid. He texts back that he's an expert snuggler. Score. We text back a few more times, and I ask him what he's going to have for dinner. He never texts back. I think nothing of it, because he sometimes doesn't text me back right away.

I go to work on Friday. I am counting down the hours until I get laid. It's been so long. I love that thrill — the dance, back and forth. The flirt. The gentle touch in public that says, "I am definitely attracted to you, and I can't wait to get you alone later." That first kiss, that leads to touching, groping, heavy breathing, and so much more. Jesus. That is my favorite game. There is nothing more thrilling in the world.

And, it's been a while. I dream about it. (Also, as I tried to type dream, Freudian slip…my fingers typed 'cream.' Ha.)

I don't hear from him all day, but we're both working, so again, I think nothing of it. I get off work and immediately hop onto the freeway. I'm already prepared to sit in traffic for over an hour. I pass time on the freeway singing at the top of my lungs.

I look at Google Maps, and the clock. I'm way ahead of schedule. At this rate, I'll be there by 4:30pm! Maybe I can actually touch up my makeup before I see Corey. Spritz some perfume, primp my hair. I decide somewhere along the way to stop for coffee, since I'm making such good time, and we'll most likely be up all night…having all the sex!

I arrive at the hotel by 4:40pm. It's either valet or self-park, but I have to visit a parking kiosk to even get into the structure. The girl asks if I am checking in.

"No, I'm staying with a guest this evening."

Wow, I kinda feel like a hooker.

"What's her name?" I don't correct the pronoun. Corey could be a girl's name, and I don't need to feel any more like a hooker than I already do.

I give Corey's full name. "And do you know when she checked in? We need that info to find the reservation."

What the hell kind of hotel can't just look someone up by name? I try to text Corey, but he isn't answering. He's still working, so I don't really expect him to.

The girl at the kiosk tells me I can park down the street at the mall, and when my "friend" is off work we can figure out the parking situation.

Fine.

I park, and text Corey: **Hey! I'm here early at the mall, so just let me know when you're off!** I head into Sephora, phone in hand so I can hear his text. I can't wait for kisses and snuggles. And sexy time.

The woman at Sephora helps me sexify my eyebrows: new gel to define them, and it's waterproof! I also pick up some eyeliner, foundation, and other necessities I've needed to buy for the last few days. Forty-five minutes and $150 later, I look like a million bucks, but I'm starting to worry. It's 5:30pm, and I haven't heard anything from my love slave.

Ok, don't panic. Maybe he's in a meeting that ran long. Don't be the crazy bitch that sends a million texts.

Good thing I brought some writing with me (mainly working on this book). I decide to set up shop in his hotel's lobby — not because it's his hotel, but because I love the lobby. It's my favorite. I find an empty seat, and take out my laptop. I start to write one of these stories (if you're curious which one, it was *New Orleans*) and suddenly I'm lost in my own world. I look at my phone. No text, and it's 6 pm.

I start to panic. Again!? Fucking stood up again!? Are you Goddamn kidding me?! What is with this shit? My face feels hot, and there is a knot in the pit of my stomach. I have an overwhelming sense of dread.

Time to call in reinforcements.

I text my friend Georgia, who lives in the area.

**Hey. Are you around? I was stood up for a date.**

She texts me back almost immediately.

**No way. Where are you?**

I tell her.

**I'll be right there.**

Good. It's the peak of traffic at this hour, so I can't go home yet. And I'm not wasting my drive down to this area without actually doing something while I'm here. My friends are the best.

I finish writing my story, and heave a big sigh. I'm still feeling super low. I send Corey a text.

**Wow, really? Ok, or not.**

I thought about reading him the riot act. Sending him a text where I tell him off. Where I let him know what a piece of shit he is. How dare he stand me up!? Doesn't he know he was going to get laid?! It was a sure thing! Why would he just not reply? I decide the rant isn't worth my time.

I walk back to my car to drop off my laptop, head down the entire way. I am ashamed. This one, however, I know is not my fault. Fuck this guy.

I drop off my laptop, and head back to one of the restaurants at the mall. Georgia texts me that she has parked just as I get seated at the table. I sit at the table, head in my hands, ready to burst into tears. What a shit day.

Just then, Georgia sits down, big smile, and proceeds to tell me about her day. She doesn't give me a chance to talk. Perfect. She knows just what to do to make me feel better — take my mind off of it completely. It's nice to lean on friends when shit gets hard.

By the end of dinner I am in a much better mood. And I still haven't heard from Corey.

In fact, I never heard from that dick again.

## WELL THAT WAS A WASTE OF MY TIME

*This date isn't going anywhere, and we both know it.*
*Can we stop pretending?*

# 94
# Crocker Club

My friend Patrick throws a fantastic birthday outing every year. It's titled the "Black and White Dinner Spectacular," if that is any indication of its fabulousness. We all dress up in extravagant clothing and head to an expensive restaurant for dinner, and then to a club afterwards.

This particular year, I was wearing a strapless thigh-length pleated black dress with a sweetheart neckline. Black satin heels adorned with feathers hugged my feet. I looked like a million bucks.

We were entering a club downtown after our amazing dinner. I'd had some wine and champagne so I was feeling good. The club was in the basement of an old bank building, and the VIP rooms were old vaults. In order to get to the club, we had to climb down a long staircase. In heels. After booze.

I was trying my best to be as graceful as possible. I got about three steps from the bottom when I heard a voice say, "Girl, if this were the Oscars, the award would go to you!"

I looked at the bottom of the stairs and smiled. Black man, sport coat, fairly tall. He proceeded to tell me I was working it. I looked him over and decided he was quite handsome, and I wouldn't mind getting to know him.

Of course, as it turns out, his table was between our table and the dance floor. As I passed by him all night, he proceeded to pull me aside every other time to chat. At one point he asked for my number. I gave it to him. By the end of the night, he was wasted. I was totally into the compliments he kept paying me. I left without saying goodbye.

He texted me the next day, and we went through the usual getting-to-know-you details: I told him where I lived. He told me he lived in the Valley. (Ew.) We texted back and forth all week, and he asked me out for a drink the next weekend.

He gave some excuse about his car not working, so I had to drive to his neighborhood to meet him. He picked a bar, and I arrived ridiculously early, because apparently there is no traffic on the 405 at that time of night on a Saturday. Who knew? He showed up, apparently having walked from his house. *In sweat pants.* He's slightly more overweight than I remember, but I'm no stick-thin super model myself, so I can't judge. He has a handsome face.

He proceeds to talk about himself. He tells me how in the past he owned his own business and traveled the world. I ask him what he does now.

"I work for a gym."

"Oh, are you a trainer?"

"I'm flattered! No, I'm a membership advisor."

This fool makes minimum wage. In sweat pants. Without a car. Winning?

I tell him about teaching. He's not impressed. I already know I don't want to see him again.

Then he asks, "So where do you see yourself in five years?" I reply that I'll be teaching. That's what I'll do until I retire. It's my passion, my livelihood, what I live to do.

"What about you?"

"Oh, I'll have a million dollars." Oh, really? How's that working out for you now, Señor Sweatpants? If you're going to have a million dollars in five years, why not start on that now? He then tells me he's in the fashion industry. He even critiques my outfit, saying my shirt is a weird cut on me.

I finish my cocktail, and tell him I need to head home, since it's getting late. He walks me to my car because it's on his walk back to his house, we hug, and I get in and drive away. He texts me later to tell him he wishes that I had kissed him.

I'm sorry Bud, that was never going to happen. I ignore his text. The next day when he texts me again, I tell him that I just don't think we're compatible and things just aren't going to work out.

I don't think I own enough sweatpants for him.

# 95
# Football

In one of my early sessions with my therapist I remarked that I knew nothing about sports. My dad wasn't into sports at all. He was more of the nerdy, engineer type who would rather play with his electronics than do any sort of physical activity.

My therapist said since I was so good at posting on Craigslist I should write a post asking someone to teach me football.

I thought there was no way I could do that. I couldn't put myself out there as the "dumb girl." I hate feeling or looking stupid. And yet, here I was, week after week, month after month, putting myself out there in the dating world. Why not just go for it? It's a good icebreaker when you aren't exactly sure how to date.

So, I posted an ad on Craigslist.

**Teach me football!**
**Want to teach me the rules to football? Let's watch a game together, and you can explain the rules to me so I can enjoy this pastime that everyone else already understands.**

Award winning stuff, I know.

Anyways, Jimmy replied to my ad and said he would love to meet with me and watch a game together. He lived in the Valley, and would meet me at a sports bar near my place, which was at least a 45 minute drive away.

I arrived at the bar at the time we had planned to meet, and sat at a table. He wasn't there yet, so I texted him to let him know I arrived. At this point in my life I wasn't comfortable sitting by myself at a bar, never mind in a sports bar. It all felt very foreign, and I'm sure I looked out of place. I tried watching the screen, but I just couldn't follow the game. So I pretended to watch the game, and waited.

And waited.

And waited. For what felt like hours. It was probably only a half hour or so, but it felt like an eternity.

Jimmy texted me to say that since it had begun to rain, he had to drive his motorcycle home and switch it out for his car. He was finally on his way.

Great.

I already feel completely out of place, and now I have to fucking wait another 45 minutes for this guy? This is pre-smart phone days, so all my phone can do is text — which takes forever because in order to type the letter c, I have to press the number 2 three times — or play that stupid snake game.

Or watch football. Ew.

And this is before the days when I was confident enough to walk up to the bar and just strike up a conversation with a total stranger. This is back when I lack self-confidence, when I think I am too fat for anyone to date me, when I think no one is attracted to me. (Yes, I now realize all of this is wrong. And that I am enough, and I am perfect just the way I am, and that the right person will come along and love me when the Universe is ready to place that person into my life. Until then, I just get to keep meeting cool random folks in bars and dating random weirdos. Rad.)

I get another drink and continue to stare at the screen. I look around the bar. It's mid-day on a Sunday, and the bar is fairly full. There is a group of guys about my age in the far corner, but I am too shy to make eye contact with them. Around the rest of the bar are fifty-somethings in jerseys watching the game, clapping and cheering when something happens on the screen.

Finally, *finally*, he shows up. He apologizes for his tardiness, and orders himself a drink.

He attempts to explain football to me, but it turns out he's not a very good teacher. All he keeps saying is "it's easy to understand," or "it's pretty self-explanatory."

Look, learning football is like learning another language. It's a whole cultural phenomenon. There are nuances to it, and if you're not familiar with it, it takes a lot of cognitive ability to understand it. If you grow up practicing then it's easy for you to understand. It feels hard-wired into your brain.

Eventually I give up trying to learn from him. I tried asking him a few questions about himself, but it's easy to see that he's not really interested in me. And that's fine. I finish my drink, the game ends, we each pay our tab and we both go our separate ways.

And I never heard from him again.

Side note: For all of you who are concerned about my understanding of American Football, don't you fret! I eventually got season tickets for my alma mater's football team, and proudly follow every single game of the season. I appreciate college football, but am still trying to get into NFL football. Maybe I should repost my ad and see if I can get a date or two for some NFL games...

# 96
# Mr. Show Tunes

Have you ever met a drama guy? You know the ones I'm talking about. The ones that are obsessed with Broadway, are into plays, and are a little bit weird? They've got big booming voices, love to act and do weird voices in public, not in a cute way, but in an annoying way.

I went on a date with someone like that. We met on OkCupid. From the beginning of our Starbucks date he was just trying way too hard to be charming.

At first, I thought maybe I could ignore some of his quirky traits. He worked for a sustainability company in the city I lived in, which was pretty cool. He showed me pictures of the building. I couldn't help but think about what a good contact he would be for the students at my school, who worked with sustainability practices.

Somehow we began to talk about karaoke. I loved to karaoke occasionally on a Friday night. Apparently he was in the karaoke circuit in LA and went multiple nights a week. Suddenly, he began to sing his karaoke song in the middle of Starbucks. Not in hushed tones, as any normal person would do in public. No, instead he felt it was a good idea to sing his "Tell Me More" from *Grease* at the top of his lungs for the entire Starbucks to hear. I'm not easily embarrassed, but for some reason this perfect stranger sitting across from me belting out show tunes made me cringe and want to hide under my latte. Besides that, *Grease* makes me cringe. This may not win me any points, but I hate *Grease.*

Anyways, the longer I sat with this guy the more I realized this was not going to work out. I was already annoyed just hanging out with him for an hour. I couldn't imagine spending a second date with him, even if he was trying to be nice.

I thanked him for the coffee, and left. I never heard from him again.

# 97
# Bicycle

Bicycle messaged me on OkCupid. He lived in Hermosa Beach, and seemed fairly laid back.

We agreed to meet at a bar for a drink. There was live music playing inside, so we sat outside. I had a mimosa, and he ordered a beer. Conversation was really casual. He shared that he had ridden his bicycle to our date, since he lived so close. I told him that was really neat, and how very environmental of him! Suddenly, he just sort of drifted away into silence. He wasn't engaged in anything I had to say.

"Dude, this music is really good," he interrupted, while I was sharing about how much I loved my job, and that my students are so amazing and special to me. Awesome. So he's clearly not listening to anything I have to say. Way to make a first impression.

I am already checked out. One of my most important things is that I'm listened to. I'm not one of those women who talks just to fill space. I choose my words intentionally, and I speak with purpose. Bicycle wants to listen to something else. That's fine, it just means he's not someone that I want to spend my time with. I allow him to listen to the music, and fill the silence as he sees fit.

When we finish our drinks, he tells me he's going to head out. He wanted to stop by the liquor store on the way home to get a drink to enjoy at home.

Oh, okay. Thanks for sharing? Apparently I'm not good enough company. You're not interested. Glad we're not wasting each other's time.

I thanked him for the drink, we said our goodbyes, and went our separate ways. I watched as he walked into the liquor shop so he could enjoy the rest of his evening alone.

Bicycle messaged me two weeks later. **Hey! Want to go for a bike ride?** It was the first time he had messaged me since we had gone out.

I was clearly just someone he wanted to pass time with. I'm unwilling to be someone's back up plan. I want to feel like a priority in someone's life. I also want to feel like the man I date is listening.

**No, thanks!** I responded.

I never heard from him again.

# 98

# The DJ

He sent me a message on OkCupid, and I clicked with him immediately. He seemed like a lot of fun. He was a DJ, and was constantly trying to get me to come out to events that he was working.

One evening he was dj-ing at an art show in Downtown LA. My friend Patrick and I were heading to the area to have dinner. We decided to stop by the art show after dinner to check it out. I knew The DJ was working at the event, so I specifically went to hunt him down.

The DJ seemed nervous to meet me. He was prepping for his set, but could hardly form sentences for how nervous he was to talk to me. He kept giving me a stupid grin. I tried to ask him questions, but it was so difficult to hear with the other DJ that was working at the time. We chatted for a few minutes, then he said he needed to go and get ready for his set. He hugged me, and we parted ways. I didn't have much chemistry with him, but at least I had met him and didn't have to wonder any longer. Besides, it was kind of nice that it wasn't a wasted trip that I spent going downtown just to see him.

Patrick and I continued around the art show. I ended up finding an amazing spray-painted art piece of John Lennon's face. I hung it above my bed for quite some time — men used to get creeped out by his face staring at them when we were fucking.

At least I got a fun memory out of the date.

# 99
# Colorado

Sometimes a girl just wants to get her needs met. I'll admit it.

I joined Tinder thinking that maybe I could find myself a little FWB (Friends with Benefits, for those of you who have been in committed relationships for a while, or who aren't up on the online lingo).

I matched with Caleb on Tinder. I don't really remember swiping right on him, or how the conversation got started. Caleb's pictures included him weight lifting at the gym (pretty typical LA Tinder profile), and one of him in a hat. He had a nicely trimmed sandy blond beard, and was wearing a hat in every single picture. He was 8 years younger than me, which absolutely goes against my dating stance, but for fucking, I guess that rule doesn't stand?

We chit-chatted quite a bit. He smoked weed pretty often, which is not something I was interested in at all. It's a turn-off in dating, but again, when you're just looking for a FWB, it's not really personality or habits that count. He also shared that he was from Colorado, and had moved out here three months ago for a construction job.

One evening I invited him out for dinner, but he said he couldn't make it (it was last minute notice, like 2 hours before I planned to go). I said that was fine, but we should meet up for dinner soon. We had moved from Tinder to texting and eventually I asked him out to dinner again.

About an hour before we were supposed to meet for dinner, he attempted to bail on me.

Him: **Hey, I don't think I can make it tonight.**

Me: **Seriously? That sucks. I'm going to grab a sandwich either way, so if you want to come, no pressure.**

There's a few minute pause. I'm wondering if he's going to bail again, if I should just get back on Tinder and find someone else to sleep with, when I get this message:

Him: **Look, I just feel like I should be up front with you. I'm younger than you and I'm not sure why you'd be interested in me. I'm really just looking for sex.**

Me: **Well, I'm not on Tinder looking for my soul mate, so....**

Him: **Oh, seriously? Glad we're on the same page. I'll see you at dinner.**

We planned to meet at my favorite gourmet sandwich shop after work. I got there first, and waited at a table outside for him. When he walked up, I thought he was definitely attractive — taller than me, with a little meat on his bones. Someone who could definitely muscle me around in the bedroom. He smelled good.

We stand in line to order and I attempt light-hearted conversation by asking about his day. He responds that it sucked. I order my meal, and pay. He asks for a beer, and so the cashier cards him. When he pulls out his ID, she comments that she's also from Colorado. They converse as she hands him his beer. I'm weirded out. He seems to have an easier time having a conversation with her than he does with me.

I find a table and take a seat. He sits across from me, sips his beer, and makes a face.

"This beer is fucking terrible!" he exclaims. "I should send it back."

"Well, go ahead, if that's what you want to do."

"I mean, I fucking paid for it. I should not have to drink this shit." He continues, as if he hasn't heard me. He complains some more, but doesn't actually send the beer back.

I try to change the subject by offering my usual barrage of questions, choosing to ignore the swearing and bad attitude. I am already internally upset and know that I am not going to see this dude ever again, for sex or dating.

For every question I ask him, he is super negative.

"My day was shitty."

"I hate California. And LA. The people here are terrible."

"I hate where I work. The people are all lame."

"Okay..." I proceed, realizing that he hates everything, "so what *do* you like?"

"I like the beach. I like weed. I like *good* beer."

I've clearly picked a winner. I take a bite of my sandwich and try my best not to roll my eyes.

He hated his commute, he hated his coworkers, and his neighbors. He didn't have any hobbies here in LA. He hated traffic (well, that one is a given). He kept comparing LA to Colorado.

"There's a lot of Mexicans here," He stated. I cringed.

"Yes, we have a lot of diversity in Los Angeles," I try to redirect his language. "There are a wide variety of Latino and Chicano folks."

I continue with my questioning, and he doesn't really ask much about me. (Ugh, total turn-off. I just want to be listened to. I don't even talk that much, but I want someone to ask me some questions about who I am. At least pretend to take an interest to try to get in my pants.)

As our conversation continues, I can't remember the exact context, but I do remember him starting a sentence, looking over both shoulders, leaning in towards me, and whispering "Black people" in that way that is clearly where someone is saying something completely racist.

My face goes completely white. "Okay, you need to stop talking like that."

"God, you LA people are so sensitive."

"No, it's just really not appropriate for you to say anything racist. Knock it off or I'm leaving."

"So, anyways, this female Asian driver...," he continues with yet another inappropriate comment, ignoring my ultimatum.

I've had enough. I will put up with a lot of things that I'm not a fan of for good sex, but not this. "Okay, I'm leaving!" I declare as I stand up and begin to gather my things.

"Oh...you were serious?" he inquires.

"Yes!" I exclaim, exasperated. "You're being racist, and it's not cool!" I storm away from the table, leaving him by himself at the table.

"Ooookaaay, bye...," he adds quietly.

I march into the bathroom. It's a long drive home, and I want to pee before I get on the road. When I return from the stall to wash my hands, the cashier happens to be in there fixing her hair.

"Well, that didn't go well!" I exclaim to her while rinsing my hands

"Oh, were you on a date?" She looks excitedly in my direction. Her eyes light up, and I can tell she wants to hear the story. I recount everything that happened over the last 30 minutes.

She looks at me with wide eyes when I tell her I walked away. "Wow, that's really brave of you. I'm so glad you had the guts to just get up and leave! I couldn't have done what you did."

I respond by telling her that my time is valuable, and I don't have time for people who aren't going to better my life in some way. I don't have time for niceties for someone who is obviously a jerk. If you are going to be a negative, racist, asshole on a date, I can't be bothered.

And I suppose it goes without saying, but I never heard from him again.

# 100
# Train Guy

*Dear Diary,*

*I'm so sick of going on dates with awkward men. Maybe that's just what I get for doing online dating? I don't know, I have some friends who have met their significant others through online dating...*

Train Guy was clearly going to be a nerd from the moment I met him. He was blond with a beard and dressed in sweaters and khakis. Some of his photos had pictures of him at Comic Con. This is the kind of guy I need to be with, not some guy in the

Entertainment Industry, or some Meat Head. I could tell he was going to be smart.

I didn't know just how awkward he was going to be. Damn you, online dating!

When we met for coffee, he was so nervous. He had just moved to LA from Oklahoma — talk about a change of pace! He worked for the railroad industry and spent the ENTIRE date talking about trains. Different types of trains, engines, model numbers, the tracks. He spent his free time building model trains.

I couldn't have been more bored. He didn't ask a single question about me. There was no way to insert myself into the conversation about trains. I like taking the Metro, but I'm not going to spend my date talking about that!

Fortunately, due to some dumb luck, the coffee shop I had picked (oh, right, because he was too awkward to even choose where to have a date) was closing, so they asked us to leave. I took that as my cue to say it was getting late, and I needed to get home.

As we walked outside, he thanked me, head down, too nervous to look me in the eye.

"Thank you for the opportunity."

My heart melted. I had just been internally rolling my eyes so hard at this man for being so obnoxious about his trains. Now, here he was, humbly thanking me for gracing him with my presence. Oh, man. I wasn't interested in going on a second date with him, but his comment repeated in my head on my drive home.

This date was not going to be my last date. I mean, I know he wasn't my guy, but maybe the lesson I was supposed to learn from this, the reason that this man was brought into my world, was for me to humble myself, and remember that not everyone is in the same place on their dating journey that I am. Some people are still at the beginning stages, where every opportunity to go on a date breeds crippling anxiety and awkward conversation. I was in his shoes ten years ago when I wasn't comfortable in my skin. I have come such a long way in my dating journey, in my life journey, in my willingness to love myself. I need to honor and embrace that, and continue to treat these awkward guys with the love and compassion I wish men had shown me in my early dating days.

I don't know where Train Guy is, but I hope he grows in his dating experiences, and finds a woman who wants to ride trains with him for the rest of their lives.

# EPILOGUE

If you're hoping that this book ends with the story of how I met the love of my life you're just going to be disappointed.

I'm still single.

Fuck.

I'm actually taking a break from the entire dating scene. I've deleted all of the apps from my phone, and I can't even stomach the idea of another coffee date at this point in time.

I can't sit here and pretend that life is all sunshine and rainbows all the time. I also can't say that every minute of being single is awful. Because you know what? My feelings and emotions change over time, with every event and every thing that happens to me.

I can say that every experience that I have had in this book, along with countless others, has helped me to understand and get clear about what it is that I'm looking for in a partner. I know what I want, and even more importantly, I know what I *don't* want. And if the Universe, or God, or whatever, is conspiring to take it's sweet fucking time to bring me the man of my dreams, then I will be patient.

Or I will sit and pout. Maybe that's what I'm doing right now. Pouting. Throwing a tantrum that he's not here yet.

But, even on my worst, most-single-est days, I would rather be single and living the life that I love than to be trapped in a relationship that doesn't make me happy.

I have spent the last few years really honing in on what I like in life, and what makes me happy. I have the freedom to do what I want, when I want, and I don't need to ask permission or check in with anyone to do it.

Probably one day soon I'll get back out there. I think it won't be in the online community. I'm not sure what that means then. A lot of men who are single (as in never married) at 35 really just want to stay single, or never want to get married. I have a friend who met her partner when she was 42. I have another friend who met her man after 198 dates. I'm not sure if it was cool or weird to find someone else who also counts her dates. And if I have to fucking go on 98 more dates, I'm not sure I'll have the strength or the patience to continue. My bullshit threshold is extremely low these days, people.

However my life ends up, whoever I do or don't end up with, I know that I'm happy where I am now. I've created this amazing life for myself — travel to Europe, French lessons, dinners with friends, Dodger games, UCLA football games, and book club.

If I can find a man I want to fit into that life, to spend those moments with, to create a life and traditions with, I will. But if I don't, I need to be okay with the idea that I will be single, and maybe I'll have a few more great loves.

After all, the future is uncertain. I need to live in the present.

## ACKNOWLEDGMENTS

This book would not have been possible without the many men I have dated, and the friends that have been there along the way.

Along those lines, I want to thank my therapist Virginia Green for encouraging me to start this book in the first place. I guess this is the best way to process — so that everyone can see it.

I also want to thank AJ for being my accountabilibuddy, and my first reader.

A huge shout out to my editor Courtney Hughes for all your amazing hard work and feedback.

Thank you to my entire Facebook community for staying up-to-date with all of my writing progress, and for encouraging me when shit felt hard.

A huge thanks to those who attended my first reading party. You all made this book feel real, and like I was a legit writer. Who knew?

Love you all.
~Desirée

## ABOUT THE AUTHOR

Desirée Kent both loves and loathes dating at the same time. As an avid dater and lovable math teacher she recently discovered a love for writing. When not drinking coffee or doing yoga, Desirée is planning her next travel adventure. You can catch her most current dating stories at www.100FirstDatesBook.com or on Instagram: @100firstdatesbook.

95310492R00197

Made in the USA
San Bernardino, CA
15 November 2018